The Randstad: A Research and Policy Laboratory

The GeoJournal Library

Volume 20

The titles published in this series are listed at the end of this volume.

The Randstad: A Research and Policy Laboratory

edited by

FRANS M. DIELEMAN

Faculty of Geographical Sciences,
University of Utrecht, The Netherlands

and

SAKO MUSTERD

Center for Metropolitan Research,
University of Amsterdam, The Netherlands

KLUWER ACADEMIC PUBLISHERS
DORDRECHT / BOSTON / LONDON

ISBN 0-7923-1649-5

Published by Kluwer Academic Publishers,
P.O. Box 17, 3300 AA Dordrecht, The Netherlands.

Kluwer Academic Publishers incorporates
the publishing programmes of
D. Reidel, Martinus Nijhoff, Dr W. Junk and MTP Press.

Sold and distributed in the U.S.A. and Canada
by Kluwer Academic Publishers,
101 Philip Drive, Norwell, MA 02061, U.S.A.

In all other countries, sold and distributed
by Kluwer Academic Publishers Group,
P.O. Box 322, 3300 AH Dordrecht, The Netherlands.

Printed on acid-free paper

Printed in the Netherlands

CONTENTS

PREFACE

In 1987 the Dutch Minister of Education and Science initiated a five-year program of urban research, Urban Networks. While Education and Science provided the lion's share of funding, the Ministry of Physical Planning, Housing and the Environment, and the Ministry of Welfare, Health and Culture sponsored more specific research projects. The aim of the program was to foster research on urban restructuring and urban problems in the Netherlands. The research was focused on contrasts between regions and social classes in the Randstad Holland, the conurbation comprised of Amsterdam, Rotterdam, The Hague, Utrecht, and several smaller cities in the West of the Netherlands (see the map on the next page). The problems of urban society in the Netherlands are most clearly manifest in this region. But the Randstad is also the seedbed of many new economic functions as well as new social and cultural trends. The region is also the playground of physical planners, whose foresight has helped to preserve its unique form: a horseshoe of cities around the Green Heart.

The research in Urban Networks was a joint effort of three Dutch centers for urban and housing research:
- Center for Metropolitan Research (CGO, University of Amsterdam)
- Institute of Geographical Research (IRO, University of Utrecht)
- Research Institute for Policy Sciences and Technology (OTB, Delft University of Technology)

Apart from these centers, researchers from other institutes participated in the program: the Faculty of Economics at the Free University of Amsterdam, the Willem Pompe Institute at the University of Utrecht, and the Bureau of Social and Cultural Planning in Rijswijk.

This year, 1992, is the last year of the Urban Networks program. From 1993 on the research network will continue to exist as the Netherlands Graduate School of Housing and Urban Research (NETHUR).

The research in the program was multidisciplinary. Specialists from the fields of economics, geography, housing, sociology, and urban planning participated in Urban Networks. About 200 publications have appeared thus far. The efforts of researchers in Urban Networks are now focused on integrating the research findings in a number of books and special issues of international journals. One of these publications is the present book.

This book reports and integrates Urban Networks research on an array of topics. The aim of the editors was to confront that research with government policy in these fields, particularly with respect to physical planning. The contributors were asked to pay special attention to the interrelations between the various processes of change in the Randstad and to relate research findings to policy endeavors.

The main issues discussed in this book are introduced in the first chapter, which highlights the history and character of the Randstad Holland. The second chapter reviews trends in Dutch urban planning policy in recent decades. The following chapters are paired to give different perspectives on four themes: housing, employment and the

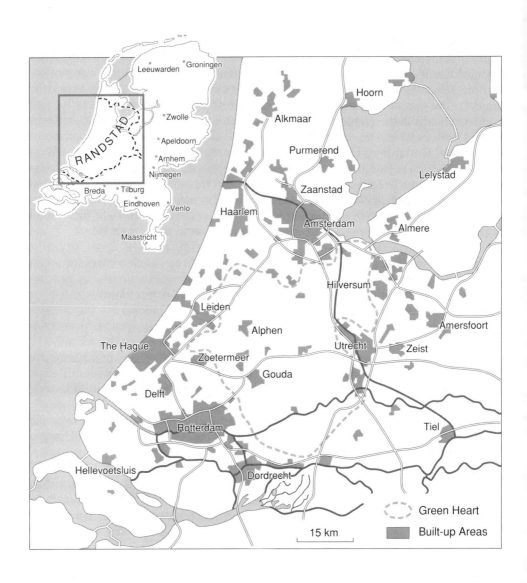

Randstad Holland

labor market, infrastructure, and the provision and use of public services in the Randstad. The first chapter of each pair is mainly research-oriented, whereas the second one elaborates on policy issues in the particular field concerned. Then, the final chapter again adopts a more general planning perspective, presenting a critical analysis of the current physical planning proposals with respect to the Randstad. We feel that this volume provides an up-to-date overview of trends in urban restructuring of the Randstad, as well as of debates about the course of physical planning in this region.

It has been a privilege to work with the authors of this book. We would like to thank them for their enthusiastic participation and valuable suggestions for improvement of the various chapters. Jan den Draak and Paul Misdorp contributed by refereeing some of the chapters. Renée Bruel, Pieter Hooimeijer, Arjen Kuenen, Karlijne Kuipers, Ilse van der Lek, Marijke Vegting and Marieke Wagener helped us to prepare the text. Translations and corrections of the English were conscientiously done by Nancy van Weesep-Smyth of Interface International. Christian Smid and Hans de Visser of Feitenbrein and Ludwig Heyden made the maps and diagrams of the book. We could not have completed the book without their help.

Most thanks, however, must go to the approximately 50 researchers who have been involved in the Urban Networks program over the past five years.

Frans M. Dieleman, Chairman Urban Networks
Sako Musterd, Coordinator Urban Networks

Utrecht/Amsterdam
January, 1992

1. THE RESTRUCTURING OF RANDSTAD HOLLAND

F.M. Dieleman & S. Musterd

1.1   The Randstad Holland

The western part of the Netherlands has been an urban landscape for centuries. Four hundred years ago, six of the ten largest cities in the country were located there. Ranked by decreasing size, these were the cities of Utrecht, Amsterdam, Leiden, Haarlem, Delft, and Dordrecht (compare Figure 1.1). The concentration of the Dutch population and of the employment opportunities in this area has only increased since then. Today, the four largest cities of the Netherlands - Amsterdam, Rotterdam, The Hague, and Utrecht - form the anchors of the horseshoe-shaped urban constellation that has become known as Randstad Holland. Over six million people inhabit this area, which thereby forms one of the largest urban regions of Western Europe.

Yet, travelers from abroad arriving by plane at Amsterdam's Schiphol Airport are more likely to get the impression that they have landed in a green, water-rich agricultural and recreational area rather than in the middle of a metropolis. They will search in vain for the skyline of towering office buildings, so characteristic of the modern big city. Nevertheless, the urban structure is very compact, in spite of the lack of office towers. And the separation of urban and rural land use is uncommonly sharp. Two factors lie at the root of this unique form of urbanization. The first is its distinct historical evolution; the second, the strong grip of physical planning on urban development since World War II.

Back in the Middle Ages, the area contained a number of cities situated on the higher grounds inland from the dunes along the North Sea coast. Some others were situated to the north of the city of Utrecht and along the main rivers, which formed the routes for most of the transportation in the area. The central part of the region was an extensive area of marshy peat bogs and was much less suitable for occupation. This central area is now known as the Green Heart of the Randstad. Utrecht is the oldest of the large cities. The site of a Roman stronghold, it developed into a trading center and reached its zenith by the twelfth century. In a later era, during the sixteenth century, Amsterdam became the staple market of the world known at the time. Until the end of the nineteenth century, Amsterdam dominated the other Dutch cities; it was at least twice the size of the second city of the country. By 1800, Amsterdam was still the fifth-largest city in Europe, after London, Paris, Naples, and Vienna.

1

F. M. Dieleman and S. Musterd (eds.), The Randstad: A Research and Policy Laboratory, 1–16.
© 1992 *Kluwer Academic Publishers. Printed in the Netherlands.*

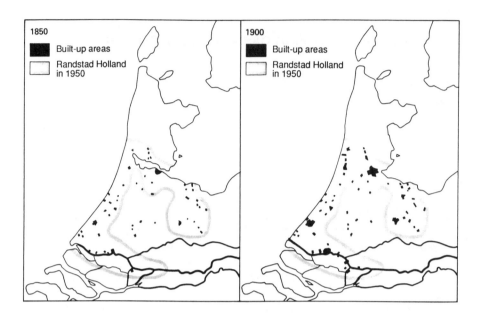

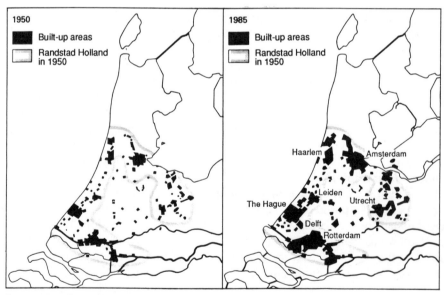

Source: Information and Documentation Center for Geography of the Netherlands

Figure 1.1   Built-up areas in the Randstad Holland, 1850 to 1985

But its function as a staple market, based on free trade, declined because of mercantilistic protection measures, while it also suffered severely from the rapid growth of London, the city's main competitor. During the Napoleonic era (until 1813), The Hague developed into the center of government. And Rotterdam boomed as the port of transit for Germany during the nineteenth century. Its situation at the mouth of the main rivers gave it a crucial advantage over Amsterdam with respect to the connections to this hinterland, which was developing economically. By 1900, Rotterdam and The Hague had rapidly closed the population gap with Amsterdam. By that point, the outlines had emerged of the urban constellation now known as the Randstad (Figure 1.1).

After 1945, Dutch physical planning came to control the development of the western part of the Netherlands. The Randstad became an important element in Dutch planning doctrine. Its name (literally: Rim City) played a key role in the policy to retain and bolster the unique form of the string of cities surrounding the Green Heart (compare Chapter 2). Hall (1966) proved to be an ardent supporter of this metropolitan form, as well as of the ways its development was promoted by the government. He held it up as an example for other rapidly developing urban regions. For a long time, Dutch politicians and scientists unanimously lauded the benefits of this form of urban development. Only recently have scientific analysts questioned the concept and the direction in which the Randstad is headed (compare Chapters 2, 4, and 11). Van der Cammen (1991) argues that it is high time for Dutch physical planning to look seriously at the work of planning authorities in foreign urban regions, such as Greater Paris, and to look critically at their own assumptions. Plesman, the founder of KLM, Royal Dutch Airlines, has been credited with coining the term Randstad when he observed the area from the air before World War II. He must have had a keen eye, because even today - as we suggested above-the urban areas take a distant second place to the greenery in the landscape that unfolds below the air traveler when flying across the western part of the Netherlands. "If only Plesman had been napping," Buursink (1991) laments in his critique of the Randstad concept, "Dutch planning would have been spared an anachronistic vision."

The Randstad covers an area of some 6000 square kilometers. This makes it more or less equal in size to Greater Paris and Greater London, for instance. Yet, in spite of this rather small spatial extent and its image as an urban ring, there is no reason to see it as a single functional entity. From a macro vantage point, it may seem to form one poly-nucleated urban structure arranged around a green core. But descending from there, this integrated entity proves to be composed of highly differentiated urban zones and separate urban regions.

A clear element in this structure is the difference between the northern and the southern parts of the Randstad. Functionally, the northern part is dominated by the service sector, while the southern part is best known for its manufacturing industry and the distribution sector (compare Chapter 5). Furthermore, although more intensive commuting flows are now emerging between Amsterdam and Utrecht, as well as between Rotterdam and The Hague, the analysis of these areas as separate metropolitan regions

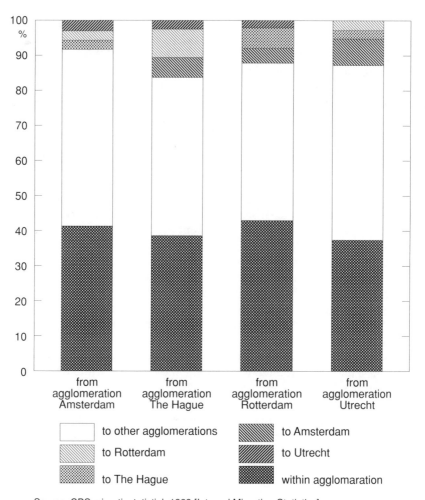

Source: CBS migratiestatistiek 1989 [Internal Migration Statistics]

*Figure 1.2   Percentages of total outmigration from each of the four big urban ag-
glomerations, reciprocal flows, and moves to other destinations*

is still the most appropriate vantage point. These urban regions are not only characterized by their own typical structural elements, but they are also barely linked in
functional terms. Cortie and Ostendorf (1986) observed that most of the commuting
takes place within each of these metropolitan regions. And also with respect to migration,
the four regions prove to be only weakly interconnected (Figure 1.2). The strongest
links among the metropolitan regions are still those formed by commercial traffic (see
Chapter 7).

So when we speak of the Randstad, we are in fact discussing the four metropolitan regions. And because these metropolitan regions are quite different from the remainder of the country, the Randstad emerges as a special region. The most important economic activities in the country are situated in the Randstad. Most of the internationally oriented firms are located there, as well as the two mainports (Amsterdam Airport and Rotterdam Harbor). In addition, the Randstad contains the national political and administrative center. But the Randstad also stands out against the rest of the country with respect to the composition of its housing stock. Especially within the largest cities, the lion's share of the housing is found in the social rental sector. This is the direct result of housing policies and physical planning practice. In addition, these cities are unique within the country because of their relatively large private rental stock. The size of the owner-occupant sector, on the other hand, is very modest, certainly by European standards. In Amsterdam, for instance, this type of housing accounts for no more than eight percent of all dwellings.

As in other countries, social problems concentrate in the big cities. Unemployment is a major characteristic. The problem of drug addiction is most compelling there. These cities harbor the largest proportion of homeless people. Forty percent of the foreign population of the country live in the four largest cities, while they account for barely eleven percent of the national population. On average, these cities have the oldest housing stock. If one can detect the formation of an underclass anywhere, then it is within their boundaries. However, because of the way in which the Dutch welfare state has been built up, there are (still) very few extreme situations (compare Chapter 6). And in spite of all these relatively unfavorable conditions, relative to the Dutch context, they are still relatively well off in comparison with many other world metropolitan regions. This applies particularly with respect to the quality of the housing stock, the magnitude of the poverty, and the range of income differentiation.

1.2   Restructuring

The Randstad may be a unique urban constellation with respect to its shape, its housing composition, and the fragmentation of its business sites. But during the past twenty years, the Randstad underwent a true metamorphosis, just like many other urban areas. As elsewhere, this was brought about by the complex interplay of demographic, economic, cultural, and political factors. But during various periods, one of these factors always predominated and thereby functioned as the engine of urban change. During the 1970s, demographic shifts attracted most attention. They caused major changes in the urban form and function. Yet, in this period, the first signs of the economic crisis appeared. However, the fundamental restructuring process of the Dutch economy, was not fully unveiled until the 1980s. Once more, this process was most readily witnessed in the cities (compare Chapters 5 and 6). During this period, the heated debate on the structure and size of the welfare state began. The measures taken to adapt the welfare state were themselves outside the realm of physical planning (housing, social security and well-being). But these policies are now having an impact on the extent of the options in this field (compare Chapters 9 and 10). The practice of physical planning in the large cities is also being affected by the discussions on the scope of the welfare state. It seems safe to predict that during the 1990s, the measures to change the structure of the welfare state will emerge as a dominant factor in urban development. Each of these topics will be discussed in the remainder of this chapter. We shall point out in which of the subsequent chapters of this book the topics are elaborated.

Residential restructuring
The extensive and selective process of suburbanization had a major impact on the urban structure of the Randstad during the 1970s. The development was mainly brought about by the rapid growth of the Dutch population in the preceding period and the simultaneous change in the dominant attitudes with respect to family formation and marriage. Between 1965 and 1985, the large cities lost a quarter of their population as people moved away. The number of people moving into the cities remained more or less stable, but this group was increasingly dominated by immigrants from abroad. Initially, the outflow was directed towards the entire range of suburban places. Later, the flow was directed towards the planned growth centers, which formed the centerpiece of the government's urban policy efforts. The net result of these developments was that the contrasts between the cities and their surroundings increased (compare Chapter 3).

During the 1980s, a change in the course of urban development became visible. Under the influence of economic factors (e.g., the oil crises of 1973 and 1978), uncertainty about the direction of personal income trends increased, and this helped to slow down the rate of suburbanization. At the same time, the category of households that are typically urban in orientation increased (compare Chapter 4). Within the Randstad, the population profiles of the cities and suburbs tended to converge (Chapter 3). This does not imply, however, that the lifestyles of the population groups also became more similar. In fact, the variation in lifestyle seems to be increasing rather than the reverse. Vijgen and Van Engelsdorp Gastelaars (1991) have shown, for instance, that with respect to the structure of their daily life, the dual-income households in suburban places are vastly different from households with a similar labor-market participation in the central cities. The former often intend to eventually start a family. And their behavior reflects this goal at an early stage.

The increasing pluralism of society as a result of international immigration has had an impact on the big cities in the Netherlands. Their population has been increasing due to a sizeable influx of foreigners. Including the people of Surinamese and Antillean descent, 24 percent of the Amsterdam population had a foreign background in 1991. In Rotterdam and The Hague, the corresponding figure was 20 percent (Muus 1991). Conflicts among population groups, residential segregation, and increasing trends of separation in education illustrate that many people find it difficult to cope with life in a multi-cultural city.

Many expect that the European cities of the 1990s will be characterized by a high rate of unemployment. They anticipate that the gap between the poor and the affluent will become more visible in the urban areas (e.g., Europe 2000). These expectations are related to the economic transformation of many cities. Frequently, the structure of the existing labor supply no longer fits the demand for labor (Sassen-Koob 1986). The adaptation of the workforce to the requirements of the new job opportunities proves to be a tedious task. It entails retraining workers who become redundant in shrinking economic sectors. Nevertheless, the experience of the big Randstad cities shows that a high rate of unemployment does not automatically coincide with increasing contrasts between the poor and the rich within their regions. On the contrary, the urban-suburban income gap seems to be diminishing despite high unemployment (Sociaal en Cultureel Rapport 1990). Until the mid-1980s, the position of the central cities eroded steadily relative to their suburban areas, but this trend changed direction along with the economic recovery. The socio-economic level of the population in the core of the central cities started to improve significantly, which diminished the contrasts with the surrounding neighborhoods within the cities, as well as with the suburban communities. This places the cities of the Randstad outside the dominant trend manifested by other European cities.

The explanation for this notable development seems to be tied to the specific structure of the Dutch welfare state. Subsidies for many services and facilities diminish the gap between the poor and the rich (Chapters 6 and 10). For instance, subsidies are available for the provision of housing as well as for the housing costs of individual tenants. Moreover, financial assistance in case of illness and unemployment is relatively generous. In addition, the Netherlands (and especially the big cities) now has the highest share of social rental dwellings of all the EC countries (Figure 1.3). With this option, considerable numbers of households from the lowest income groups can gain access to housing of a decent quality (compare Chapter 4). But the perspectives for the future are less positive. The financial problems engendered in the attempts to keep the provisions of the welfare state intact have expanded (Chapter 6). One of the current strategies to head off the problems is to engage the private sector to a considerable degree and to emphasize the economic functions of the cities. Previously, efforts to adapt the built environment of the big cities relied on urban renewal, emphasizing the residential functions and the needs of the 'sitting' population. But recently, policy has shifted towards promoting economic revitalization.

One of the characteristic features of the Netherlands is that in certain sectors, such as housing, its public policies have always included strong spatial goals. The implementation of spatial policy was facilitated by the large numbers of social rental dwellings that were built. Obviously, public control over residential construction is then strong. Chapter 4 shows that this link between housing and spatial planning determined the image of the growth center policy, the urban renewal policy, and the 'compact city' policy. Often, the planning goals that the authorities set were actually achieved (Chapter 2). But as far as the functioning of the created residential environments is concerned,

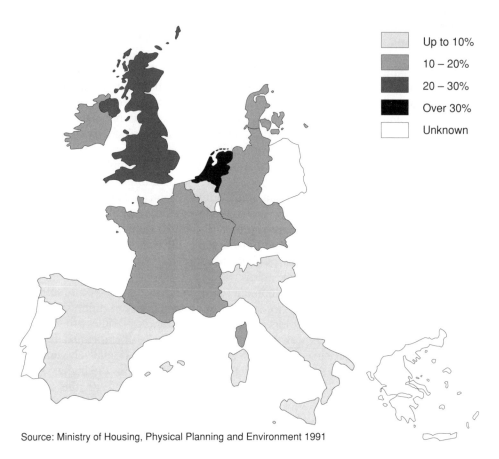

	Up to 10%
	10 – 20%
	20 – 30%
	Over 30%
	Unknown

Source: Ministry of Housing, Physical Planning and Environment 1991

Figure 1.3   Social rental dwellings in EC countries, percentage of total housing stock

the success of the policy is not always unequivocal. Many of the sites of the growth centers are too peripheral, are not attractive as business locations, and result in large commuting flows. The urban renewal activities targeted to the problems of the neighborhoods have not brought the desired degree of social improvement. And finally, the 'compact city' policy is based on simplistic assumptions concerning the ease with which large categories home-seekers can be bound to the central cities.

Economic restructuring
There is a clear demarcation of land use between urban activities, on the one hand, and agriculture and open-air recreation, on the other. Nevertheless, the location of employment opportunities in the Randstad is very fragmented. For example, not a

single real 'downtown' with a concentration of office activities, has been developed in the cities of the Randstad. This is partly due to the dispersal of the residents and the jobs among so many cities. But the policies of the local administrations are also to be blamed for the lack of real downtown areas. In the trend to find new uses for aging commercial and industrial areas in the centers of the cities of the Randstad, priority has been given to the construction of dwellings instead of commercial buildings. In addition, the erection of very tall office buildings has been prevented by the authorities, who seek to preserve the character of the historic cores. But even when offices are constructed at the edge of the city, tall buildings are seldom permitted. The province of North Holland, for instance, recently blocked the development of such a building near the Slotervaart railway station in the southwestern part of Amsterdam. But the policies differ among the cities. Rotterdam lost its historic core in the bombardments of the city at the outbreak of World War II. Thus, the construction of offices in the heart of the city is more welcome there than in Amsterdam. But the development of a downtown characteristic of the service city is not likely anywhere in the Randstad before the year 2000, even though the big cities now plan to stimulate employment opportunities in their city centers (compare Chapters 2 and 11).

The economic restructuring of the previously strong manufacturing-based urban labor market into a service economy has resulted in a further decentralization of employment in the Randstad. In 1950, 40 percent of all employment in Amsterdam was still provided in the manufacturing sector. Currently, this share has dropped to 14 percent (Jobse & Needham 1988). The shift has caused a large proportion of the jobs to disappear from Amsterdam's inner city.

Nevertheless, the restructuring of the urban economy has had a much less severe impact on the big cities in the Netherlands than elsewhere; for instance, in the areas that were the cradle of the Industrial Revolution, such as Liverpool, Leeds, and Birmingham in Britain, the cities of the German Ruhr region, and those of the Walloon region in Belgium. The economic profile of the Dutch cities had never been so strongly 'Fordist-industrial'. For centuries, trade has been relatively important. And this buffers the impact of the economic transformation to a much larger extent than elsewhere.

The expansion of employment opportunities that has been registered since the second half of the 1980s is mostly based on developments in business services and social services (compare Chapters 5 and 6). Especially the northern part of the Randstad has benefited from this growth, whereby the area around Schiphol Airport has been the main beneficiary. This area exhibits a characteristic pattern. The new employment opportunities have not been created in the old central cities but rather on the edges of the metropolitan areas. This strong tendency to site new employment on the urban periphery casts doubt on the feasibility of the new urban development policies proposed by the big cities' administrations. They have recently formulated plans to promote their inner cities as locations for international business services. Given the recent developments witnessed in the Randstad, but also in other metropolitan areas, the question of whether the administrations have identified the appropriate spatial scale has taken on a new urgency. To be able to participate in the European league, we should not lose sight

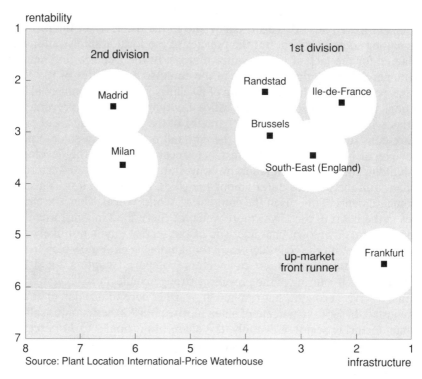

Figure 1.4   *Position of the seven top-ranking European metropolises in terms of rate of return on capital investment and infrastructure*

of the fact that urban economic functions are no longer the exclusive prerogative of central cities in metropolitan areas.

It is clear that the Randstad as a whole occupies a special position in the amalgam of developments in the Dutch economy. In this respect, internationalization is the key concept. De Smidt (Chapter 5) shows that the position of the Randstad in the field of international competition for new jobs is relatively strong in comparison with that of other European metropolitan areas. A recent study of international plant locations by the consultancy firm Price Waterhouse corroborates his interpretation (compare Figure 1.4). The regions still holds a number of trump cards, such as the plentiful supply of inexpensive yet modern business premises, the low cost of living, and the widespread fluency in foreign languages among the population. But De Smidt also indicates that the Randstad is actually too small to be able to meet the European challenge successfully. He concludes that the neighboring provinces to the east and southeast of the Randstad should be allowed to play an important role.

Increasingly, the development of urban areas depends on their position within the international networks of cities. To be able to play their role, they have to have an adequate infrastructure. In this regard, the Randstad leaves much to be desired. An entirely new vision and corresponding policy is needed, as argued in Chapters 7 and 8. The Netherlands does have a strong position with respect to water-borne transportation, based on the key role of the port of Rotterdam. Likewise, the trucking sector is well developed. But investment in rail freight has been deficient. In addition, the rate of investment in public transportation has been consistently low. Figure 1.4 also shows that the position of the Randstad in terms of infrastructure is not very strong.

The new international playing field demands the realization of mega-projects, also with respect to logistic systems. The efforts must be carried out at varying levels of scale, because each transportation mode has a unique spatial horizon. Much of the freight transportation is international in scope. Commuting is mostly limited to a regional scale, and business traffic is interregional. A complicating factor concerning major investments in infrastructure is their impact on the quality of the environment. The limited space in the Randstad implies that the area can fill up easily. By improving the accessibility of the mainports, road traffic will increase, despite all good intentions to stimulate rail transportation. There are still no adequate solutions for the environmental problems these infrastructural investments will entail, and the current policy intentions are rife with conflicting goals.

Because so many policies aim at bolstering the economic position of the Randstad, the total mobility is being stimulated, including the use of the private car. Automobile traffic is bound to increase further, for the transportation of goods as well as for commuting, because no satisfactory alternative is readily available (compare Chapters 7 and 8). But the government is trying to reduce this mobility by means of user fees and taxation, to safeguard the environment. At the same time, the economy must not suffer from these measures. On the one hand, there is now broad support for investments that can link the Randstad into the European network of high-speed rail transport, as these would enhance the competitive position of the Randstad. But on the other hand, investments in a dense and efficient public transportation system within the metropolitan regions remain limited, while the overwhelming share of mobility takes place within a relatively small area. The limited and tardy investments in an adequate system of public transportation also exert a negative effect on the overall development of the urban system of the Randstad. The location of employment is therefore increasingly focused on the road system. The provision of public transportation has thereby taken a passive role, catering to the developing structure rather than steering its direction. But well-planned infrastructure can guarantee that residential and employment concentrations actually end up where they were projected. In our opinion, residential construction has had to take too much responsibility for shaping the Randstad. This has not been sufficiently supported by investments in the public transportation network.

The welfare state

Dutch society has been quite successful in its attempts to link economic growth and a high level of public services. The government has been able to achieve this on the basis of a level of public taxation that is high even by European standards. This tax revenue has been used for a redistribution of income, for subsidies, and for relatively high levels of social benefits. In addition, the government has played a major role as employer. Among others, Kloosterman and Lambooy deal with this issue (Chapter 6). They show that the substantial role that the Dutch government plays in the redistribution of welfare forms the basis for the high 'quality of life' in Dutch cities. They believe that this is one of the possible explanations for the lack of real social problems in the big cities.

The welfare state is under siege, however. Many people believe that the total care package has grown too voluminous, and that the marginal effect of additional programs has become minimal. The scientific advisory council for government policy established that the socially deprived and non-active population is showing signs of impeded social mobility (Wetenschappelijke Raad voor het Regeringsbeleid 1990). People have become too dependent, too passive, and too accustomed to being on the receiving end. In order to break through such attitudes, it was proposed to expect individuals to show more initiative. In addition, the role of the local community in providing for their economic and social well-being is expected to increase. The local authorities are expected to trade in their welfare approach for the currently fashionable entrepreneurial model. Obviously, this is not only the consequence of a change in thinking about welfare provision. The need to decrease government spending and diminish the budget deficit on the part of the national government is also involved.

The discussion can be depicted schematically (Figure 1.5). The figure indicates that there might be an optimum level in the total volume of public care for society, and that the Netherlands has passed that point. Then public involvement will start to be counter-productive. The challenge is now to stop the retreat of government from turning into the total demolition of the welfare state. Thatcherism and Reaganism have taught us about the negative social effects when the pendulum is allowed to swing too far towards the free market economy. The recent commotion in Great Britain about the consequences of the conversion of social rental housing to owner-occupant dwellings provides a case in point. Many of the buyers of council housing have fallen upon hard times financially, as a consequence of the recent economic recession. Now the authorities do not know how to solve these problems, which were created by earlier policies. The experience gained in countries such as Great Britain and the United States with respect to (re)emphasizing the market is not really encouraging. The increasing problem of homelessness is closely connected with it. So is the widening gap between the 'haves' and the 'have-nots', which has now reached painful proportions, especially in the big cities. In the long run, the social costs incurred when a government retreats too far might in the long-run easily outweigh the short-term economies gained by reducing public involvement.

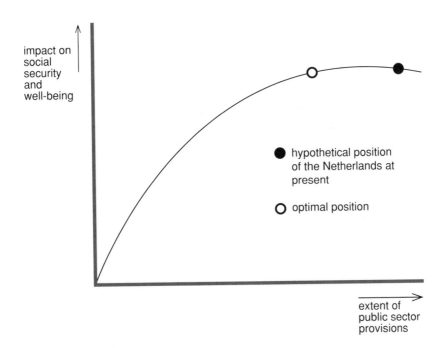

Figure 1.5   *Hypothetical association between the extent of public sector provisions and their impact on level of social security and well-being*

In the context of the supply and use of public services and facilities in the Randstad, Chapters 9 and 10 also discuss the welfare state. It is shown that a shift from equity to efficiency goals is currently under way. This corresponds to the role of a more efficient and modest public sector that operates in the background. But cuts in spending and improved control of expenditures are not the only factors that lead to changes in the supply of services and facilities and their use. Macro factors, such as spending cuts and the application of principles from business economics, join the individual, micro-level factors in their impact on the changes in supply and demand. In addition, the changes in the demographic structure of the population, as well as shifts in cultural attitudes and the buying power of the public, lead to new ways in which people will utilize facilities and services.

There is consensus on the best way to make the welfare state function more efficiently: by decentralizing responsibilities from higher to lower authorities. This dim view of the performance of the voluminous central government in a range of fields is shared by many in the public sector. Lower levels of government are in principle better equipped to observe the need for public support and the shifts that occur in this respect. They can more easily adapt to such changes. Evaluations of various experiments with the transfer of responsibilities show that the municipal authorities take their new tasks very seriously. They even manage to generate extra financial support to compensate for the rapid decline of essential services.

The present discussion of administrative decentralization in the Netherlands focuses on two core issues: the demarcation of the jurisdictions of local governments, and the financial relationship between central government and the municipalities.

Currently, the question of how to adapt the administrative structure to the modern urban reality, at the local and the regional level, is a politically sensitive issue (Chapters 2 and 11). The present administrative structure consists of three levels: state, province, and municipality. In principle, this is a straightforward structure of government, but in practice it is not so simple. Four provinces are involved in the affairs of the Randstad, which coincides with their territory or a part of it. In addition, the four biggest cities of the Netherlands are intimately involved, as well as some 200 municipalities. In addition, there are several hundred formal agreements of intermunicipal cooperation, as well as numerous formal bilateral agreements between administrations of different levels. Altogether, this virtually guarantees the lack of an integrated policy for the Randstad.

Many central government programs are implemented by municipal agencies. But in many cases, the municipalities no longer coincide with the functional entities in which urban life takes place. Neither the housing market nor the labor market operate locally, but rather at a regional scale. The same can be said of the service area of many of the urban facilities. This works to the detriment of the big cities, which are usually required to provide the full range of facilities. They have lost much of their wealthy population and many of their businesses, and they can barely afford to provide for the needs of those who remain. No wonder they are protesting against the present situation most vociferously.

The debate on the administrative structure is also linked to the organization of taxation in the Netherlands and the way in which these funds are eventually redistributed. Most taxes are levied by the national government; municipalities find themselves dependent on the state with respect to policy formulation. Many local authorities believe they have been reduced to the role of the counter where the population can collect nationally arranged benefits. Consequently, their role as a level of government with its own responsibilities has been curtailed (compare also Chapters 2, 10, and 11). So far, the national government has redistributed the funds. It gives more financial support to the municipalities where the problems accumulate and where the socio-economically deprived population is concentrated. The central cities of the metropolitan regions thereby receive proportionately more than the other communities. But the chorus of voices clamoring for more municipal responsibility to generate their own income is ever expanding.

Over the past few decades, several attempts have been made to redesign the administrative structure as well as the tax code. Now, the time seems ripe for a fundamental change, which will result in some form of metropolitan government. That administration will be made responsible for a range of policy fields: spatial planning, housing, traffic and transportation, economic affairs, environmental protection, the provision of jobs, education, recreation, and tourism. This regional government will probably not have jurisdiction over the entire Randstad but only over the individual metropolitan areas. It would be possible to adopt a new tax code, giving the municipalities the responsibility to generate a greater proportion of their income. However, this change pose new dilemmas. One of the most important dilemmas is the inherent contradiction between two dominant tendencies. On the one hand, there will be increased administrative cooperation among the municipalities within a metropolitan region, which is necessary to develop a profile for the outside world, including foreign countries. On the other hand, the competition among the municipalities within a region will increase in order to achieve a sufficient level of tax income.

1.3   The present decade

The outgrowth of the Randstad during the present decade will be determined above all by the way in which the Dutch welfare state will be adapted, as was argued above. Just like in the past, when the demographic transition and the economic restructuring were responsible for the changes, the effects of the modified and less comprehensive welfare state will be most visible in the big cities. If, for instance, the system of individual rent subsidies will be retained, this will bring greatest benefit to the inhabitants of the central cities. Most of the rental dwellings are to be found there, as well as large numbers of people with low incomes. Conversely, if the program is abolished, the central cities will be hit the hardest.

During this decade is should also become clear whether or not physical planning will be able to safeguard the basic structure of the Randstad. It has been able to do so during the past few decades, when virtual revolutions in the population structure and the economy took place. Now physical planning will have to deal with the changing context of a retreating government and the increasing influence of the market sector. A successful outcome is all but guaranteed. If, for instance, the housing sector will be dominated by the owner-occupant sector, and if Amsterdam's Schiphol Airport will develop into a true mainport, the present policy to protect a very extensive Green Heart in the center of the Randstad will not be very realistic (compare Chapter 11). But for the time being, the Minister of Housing, Physical Planning, and the Environment seems to be more determined than ever to continue implementing the policies of the past.

References

Buursink, J. (1991), Randstad: voorbeeld van mannelijk machtsdenken. Rotterdam: NRC-Handelsblad.

Cammen, H. van der (1991), Ile de la Cité ligt ergens bij Zwammerdam. NRC Handelsblad, 16-4-91, p. 8.

CBS (1989), Migratiestatistiek. Voorburg/Leiden: CBS.

Cortie, C. & W. Ostendorf (1986), Suburbanisatie en gentrification: sociaal-ruimtelijke dynamiek in de Randstad na 1970. Geografisch Tijdschrift 20, pp. 64-83.

European Community (1991), Europe 2000. European Community Document. Brussels: European Community.

Hall, P. (1966), The World Cities. London: Weidenfeld & Nicholson.

Jobse, R.B. & B. Needham (1988), The economic future of the Randstad Holland. Urban Studies 25, pp. 282-296.

Muus, Ph. J. (1991), Migration, Minorities and Policy in the Netherlands; Recent Trends and Developments. Report for the Continuous Reporting System on Migration (SOPEMI) of the OECD. Amsterdam: Department of Human Geography, University of Amsterdam.

Sassen-Koob, S. (1986), The new labor demand in global cities. In: M.P. Smith (ed), Cities in Transformation: Class, Capital and the State, pp. 139-171. Beverly Hills: Sage Publications.

SCP (Sociaal en Cultureel Planbureau) (1990), Sociaal en Cultureel Rapport 1990. Rijswijk/'s Gravenhage: SCP/VUGA.

Vijgen, J. & R. van Engelsdorp Gastelaars (1991), Een gevarieerd bestaan; het gebruik van tijd en ruimte in het dagelijks leven van enkele 'oude' en 'nieuwe' groepen binnen de Nederlandse bevolking. Werkstukken Stedelijke Netwerken 28. Amsterdam: Stedelijke Netwerken.

WRR (Wetenschappelijke Raad voor het Regeringsbeleid) (1990), Van de stad en de rand. Rapport 37. 's Gravenhage: SDU-Uitgeverij.

Prof.dr. F.M. Dieleman
Faculty of Geographical Sciences
University of Utrecht
P.O. Box 80.115
3508 TC Utrecht
The Netherlands

Dr. S. Musterd
Faculty of Environmental Sciences
University of Amsterdam
Nieuwe Prinsengracht 130
1018 VZ Amsterdam
The Netherlands

2. THE RANDSTAD: PLAYGROUND OF PHYSICAL PLANNERS

H. van der Wusten & A. Faludi

2.1 Introduction

The 'Randstad' is a planners' playground as no other. The turf is theirs in that planners have created the very concept. Randstad is central to the self-image of Dutch professionals and has for a long time been basic to national planning. Ever since its acceptance as the core of Dutch 'planning doctrine' (Faludi 1989; Alexander & Faludi 1990; Faludi & Van der Valk 1990), planners have continued to nurture the Randstad concept. The success of this notion is remarkable. Randstad is not only a familiar term in the international planning literature, the word has also entered everyday Dutch. Surely, this is a sign that the planning concept has been a success. In fact, it has been so successful that planners find it hard to modify, let alone abandon the concept. In a way they are the prisoners of their own brainchild. However, there is change in the offing. In this essay we weigh the arguments for and against the Randstad continuing to be the planners' favorite playground.

'Randstad' as a concept forms part of a whole complex of ideas. Within this complex, it is essential to understand the dialectic relationship of the Randstad concept with two others.

First, there is the relationship between the Randstad, often described as the Western Netherlands, or simply 'the West', and the rest of the country. Everything outside the Randstad is literally that: the remainder. The Randstad is densely populated, the rest is well endowed with open space; the Randstad suffers from overcrowding, the rest has amenity; the Randstad is the dynamic power house of the Dutch economy, the rest is in need of assistance; the Randstad is urbane, the rest somewhat inward-looking. The point is not that all of this is true, but that these are the connotations the term 'Randstad' evokes. Conventionally, the policy response has been dispersal to rectify imbalances between the Randstad and the rest of the country. However, since the mid-1980s, the Randstad is more of a national asset and the focal point for extra investments.

Second, there is the relationship between the Randstad and the 'Green Heart'. In this context, the meaning of the term shifts to denote the unique urban form of the Western Netherlands. Just as London's 'Green Belt' would be unthinkable without the conurbation it contains, so does the Green Heart imply an urban form. The Randstad

F. M. Dieleman and S. Musterd (eds.), The Randstad: A Research and Policy Laboratory, 17–38.
© 1992 *Kluwer Academic Publishers. Printed in the Netherlands.*

concept owes its appeal to the fact that, by containing urban development on the rim around an open area in the middle, it preserves what is perceived as a unique amenity. Thus, the Green Heart is necessary to understand the Randstad as an urban form. Following the classic English book on Dutch planning by Burke (1966), Van der Valk (1991) talks about the 'Randstad/Green Heart metropolis'.

The notion of a Randstad/Green Heart metropolis dates from the 1920s. It became firmly established in the 1950s. The array of urban settlements eventually labeled the Randstad is exceptional, not only for its shape but also for the absence of a predominant center.

The concept was a striking success, both nationally and internationally. Its international reputation was greatly enhanced by its inclusion among the 'world cities' in a famous book with the same title by Peter Hall (1966). Randstad as a concept experienced a powerful comeback during the debates of the late 1980s concerning urban restructuring within the context of an overall national strategy in the face of growing international competition (Dijkink & Van der Wusten 1990).

This chapter reviews the literature on the current status and possible future of the Randstad/Green Heart as a planning concept and its significance in the ongoing debate concerning the system of Dutch government and administration. In Section 2.2 we look at ways in which the Dutch planning system has acted upon the notion of the Randstad/Green Heart as a basic concept and how the concept is likely to develop. Section 2.3 deals with the system of government and administration in the Randstad. Physical planning is part of that system particularly concerned with the ordering of land uses. The system as a whole provides conditions for physical planning, e.g. by allocating responsibilities, but also by shaping the interests and preferences of all political actors with respect to the spatial order that physical planning seeks to affect. Consequently physical planning is intimately linked to other parts of the system of government and administration in a spirit of competitive cooperation. Section 2.4 draws conclusions with respect to the dynamics of physical planning and of governmental reform.

The empirical validity of the Randstad concept has always been somewhat in dispute. However, the concept has held its own. It has guided the actions of physical planners and has been invoked as a frame of reference in the search for a better system of public administration at the same time. Randstad as a description of reality has occasionally been remolded without having lost its significance, which is why Zonneveld (1991) locates the concept within the 'hard core' of the Dutch 'conceptual physical planning complex'. This position is analogous to Lakatos's notion of a 'negative heuristic' within a 'research programme'. (See also Korthals Altes 1991).

2.2   Physical planning

Dutch national physical planning is quite unique in having fifty years of cumulative experience (Faludi 1991a). So as a function of government, planning is well established, with a National Physical Planning Agency advising a minister responsible for physical planning. The minister works through, among other institutions, a Cabinet Committee on Physical Planning and the Environment. The institutional setup has its roots in regulations passed in 1941 and promulgated, albeit in modified form, in the Physical Planning Act of 1965 as amended in 1985. National planning has forged links with provincial and, indirectly, with local planning. In the 1960s and early 1970s, physical planning held a fairly central position within the apparatus of national government. Dekker (1989) argues that planning in each of the European countries that he has studied is linked to a specific policy field and that this field differs from country to country. In France planning refers primarily to industrial policy, in West Germany to financial policy, and in Sweden to labor-market policy. In this sense, physical planning is the primordial field of Dutch planning where planning professionals simply call themselves 'planoloog' ('planner'; for an explanation of Dutch terminology in English see Needham 1988), without feeling the need to specify their policy field.

Since the 1970s the meaning of planning has been in dispute, and physical planning has lost some of its appeal. This reflects the veritable maelstrom of change through which the Dutch welfare state has been passing. Kreukels discusses these developments in Chapter 11. Physical planning is now seeking to forge new coalitions to meet the emerging challenges and trying to demonstrate its relevance to issues of great public concern, like the environment, the international position of the Dutch economy against the backdrop of 'Europe 1992', and the like. So the present is a time of uncertainty for planners.

The Randstad/Green Heart complex of ideas has always been central to Dutch national physical planning. There has never been an administrative authority other than central government responsible for the Randstad as a whole. (As we shall see, now the first inter-governmental agency has been set up, involving the four provinces of the Randstad: North and South Holland, Utrecht, and Flevoland).

Dutch planning folklore says that the word Randstad was coined by Plesman, prewar director of KLM, the Dutch national airlines. It is said that he more than anybody else was in a position to perceive the pattern of urbanization in the Western Netherlands for what it was: a ring of towns and cities around a relatively open area. Being involved in the search for a national airport location, Plesman was also compelled to think in terms of overall settlement patterns. However, Van der Valk (1990, 1991) points out that the engineer-planner Van Lohuizen had identified this pattern as early as the 1920s. In 1924, the International Garden Cities and Town Planning Association (now the International Federation for Housing and Planning) held its annual conference in Amsterdam. This was a watershed in the development of Dutch strategic planning. Among other things, the idea of national planning aiming to preserve large-scale open space was floated at this conference (Van der Valk 1982). At the same conference, Van Lohuizen exhibited a map showing the intensity of urbanization per municipality in the Western Netherlands. What emerged was the distinctive ring-shaped pattern that we now call the Randstad. This map featured at various exhibitions. Van der Valk surmises that Plesman (who was interested in planning matters) may have seen this map and drawn inspiration from it.

However, initially the distinct shape of the Randstad received less attention from planners than the relation between the Randstad and the rest of the country. Before World War Two, professionals had already become concerned about overcrowding in the western part of the Netherlands, where most industrial development was taking place. At the heart of this concern was a distinct anti-urban bias. It was felt that no Dutch city should be allowed to grow beyond one million inhabitants. In addition, open space in or near urban areas had to be preserved. Migration to the western Netherlands should be controled to prevent this open space from disappearing.

This became the main theme of the evolving rationale of national physical planning, which was established in 1941 under German tutelage (but in pursuance of ideas formulated before the German occupation; see Michels 1978; Siraa 1989; Faludi 1991a; Postuma 1991). The key to preserving a reasonable balance was to control industrial location. Only industries strictly dependent on port facilities should be allowed to locate in the West. The idea was to require industrial development certificates, like in Britain. Bakker Schut, the first director of the national planning agency, advocated this with great force immediately after the war (Postuma 1991; Witsen 1991).

However, the planners were never given control over industrial location. (Another scheme, formulated in the 1970s, was intended to direct industrial location through a system of levies and subsidies but was never implemented.) In 1949, Bakker Schut was succeeded by Vink as the director of planning. The minister responsible for planning was In 't Veld (who had written an Ph.D. on a related subject). He was the first minister who, rather than restricting himself to his other responsibilities like housing and reconstruction, showed an active interest in planning. Between them, the minister and the planning director resolved to demonstrate the likely effects of unbridled growth in the western part of the Netherlands. Accordingly, the Commission for the Western Netherlands was formed, including representatives of the major cities and the provinces concerned (Ahsmann 1990; Van der Valk 1991). This was a momentous event in the development of Dutch planning. A working party set up under the auspices of this commission comprised the pick of the planning profession. It formulated the Randstad-Green Heart doctrine, and with it the rationale for Dutch national planning.

It took surprisingly long before this doctrine was fully developed, let alone accepted outside the inner circle of professionals. The Commission for the Western Netherlands deliberated for eight years, eventually publishing its recommendations in 1958. Meanwhile, they had published an important brochure called 'The West of the Country and the Rest of the Netherlands' in 1956. This had led to growing political concern for national planning. A parliamentary motion was carried inviting the government to outline its planning policies. So the recommendations of the Commission for the Western Netherlands became government policy, formulated in the 1960 'Report on Physical Planning in the Netherlands' (later to be dubbed the 'First Report'). Siraa (1989) claims that this report resulted in parliamentary pressure for provisions to be included in the Physical Planning Act (then under consideration); these provisions form the basis of the present Dutch system of national planning.

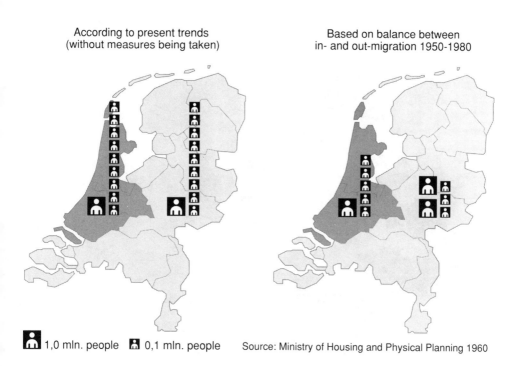

According to present trends
(without measures being taken)

Based on balance between
in- and out-migration 1950-1980

🖣 1,0 mln. people   🖥 0,1 mln. people   Source: Ministry of Housing and Physical Planning 1960

Figure 2.1   Assumptions regarding population dispersal 1950-1980

The main emphasis in the Commission's report and in the ensuing government policy was on population dispersal (Figure 2.1). This was to be achieved not by restraining industrial location in the western part of the Netherlands. Rather, dispersal was to be stimulated by providing incentives to problem areas and by decentralizing government institutions to places like Apeldoorn, Deventer, and Zwolle. (In the meantime, a branch of the National Physical Planning Agency has been relocated to Zwolle in pursuance of this policy.) Later on, more peripheral places, like Groningen in the North and Heerlen in the South, were added to the list. As indicated, dispersal was a response to the perception of the Randstad as full and the rest of the country as empty. However, the Commission for the Western Netherlands also announced other policies relating to the shape of the Randstad. The ingredients of this policy were: to prevent existing settlements from coalescing; to preserve the agricultural area (soon to be known as the Green Heart) in the middle; and to guide growth in an outward direction (Figure 2.2).

The population growth was higher than expected and suburban development was intensifying. This meant that the pressure on the Western Netherlands increased even

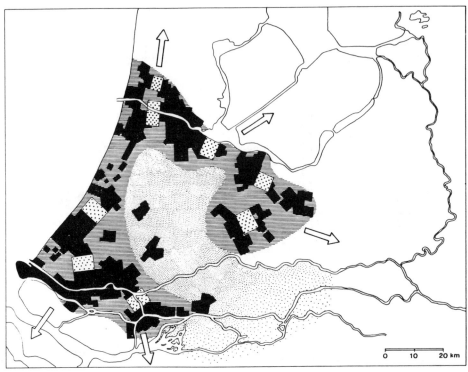

Randstad Holland

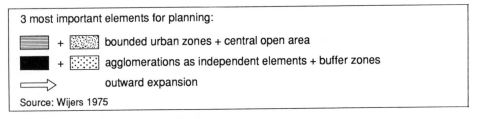

Figure 2.2   The Randstad/Green Heart idea

further. The danger was that continued growth might alter the distinct shape of the Randstad. J.P. Thijsse had already given the Commission for the Western Netherlands a graphic illustration of what the consequences of development in the Green Heart would be: an ocean of houses reaching from north to south and east to west (Figure 2.3). To stem the tide, the 1960 report was followed by the 'Second Report on Physical Planning in the Netherlands' in 1966. Glasbergen and Simonis (1979) describe it as basic to Dutch national physical planning. Needham and Dekker (1988) see it as coming closest among Dutch planning documents to being a national plan.

Source: De Ranitz 1964

Figure 2.3   Doom scenario by the chief planning consultant of the Commission for the Western Netherlands

The 'Second Report' spelled out policies for accommodating the 20 million Dutch inhabitants foreseen for the year 2000. A sizable part of the excess due to natural growth was expected to leave the West. Soon, commentators pointed out that this was hardly feasible (KNAG 1967, passim). At the same time the 'Second Report' took a powerful stand against suburban sprawl. Of course, the danger of suburban growth was particularly virulent in the Green Heart. The Green Heart is easily accessible from the major cities

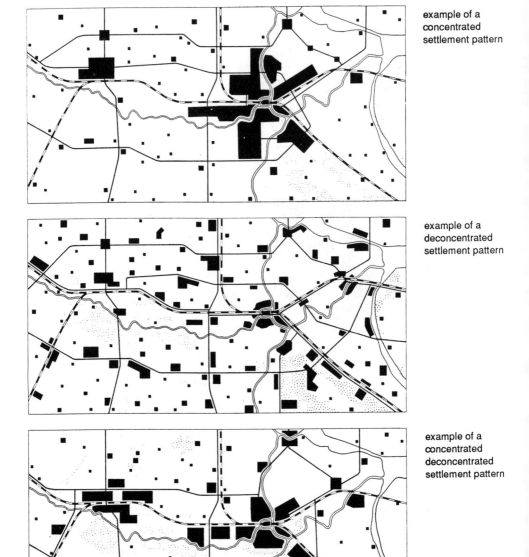

example of a
concentrated
settlement pattern

example of a
deconcentrated
settlement pattern

example of a
concentrated
deconcentrated
settlement pattern

Source: Ministry of Housing and Physical Planning 1966

Figure 2.4   Concentrated deconcentration

of the Randstad. The struggle against suburbanization became synonymous with the policy of keeping the Green Heart open. The goal was to prevent the towns and cities of the Randstad from forming one amorphous mass of houses covering the western part of the Netherlands like a seamless garment.

The battle cry of the Second Report was 'concentrated deconcentration'. This oxymoron expresses a seemingly contradictory policy: allowing people to live in suburban environments but concentrating such development in a number of specially designated overspill centers (Figure 2.4). The idea closely resembled the 'expanded towns' policy in Britain, with two genuine 'new towns', Lelystad and Almere, on reclaimed land in the polders (Constandse 1980) thrown into the bargain. 'Concentrated deconcentration' was to take place within the framework of 'city regions' comprising donor cities and overspill centers alike.

The proposed policy required coordination from the center at a critical point in time. It coincided with the coming into force of the new Physical Planning Act in 1965, when the planning system became decentralized. Since then, national and provincial plans are merely indicative and not binding, as they used to be. The plans allow few reserve powers for higher authorities to ensure that wider concerns are observed by lower levels of government.

Glasbergen and Simonis (1979) analyze the pressures on small municipalities in the Green Heart to develop at rates far in excess of indigenous need. Their conclusions cast doubt on the feasibility of stemming the tide of suburban growth. Ottens (1976) draws similar conclusions. The Green Heart was the most dynamic area in the country, making a mockery of the policy to keep it open.

The irony is that, as soon as these studies were published, growth management did become more effective. Growth management entailed a two-pronged attack on suburban sprawl. The provinces became convinced of the need to effectively check plans of municipalities in the Green Heart catering to more than indigenous need. The other attack involved a positive policy of providing alternatives in, as they were now called, growth centers (Faludi & Van der Valk 1990, 1991; Nozeman 1990). An inter-departmental commission began to effectively channel a great many subsidies for housing, infrastructure, welfare facilities and the like to the growth centers. At long last, the planners were given instruments to direct some developments: if not industrial location, then at least housing and attendant facilities.

This has been successful. An important stepping stone in bringing this about has been the Third National Physical Planning Report. This report (especially Part 2, called the Urbanization Report, published in 1976) was more down to earth than the Second Report. Up until the mid-1980s urban development in the Randstad largely followed the patterns set out in the Urbanization Report. As Faludi and Van der Valk (1991; see also Galle 1990) point out, there are more than half a million witnesses to its success. This is the number of people who have moved to where national planning policy has said they should in pursuit of the Randstad/Green Heart idea. In effect, the 'growth centers' became the cornerstones of Dutch planning doctrine (Faludi & Van der Valk 1990).

Let us pause here to reflect on the secret of this success. Undoubtedly one of the key factors has been massive public investment in the growth centers when private investment in housing was at a low. The proportion of subsidized housing during the economic crisis of the early 1980s was a staggering 90 percent plus. (The present policy is to reduce this percentage to a 'mere' 50 percent by 1995.) Growth centers were sometimes located in places that were difficult and costly to develop. The areas remaining in and around the Randstad, which were cheaper to develop, were mostly woodlands and areas of natural beauty. It is generally accepted that these should be preserved as recreation areas and open space. So funds were made available to take care of the extra expenditure incurred in servicing marshy land in some of the growth centers. Traditionally, assembling land and preparing it for development are tasks of the municipal government, but in these cases the central government felt compelled to come to the assistance of the growth centers.

Housing subsidies and funding for land assembly, infrastructure and facilities provided the preconditions for the success of the growth centers policy. However, these preconditions had existed for some time. What was unique in the late 1970s and early 1980s was the widespread consensus concerning the desirable pattern of urbanization and how to achieve it. Consensus building, rather than the issuing of directives, was (and indeed still is) the dominant mode of Dutch planning. Its capacity for consensus building is one of the three criteria for success that Alexander and Faludi (1990) apply to planning doctrine (the other two being empirical validity and comprehensiveness and consistency in elaborating the metaphoric core responsible for its consensus-building capacity). The mechanisms for consensus building in Dutch planning are discussed by Van der Heiden et al. (1991). They range from the planning inspectorate acting as an intermediary between national, provincial and municipal planning at one end of the spectrum to interdepartmental committees, frequent informal meetings, conferences and the like.

The Randstad/Green Heart concept has been so successful in building consensus that it would be difficult to undo it. Yet since the mid-1980s, some planners have been toying with this idea. There have been attempts to get away from the classic doctrine centering on the location of new urban development. Planners have sought to redefine their tasks and approaches, focusing on new issues like communications technology and environmental pollution. Above all (like immediately after the War), planners want to focus more on the restructuring of the Dutch economy, but now against the backdrop of 'Europe 1992'.

Particularly the Green Heart, both figuratively and literally the core of the Randstad concept, has become something of an article of faith. One minister after the other feels compelled to restate his commitment to preserving the Green Heart. A small band of mavericks is questioning the continuing wisdom of this policy. Van der Cammen (1991) points out that the 'Ile de la Cité of the Netherlands is at Zwammerdam', an insignificant place in the Green Heart. He thereby draws attention to the fact that the Dutch pattern of urbanization is a far cry from what economic logic would dictate. Van der Cammen thereby reopens a debate that raged within the Commission for the Western Netherlands in the 1950s. Their report includes a dissenting opinion by the representative of the Ministry of Transport and Waterways arguing that keeping the Green Heart open was wasteful. Nevertheless, the doom scenario of the Western Netherlands as one continuous sea of development, as sketched by the Commission's planning adviser, the urban designer Thijsse, had swayed the rest of the Commission against recommending such a course of action.

Van der Cammen is not the only one to question the validity of the Green Heart. An Amsterdam politician, Schaefer, exclaimed that there are "too many cows and not enough houses" in the Green Heart. There is probably truth in the contention that the Green Heart, and with it the Randstad policy, needs to be reconsidered. To preserve agricultural land close to urban agglomerations made sense in the 1950s when memories of wartime shortages were still vivid. Dutch agriculture has since become an efficient source of foreign exchange. However, the perception of the agricultural sector has shifted. What Schaefer expressed so clearly is that agriculture is held responsible for over-production and for a great deal of pollution. It seems certain that some agricultural land will be turned over to other uses. Dairy farming in the Green Heart is hard pressed anyway. Greenhouses are mushrooming instead, but they hardly enhance the beauty of the Green Hart. So why preserve it?

The complement to the Green Heart, the Randstad, is also becoming something of a liability. There have been attempts to modify it. The Fourth National Physical Planning Report, which came out in the late eighties, introduced a couple of new concepts that potentially dilute the Randstad concept. One is the 'Western Part of the Randstad', the other the 'Central Netherlands Urban Ring'.

Usually, the Randstad is divided into a Northern Wing (with Amsterdam and Utrecht as the main cities) and a Southern Wing (revolving around the Hague and Rotterdam). Conventionally the cities mentioned are referred to as the 'four big cities'. Between them, Amsterdam, Rotterdam, the Hague and Utrecht house a sizable proportion of the population of the Randstad. They also experience most of the typically urban problems: unemployment, concentration of ethnic minorities, and so forth.

Now, the Fourth Report has identified a number of international 'top locations' as foci of public and private investments. The feeling was that four top locations was too many. Developers even suggested that on the scale of the Netherlands only one top location, Amsterdam, made sense. Be this as it may, Utrecht was demoted to being the 'largest of the medium-sized towns', the status of top location being reserved for Amsterdam, Rotterdam and the seat of government, The Hague. As a complement to this, the 'Western Part of the Randstad' (sometimes dubbed the 'Western Wing') was introduced to designate an area of great functional interdependence.

As a next step, major towns, some of them outside the Randstad, were designated as the 'urban nodes' with priority status for investments. Most of the urban nodes were identified as forming part of the 'Central Netherlands Urban Ring'. This ring extended way beyond the Randstad. The 'Central Netherlands Urban Ring' (and not as before the Randstad) was identified as the economic core of the Netherlands. Parallel to this, an effort was made to redefine the Green Heart as forming part of a broader concept, the 'Open Central Area'. Between them the 'Western Part of the Randstad' and the 'Central Netherlands Urban Ring' seemed to spell the end of the Randstad/-Green Heart as the core of Dutch planning doctrine. They amounted to a new super structure to replace the existing principle of spatial organization.

However, the Randstad/Green Heart idea proved resilient. The notion of a 'Western Wing' got little support (Zonneveld, forthcoming). The interrelations between Amsterdam and Utrecht were emphasized instead. Above all, the present left-of-center government (with the Labor Party as the new coalition partner joining the 'pivotal party', the Christian Democratic Accord, which as always continues to form part of the governing coalition; see Gladdish 1990) had inherited the Fourth Report from its right-of-center predecessor and wanted to leave its mark on it. So it was decided to supplement the Fourth Report with the 'Fourth Report Extra'. The latter report amplified and in some cases rendered more stringent the policies expressed in the previous one. As regards Randstad/Green Heart, it gave more emphasis to both these concepts as part of a general drive towards environmentally sound urban consolidation policies. Thus, the sizable additional housing need in the Randstad (estimated at 700,000 units between now and 2015) is to be met by developing neither outside the ring (the old policy of deflecting growth away from the Randstad, which led to increased mobility), nor inside the ring (which would mean further encroachment upon the Green Heart), but 'on the ring'. This means consolidating and enforcing existing patterns of urban growth. By the same token, for the first time in Dutch history, the 'Fourth Report Extra' draws a firm boundary around the Green Heart, thus defining the precise area to be protected. It has been suggested that even agreed-upon plans catering to further growth within the Green Heart might be rescinded.

As far as this rather Draconian measure is concerned, government had to compromise. For our purposes, this is neither here nor there. What the Fourth Report Extra signals is that the Randstad/Green Heart idea has reached a crucial stage in its development. With the concepts being sharply defined, current policies will either make or break them.

In this respect, it is relevant to mention that the preconditions are less favorable than before. Central government wants to relinquish its dominant role in housing. Central government powers and resources are being devolved to the provinces and the larger municipalities (Van der Schaar, 1991). With this the fate of Dutch twentieth century planning doctrine hangs in the balance. Developments in the near future will be interesting for the light they throw on the power of planning concepts (Zonneveld 1991) and the metaphors of 'rule and order' (Faludi 1991b) on which they are based.

In an extraordinarily frank interview on the occasion of the publication of the 'Fourth Report Extra', Den Dunnen, then national planning director, revealed the present ambiguities:

"Really, we are not talking about the Randstad any more, we are talking about the Central Netherlands Urban Ring... However, you must, of course, never throw away well-known concepts." (Ten Cate, 1991, pp. 21).

He said this while the 'Fourth Report Extra' emphasized building 'on the ring' (i.e. the Randstad)! It seems that, if planners had their way, they would like to abandon the Randstad, and maybe also the Green Heart, replacing them by concepts more attuned to present needs. However, planners are well aware of the enormous investments that have been made in the consensus surrounding these two concepts. This is just as well. We have identified their ability to generate consensus as one of the chief advantages of easily understood concepts like the Randstad and the Green Heart. On the other hand, of course, the planning doctrine based on them must not run foul of other criteria, like validity and comprehensiveness and consistency. This is the dilemma that Dutch national planning currently faces.

2.3   Fragmented government and spatial order

Physical planning is one of the many functions of government. In this section we discuss the Dutch system of government and administration as it relates to the aim of physical planning: the ordering of land uses, which is a major contribution to the spatial order of society. The overall system is relevant as it provides a function for physical planning proper. In return, views propounded by the agencies concerned with physical planning may well permeate far outside the bounds of physical planning. This seems to have happened at the apogee of physical planning in the 1970s. In addition the way the system of government and public administration is shaped regarding the number of tiers of government, number of units, territorial shapes, and overall distribution of powers and responsibilities reflects and conditions interests of political actors with respect to the preferred spatial order. It is this last relation that primarily concerns us here. Regardless of the way physical planning proper operates, the shape of the system of government and public administration will affect the spatial ordering of land uses, not to mention the role of politically relevant actors outside the public sphere.

In essence, present constitutional arrangements date from after the revolutionary turmoil of 1848. Actually, to describe the changes that took place as revolutionary is an exaggeration. What emerged reflected a longstanding tradition of federal government dating from the days of the Dutch Republic, the unitary regime under French rule and the subsequent fairly autocratic reign of the House of Orange since 1813. Its final form was inspired by the liberal spirit of the day. A liberal constitution and a series of organic laws ensued, leading to a three-tier system of government. Between them, central government and the municipalities took the lion's share of powers and responsibilities. The provinces received some delegated powers of control over municipalities. The whole country was covered by a seamless garment of provincial and municipal jurisdictions (Blaas & Dostal 1989).

As the scope of government increased, more and more powers and responsibilities came to be shared between central government and the municipalities. This took different forms depending on the particular field of policy. Often it was the municipalities that initially assumed new responsibilities. Subsequently, central government responded by imposing general rules on the one hand and accepting overall financial responsibility for service provision on the other. However, in most instances central government channeled the necessary funds through the municipalities.

On all levels the scope of government increased tremendously in the period 1870-1930. Budgets, personnel, and the nature of government bureaucracy were transformed during those decades (Kraemer 1966; for a detailed study of some municipalities see Raad-schelders 1990). The notion of the role of the state changed from that of a night watchman to the idea of the welfare state. However, the basic elements of the system installed after 1848 did not change. Central and local government became more intimately related to each other. In 1929 a fundamental rearrangement of their financial relations was enacted. Municipalities lost nearly all their autonomous powers of taxation. They became utterly dependent on transfers of funds generated by taxes levied by central government. However, a large part of government expenditure continued to be channeled through the municipalities.

The original purpose of the 1929 tax reform had been to do away with excessive local tax differences. In parts of the Randstad particularly, suburban growth during the preceding decades had resulted in such imbalances. Initially, preferences for suburban living and consequent changes in local taxes conditioned further changes in the land use distribution and the spatial order of urban society. Suburban growth presented a further complication in intergovernmental relations. Increases in scale occurred along various dimensions of social life, the territorial dimension being one of them. To be able to make use of economies of scale, service providers and utility companies demanded intermunicipal cooperation.

The increase in scale of urban society gave rise to a whole series of ideas as regards the optimal structure of local and regional government. They were purported to solve various problems resulting from this mismatch that negatively affect the spatial order of society: inefficient scale of service provision, inducement of spatial inequalities, disregarding negative external effects, free-rider behavior, and poor coordination of mutually advantageous projects. Many took the form of more intensive 'horizontal' relations across municipal boundaries or a differently constituted set of local units: intermunicipal cooperation, annexation, large-scale mergers accompanied by territorial decentralization within central cities, an additional tier of metropolitan government, subdivision of provinces with more operational powers and responsibilities. All these ideas have been floating around for over half a century. Yet only the first two ideas have borne fruit. Depending on how one defines such an arrangement, the number of intermunicipal agreements varied between 764 and 1250 in 1981 (Derksen & Korsten 1989). More recently Bussink et al. (1990a) counted 196 cases of recently instituted (since 1985) intergovernmental cooperation very often involving municipalities. They limited their attention to instances relevant to physical planning. It should be added that many of these were feathery in terms of definite commitments. The number of municipalities decreased from 1209 in 1851 to 714 as of January 1, 1988. The rate of annexation has been slowly increasing (data in Derksen & Korsten 1989).

The Dutch system of government has in its basic provisions been extremely resistant to structural change (WRR 1990). Among other things, this stems from the constitution and organic laws making the procedures for change cumbersome. Thus, changing the jurisdiction of a municipality requires an act of parliament. Dutch political culture is also very conservative as far as the basic features of the system are concerned. The common view is that this is the result of a centuries-long tradition of seeking broadly based consensus in a country with otherwise strong denominational divisions (Daalder 1981). At the same time the traditional international openness and position at the juncture between German, French, and British influence - in the postwar era superseded by an overriding American influence - has resulted in an often highly volatile climate of opinion based on short-lived preferences for this and that. The combination of stable structures and changing preferences on the issues of the day can at times be perplexing (Dijkink 1990).

We have seen that major changes took place until the 1930s. From the 1930s to the 1980s, the system of government and public administration continued to expand at a tremendous rate, basically within the same type of overall organization. Notwithstanding many proposals to that effect, there was again no structural change. During the 1960s and 1970s, the Dutch system of government and administration reached historically unprecedented levels of interweaving of the various tiers of government (Vonhoff 1980, De Beus & Van Doorn 1984, Vonhoff 1985, Tjeenk Willink 1983-1986). At the same time, government had become highly segmented between policy realms. Rather than looking sideways, their financial dependence and the need for vertical coordination compelled actors at the municipal level to look more to actors in the same policy community at provincial and national level.

Physical planning was one of the policy communities that succeeded occasionally, and up to a point, in implementing strategic policies, with the growth-center policy discussed in the previous section being an obvious example. Naturally, such efforts were often blocked by other policy communities. This has been likened to tribal warfare between government departments and their supporters at other levels of government. For the spatial order of urban society, this results in weak links between some of its component parts that are functionally related. Physical planning had traditionally far more control as regards land use for housing purposes than for major infrastructure and concentrations of employment like industrial estates. This obviously resulted in unintended commuter flows.

Horizontally, between municipalities, things were different. As we have seen, many forms of cooperation existed. However, there was also much reluctance to enter into binding agreements in cases where coordination was called for. Despite their pretensions to that effect, the success of the provinces in coaxing municipalities into entering such agreements was limited (examples of successful provincial coordination in Eiff 1991; of hardly satisfactory performance in Groenendijk 1990). Consequently municipalities with differing population bases and therefore differing interests as to the use of their land were very slow in taking account of the interests of other municipalities.

Toonen (1987) concludes that since 1848 the Dutch system developed from a polycentric one, wherein many fairly autonomous actors at various tiers of government had to mutually adapt to each other. It developed into a pluralist one, in which one state machinery has to be managed by a variety of actors. It eventually aspired to a monocentric system, in which a single center of power manages the state machinery overall. However, the monocentric arrangements of the 1960s and 1970s have failed. Assumptions underlying a centrally managed system of government often prove to be unrealistic. The arrangements fail for lack of central steering capacity per sector and for lack of coordination between various central government departments. This failure, if anything, is more pronounced there than in the municipalities (where coordination is also a problem). This has led to tensions, especially in the wake of the economic recession and the general reevaluation, particularly strong in the Anglo-American world, of the welfare state.

Since the early 1980s we have seen renewed and substantial efforts to change the structure of government and administration in its vertical dimension. They take various forms: cost-savings by simply discontinuing or privatizing service provision; efficiency drives accompanied by efforts to redefine central-local relations in terms of fewer but more strategic and more binding agreements coupled with decentralization of powers and responsibilities. This could result in a new 'polycentric state', though inevitably with infinitely more inter-linkages (for a spirited defense of such a development, see Van Leeuwen 1989). Against this background, it seems unlikely that further development of the Randstad/Green Heart complex of ideas as a spatial policy will be high on the list of strategic priorities. We return to this below.

This leaves the problem of horizontal intergovernmental relations. The topic resurfaced on the political agenda of the late 1980s, starting with the report of the Montijn Commission (1989). This stems primarily from a powerful and sustained lobby of the larger municipalities within the Randstad. Despite much skepticism in light of the fate of earlier efforts, the years to come may see a new government structure evolving at the lower tiers, especially in urban regions. This will entail new units at metropolitan level fulfilling a limited number of strategic tasks, such as the planning of major housing schemes and infrastructure together with the provision of serviced land for such purposes. The four big cities will probably continue to pursue a policy of internal decentralization that most of them have pursued for a number of years, particularly Amsterdam (Van Goor 1989). Some central cities that urgently need new land for development will probably be granted some extra territory through annexation.

The sustained campaign lasting a number of years in those areas where metropolitan government is an issue (in the Randstad this relates to the major cities and their hinterland) has perhaps led to sufficient consensus about the need for new forms of metropolitan government from 1993 onwards. However, decisive steps still have to be taken and there is a long tradition of inconsequential brinkmanship in these matters. The process has been carefully monitored, encouraged and guided by the Ministry of Home Affairs. The trajectories that various metropolitan areas will follow differ somewhat (Ministerie van Binnenlandse Zaken 1990, 1991; Bussink et al. 1990b). The process is complicated by the efforts of various central government departments to install their own decentralized sectoral planning and policy institutions at metropolitan/-regional level. Slightly differing boundaries take shape, and a plethora of new authoritative institutions and arrangements does not facilitate overall coordination at metropolitan level. This development now occurs in various policy sectors e.g. social housing, public transport, police.

So on the one hand, central-local relations are becoming somewhat less intricate (which does not necessarily mean less tight). On the other hand, horizontal links forged under various guises are becoming more complex. Even more important, horizontal coordination within metropolitan areas is becoming mandatory. Against this background, the Randstad will probably not be one metropolitan area but comprise a set of four of such areas. These metropolitan regions are more closely interwoven in some respects (commercial services) than in others (housing/labor markets) (Knol & Manshanden 1990).

Perhaps we can discern a pattern in this long-term development. Initially municipalities were very much on their own. Of course, there were some differences between them as to size and centrality. However, from the point of view of the system of government, at that stage centrality was less important than later on. As the scope and the scale of government involvement increased, not only an increase in intergovernmental relations occurred, but the socio-economic composition of various municipalities became more differentiated at the same time. The out-migration from the cities of people looking for more adequate housing was selective as to income (the alternative of large-scale redevelopment of the center for high-income groups was disregarded in the Netherlands, as indeed it was in Britain, but not in Paris and Rome; see Wagenaar 1992). As a result, private services in the central cities lost customers; welfare services for the poor attracted relatively more customers, creating a heavier burden on the municipal budget. Other public services catering to the well- to-do had to be maintained despite the fact that they were a burden on local budgets, to which clients from other municipalities did not contribute. The local tax base faltered and tax rates had to be increased in order to maintain the level of income of local government. This induced further out-migration of high-income groups who could afford to do so, thus further degrading the tax base. So the vicious circle went on and on.

A major incentive for the 1929 tax reform had been the desire of central government to stop this process and to suppress the ensuing urge of the major cities for annexations in order to maintain their tax base (Terhorst & Van de Ven 1990). What has basically happened after 1930 is an ever-increasing dependence of local on central government for its income plus a further differentiation between central cities and suburbs. There has been a general acceptance on both sides that their respective populations would become more and more homogeneous as regards socio-economic composition. Central government felt compelled to direct more and more funds to the central cities in order to compensate them for the extra expenditure caused by their centrality on the one hand and their relative impoverishment on the other.

New arrangements now under discussion should induce municipalities to look after themselves by maintaining their tax base (WRR 1990). The poorer central cities must call a halt to developments that have been going on for quite a number of decades. This does not apply to the wealthier suburbs. Here the internal debate is between professional administrators, who have a vested interest in further growth, and local interests, wishing to preclude any change in their living environment that in their opinion is for the worse. Such different perspectives notwithstanding, the area-wide metropolitan authorities will have the unenviable task to cajole, induce, enforce, negotiate, and build consensus around strategic planning goals. This will by no means be easy (for some of the difficulties concerning local tax rates see Dekker et al. 1991).

As new forms of metropolitan governance get underway in parts of the Randstad, the role of the provinces will become more circumscribed. The Randstad provinces are now lobbying for an authority on the level of the Randstad as a whole. Alternatively, they are looking at joint arrangements for the Green Heart. One never knows, but it seems unlikely that such an authority will come to pass. However, more concrete steps are being taken, and it is just as well to take note of those. What we mean is the setting up of the first inter-governmental agency involving the four provinces of the Randstad: North- and South Holland, Utrecht and Flevoland. Obviously it is still too early to judge its effect on the future of the Randstad/Green Heart.

2.4   Final remarks

The Randstad/Green Heart has been the core of a successful doctrine of physical planning. Its future now hangs in the balance. The case for a declining role of the Randstad/Green Heart dual concept during the next few years can be argued as follows. Continued relevance depends on consensus among planners and the missionary appeal that strategic planning doctrine maintains outside the profession. As we have seen, the doctrine's position within the profession has become somewhat more circumscribed than previously. The position of physical planning within public administration has weakened. Likely structural developments in the field of government and public administration aiming at decentralization do not exactly strengthen the Randstad's relative position vis-à-vis its constituent parts. For some time to come, the 'Randstad' may continue to be seen as an international trademark of Dutch planning. As an ideal it may very well lose its appeal internally and become even more diffuse in reality than it has been in the past.

On the other hand, a revival of the Randstad/Green Heart idea can certainly not be excluded. If anything, the current 'Fourth Report Extra' represents a strengthening of both the Randstad and the Green Heart concept. Indeed, in order to reduce mobility and preserve the environment, government commitment to upholding these concepts now seems so strong that we can speak of a renaissance of traditional planning ideas. The Randstad provinces have reacted forcefully to the 'Fourth National Physical Planning Report', presenting joint proposals for the further development of the Randstad. At the same time it must be said that heightened expectations of government policy will either make or break the doctrinal heart of such policies. Imagine that, despite a high level of commitment to this policy, planners do not effectively curtail suburban growth in the Green Heart. Surely the result would be a credibility gap of massive proportions.

References

Ahsmann, R. (1990), De Werkcommissie: Een historisch onderzoek naar de Werkcommissie voor het onderzoek naar de ontwikkeling van het Westen des Lands (1951-1958). Werkgroep PSVA publicatie 10. 's-Gravenhage: NIROV.

Alexander, E.R. & A. Faludi, (1990), Planning Doctrine: Its Uses and Applications. Working Papers 120. Amsterdam: Planologisch Demografisch Instituut, Universiteit van Amsterdam.

Blaas, H. & P. Dostal (1989), The Netherlands: changing administrative structures. In: R. Bennett (ed), Territory and Administration in Europe, pp. 230-241. London: Pinter.

Beus, J.W. de & J.A.A. van Doorn (eds) (1984), De interventiestaat. Meppel: Boom.

Burke, G.L. (1966), Greenheart Metropolis: Planning the Western Netherlands. London: Macmillan.

Bussink, F.L., E.C.M. van der Hulst & A. van Marwijk (1990a), Nieuwe samen werkingsverbanden in het openbaar bestuur I,II. Verkenningen 59 (a&b). Amsterdam: Planologisch Demografisch Instituut, Universiteit van Amsterdam.

Bussink, F.L., E.C.M. van der Hulst & C.M.M. Wortelboer (1990b), Bestuurlijke samenwerking in stedelijke gebieden. Verkenningen 60. Amsterdam: Planologisch Demografisch Instituut, Universiteit van Amsterdam.

Cammen, H. van der (1991), Ile de la Cité ligt ergens bij Zwammerdam. NRC Handelsblad, 16-4-91, p. 8.

Cate, F. ten (1991), Roel den Dunnen: In de Vierde Nota Extra wordt de grens van het Groene Hart waanzinnig scherp getrokken, dat mag niet verloederen. Binnenlands Bestuur, 18-1-91, pp. 20-22.

Constandse, A.K. (1980), New Towns: Almere and Lelystad in the Netherlands. In: Working Party on New Towns, New Towns in National Development. International Federation for Housing and Planning, pp. 113-117. 's Gravenhage.

Daalder, H. (1981), Consociationalism, center and periphery in the Netherlands. In: P. Torsvik (ed), Mobilization, Center-Periphery Structures and Nation-Building: A volume in Commemoration of Stein Rokkan, pp. 181-240. Oslo/Bergen: Universitetsforlaget.

Dekker, P. (1989), Overheidsplanning in West-Europa. Sociale en Culturele Studies 10. Rijswijk: SCP.

Dekker, A., P. Terhorst & J. van de Ven (1991), Bestuurlijk-territoriale geleding en belastinghervorming in grootstedelijke gebieden: nieuwe variaties op een oud thema. Werkstukken Stedelijke Netwerken 33. Amsterdam: Stedelijke Netwerken.

Derksen, W. & A.F.A. Korsten (1989), Lokaal bestuur in Nederland. Inleiding in de gemeentekunde. Alphen aan den Rijn: Tjeenk Willink.

Dijkink, G.J.W. (1990), Beleidenissen. Politieke en ambtelijke cultuur in Nederland 1965-1990. Groningen: STYX.

Dijkink, G.J.W. & H. van der Wusten (1990), Global competition as an argument in local development policy: the case of Randstad. In: A. Kuklinkski (ed), Globality versus Locality, pp. 329-338. Warsaw: Institute of Space Economy, University of Warsaw.

Eiff, V.L. (1991), Beleid voor bedrijfsterreinen. Een politiek-geografische studie naar betrekkingen in het openbaar bestuur bij het lokatiebeleid voor bedrijfsvestiging in stadsgewesten. Nederlandse Geografische Studies 126. Amsterdam: KNAG/Instituut voor Sociale Geografie, Universiteit van Amsterdam.

Faludi, A. (1989), Perspectives on planning doctrine. In: A. Faludi (ed), Keeping the Netherlands in Shape. Built Environment 15, pp. 57-64.

Faludi, A. (1991a), Introduction. In: A. Faludi (ed), Fifty Years of Dutch National Physical Planning. Built Environment 17, pp. 5-13.

Faludi, A. (1991b), "Rule and Order" as the Leitmotif: Its past, present and future meaning. In: A. Faludi (ed), Fifty Years of Dutch National Physical Planning. Built Environment 17, pp. 69-77.

Faludi, A., Valk, A.J. van der (1990), De groeikernen als hoekstenen van de Nederlandse ruimtelijke planningdoctrine. Assen: Van Gorcum.

Faludi, A., Valk, A.J. van der (1991), Half a million witnesses: The success (and failure?) of Dutch urbanization strategy. In: A. Faludi (ed), Fifty Years of Dutch National Physical Planning. Built Environment 17, pp. 43-52.

Galle, M. (1990), 25 Years of Town and Country Planning Achievements. The Hague: Ministry of Housing, Physical Planning and Environment/National Physical Planning Agency.

Gladdish, K.R. (1990), Governing the Dutch. Acta Politica 25, pp. 389-402.

Glasbergen, P. & Simonis, J.B.D. (1979), Ruimtelijk beleid in de verzorgingsstaat: Onderzoek naar en beschouwing over de (on)mogelijkheid van een ruimtelijk beleid in Nederland. Amsterdam: Kobra CV.

Goor, J.G.B.M. van (1989), Binnengemeentelijke decentralisatie en deconcentratie in Amsterdam, Rotterdam, Den Haag en Utrecht; een inventarisatie. 's Gravenhage: WRR.

Groenendijk, J.G. (1990), Coordination of urban economic development policies. Tijdschrift voor Economische en Sociale Geografie 81, pp. 289-298.

Hall, P. (1966), The World Cities. London: Weidenfeld & Nicholson.

Heiden, N. van der, J. Kok, R. Postuma & G.J. Wallagh (1991), Consensus-building as an essential element of the Dutch planning system. Paper given at the joint ACSP/AESOP conference Planning Transatlantic held at Oxford, 8-12 July.

KNAG (1967), Handelingen KNAG Symposium naar aanleiding van verschijnen Tweede Nota. Leiden: Brill.

Knol, H. & W. Manshanden (1990), Functionele samenhang in de noordvleugel van de Randstad. Nederlandse Geografische Studies 109. Amsterdam: KNAG.

Korthals Altes, W.K. (1991), Statica en dynamica van planningdoctrines: Over plaats, functie en verandering van duurzame denkbeelden in de ruimtelijke ordening. Working Papers 135. Amsterdam: Planologisch Demografisch Instituut, Universiteit van Amsterdam.

Kraemer, P.E. (1966), The Societal State. The Modern Osmosis of State and Society presenting Itself in the Netherlands in Particular. Meppel: Boom.

Leeuwen, L. van (1989), De gemeente centraal. Om de doeltreffendheid van het binnenlands bestuur. Assen/Maastricht: Van Gorcum.

Micheels, S. (1978), De instelling van de Rijksdienst voor het Nationale Plan: 15 mei 1941. In: A. Faludi & P. de Ruijter (eds), Planning als besluitvorming, pp. 138-151. Alphen aan den Rijn: Samsom.

Ministerie van Binnenlandse Zaken (1989), Grote steden, grote kansen. 's Gravenhage: SDU-Uitgeverij.

Ministerie van Binnenlandse Zaken (1990), Besturen op niveau: deel 1. 's Gravenhage: SDU-Uitgeverij.

Ministerie van Binnenlandse Zaken (1991), Besturen op niveau: deel 2; Bestuur en stedelijke gebieden. 's Gravenhage: SDU-Uitgeverij.

Needham, B. (1988), Continuity and change in Dutch planning theory. The Netherlands Journal of Housing and Environmental Research 3, pp. 5-22.

Needham, B. & A. Dekker (1988), The Fourth Report on physical planning in the Netherlands. The Netherlands Journal of Housing and Environmental Research 3, pp. 335-344.

Nozeman, E.F. (1990), Dutch new towns: triumph or disaster? Tijdschrift voor Economische en Sociale Geografie 81, pp. 149-155.

Ottens, H.F.L. (1976), Het Groene Hart binnen de Randstad. Assen: Van Gorcum.

Postuma, R. (1991), The National Plan: The taming of a runaway idea. In: A. Faludi (ed), Fifty Years of Dutch National Physical Planning. Built Environment 17, pp. 14-22.

Raadschelders, J.C.N. (1990), Plaatselijke bestuurlijke ontwikkelingen 1600-1980. Een historisch-bestuurskundig onderzoek in vier Noord-Hollandse gemeenten. 's Gravenhage: VNG-Uitgeverij.

Schaar, J. van der (1991), Volkshuisvestingsbeleid: een zaak van beleid. Utrecht: Het Spectrum.

Siraa, H.T. (1989), Een miljoen nieuwe woningen; de rol van de rijksoverheid bij wederopbouw, volkshuisvesting, bouwnijverheid en ruimtelijke ordening (1940-1963). 's Gravenhage: SDU-Uitgeverij.

Terhorst, P. & J. van de Ven (1990), The territorial strategies of Amsterdam. Tijdschrift voor Economische en Sociale Geografie 81, pp. 267-279.

Tjeenk Willink, H.J. (1983-1986), Jaarberichten regeringscommissaris Reorganisatie Rijksdienst. 's Gravenhage: SDU-Uitgeverij.

Toonen, Th.A.J. (1987), Denken over binnenlands bestuur. Theorieën van de gedecentraliseerde eenheidsstaat bestuurskundig beschouwd. 's Gravenhage: VUGA.

Valk, A.J. van der (1982), Planologie en natuurbescherming in historisch perspektief, Werkgroep PSVA publicatie 2. 's Gravenhage: NIROW.

Valk. A.J. van der (1990), Het levenswerk van Th.K. van Lohuizen 1890-1956: De eenheid van het stedebouwkundige werk. Delft: Delftste Universitaire Pers.

Valk, A.J. van der (1991), Randstad-Green Heart Metropolis: invention, reception and impact of a national principle of spatial organization. Built Environment 17, pp. 23-33.

Vonhoff, H.J. et al. (1980), Rapport commissie Reorganisatie Rijksdienst. 's Gravenhage: SDU-Uitgeverij.

Vonhoff, H.J. et al. (1985), Carnavalstocht der planprocedures. Adviescommissie Binnenlandse Zaken Sanering Planprocedures. 's Gravenhage: SDU-Uitgeverij.

Wagenaar, M. & R. van Engelsdorp Gastelaars (1986), Het ontstaan van Randstad, 1815-1930. Geografisch Tijdschrift 20, pp. 14-29.

Wagenaar, M. (1992), Conquest of the center or flight to the suburbs? Divergent metropolitan strategies in Europe, 1850-1914, Journal of Urban History (forthcoming).

WRR (Wetenschappelijke Raad voor het Regeringsbeleid) (1990), Van de stad en de rand. Rapporten aan de Regering 37. 's Gravenhage: SDU-Uitgeverij.

Witsen, J. (1991), Five decades, five directors: The National physical Planning Agency 1941-1991. A personal view. Fifty years of Dutch National Physical Planning. Built Environment 17, pp. 61-68.

Zonneveld, W. (1991), Conceptvorming in de ruimtelijke planning: Patronen en processen. Planologische Studies 9A. Amsterdam: Planologisch Demografisch Instituut, Universiteit van Amsterdam.

Zonneveld, W. (1992), Naar een beter gebruik van ruimtelijke planconcepten: Wenken voor conceptvorming. Working Papers (forthcoming). Amsterdam: Planologisch Demografisch Instituut, Universiteit van Amsterdam.

Prof.dr. H. van der Wusten
Faculty of Environmental Sciences
University of Amsterdam
Nieuwe Prinsengracht 130
1018 VZ Amsterdam
The Netherlands

Prof.dr. A. Faludi
Faculty of Environmental Sciences
University of Amsterdam
Nieuwe Prinsengracht 130
1018 VZ Amsterdam
The Netherlands

3. CHANGES IN THE RESIDENTIAL FUNCTION OF THE BIG CITIES

R.B. Jobse & S. Musterd

3.1   Introduction

Dynamism is one of the most apparent characteristics of the big city. Everyone is used to the fact that there is a continuous flow of demolition, construction, and reconstruction, that people move into the city, change their address within it, or move away. Consequently, their high mobility, at least by Dutch standards, sets the big cities apart. Nevertheless, dynamism does not always imply fundamental changes in functions and structure. By today's norms, for instance, Amsterdam showed extremely high mobility rates during the period between the two World Wars. In some neighborhoods and housing market segments, between 25 and 35 percent of the dwellings turned over annually. Yet at the level of the neighborhood, this did not cause dramatic changes in the age composition of the population in most cases, or of their social status levels (Jobse 1988).

Although the residential mobility rate decreased substantially after World War II, the effects of mobility have exerted a considerably greater impact than before because of the selective character of this mobility (Van Engelsdorp Gastelaars & Heinemeijer 1985). Both at the level of the neighborhood and at that of the city as a whole, the inmigrants and outmigrants are so different from each other that significant changes in the population composition have been recorded since 1960. Consequently, the big cities have seen a notable change in their residential function since then.

The 1960s marked a transition in the development of many Western European cities (Urban Europe 1982). The large cities of the Randstad are no exception in this respect. The function of these cities within their regional housing markets has changed dramatically during the past thirty years. Around 1960, the demographic and socio-economic composition of the population of the big cities was indeed different from that of the country as a whole, and also from that of the adjacent municipalities, but the differences were not extreme. The large cities were still the place of residence for large segments of the higher-, the middle-, and the lower-income groups, for the young, the elderly, and the middle-aged, for families and for single persons.

After 1960, this situation was drastically altered because of societal change, selective residential construction and a very specific urban renewal policy, processes of urban decline, and the increasingly negative image of the cities. The big city as a whole, and

F. M. Dieleman and S. Musterd (eds.), The Randstad: A Research and Policy Laboratory, 39–64.

more specifically large parts within it, no longer houses a cross section of the Dutch population, but rather specific population categories (Jobse 1986; Schouw & Den Draak 1986, 1991). The big cities have become increasingly heterogeneous, and in comparison to the Netherlands as a whole, now form atypical social environments. The populations of Amsterdam and, to a lesser extent, Rotterdam show major imbalances (WRR 1990, p. 23). Approximately half the population of the big cities consists of such groups as the unemployed, the handicapped, single-parent families, poor elderly, and ethnic minorities, categories which partly overlap. The economically non-active are also very typical. Of the population between 15 and 64 years of age, almost half are not yet or no longer active in the regular labor market (Van den Berg et al. 1988).

3.2   Long-term developments and policy: 1960-1990

Large-scale and almost uncontrolled suburbanization took place until the first half of the 1970s. In this period, the foundations were laid for the present contrasts between the suburbs and the big cities. The new inhabitants of the suburbs were predominantly families with an above-modal income. They could not only afford to buy a house in an attractive environment, but they could also pay the commuting costs to get to and from their jobs in the central city.

During the second part of the 1970s, the public authorities reacted to this unplanned suburbanization by formulating their deconcentration policy, in which growth centers played a central role (compare Chapters 2 and 4). An attempt was made to tame the spontaneous development, and this policy was partially successful (Faludi & Van der Valk 1990).

In addition, the urban development of the 1970s was profoundly affected by economic factors. The two oil crises, at the beginning and the end of the 1970s, led to a substantial decline in residential mobility (the migration of people moving with their households between municipalities dropped by some 20 percent), but caused above all great uncertainty. A period of recession had begun, heralded by the famous words of the social-democratic Prime Minister Den Uyl: "It will never again be like it was before." Among other manifestations, this expressed itself in the residential construction output. The owner-occupier sector was especially hit-hard at the end of the 1970s. And because this sector was overrepresented in the suburbs, these areas were affected most. The economic development and the crisis of the owner-occupier sector also slowed down the development of the growth centers. This turn-around occurred just when the construction programs of these municipalities had finally taken off, around 1980 (Jobse et al. 1991).

The changes in direction of the spatial development policy to promote the central cities were possibly even more detrimental to the growth centers than to the suburbs - at least for some of them, for which this policy reversal came too early. Nevertheless, this was not an autonomous policy decision, against the trend of spatial development, but a timely reaction of the public authorities to developments that had already begun (Musterd et al. 1991).

The transition is undisputedly rooted in the (global) economic restructuring. But in addition, there is a growing individualism, which corresponds to people's increasing need for self-actualization. This, in turn, is connected to a growing assertiveness and many expressions of the desire for emancipation of individuals. One of the consequences of these changes is the rising demand for so-called flexible labor and a considerable increase in the participation rate of women in the workforce. On top of that, the size of the average household continued to decrease. These changes had a major impact on the population composition of regional housing market areas.

The net effect of these changes boosted the big cities. The 'compact-city policy' followed on the heels of these processes. The position of the cities in the national migration pattern was strengthened. In combination with the continued influx of foreigners, which had been continuously strong since the mid-1970s, this meant that during the second half of the 1980s, the big cities saw their population increase (Figure 3.1).

As far as the national migration pattern is concerned, these developments were detrimental to the growth centers. The suburbs enjoyed a renewed interest once the economy improved and the market for owner-occupier housing climbed out of its recession. The appeal of the suburbs acts as a counterforce, which results in migration effects when the economy peaks. This shows up in the statistics for the end of the 1980s, when the net outmigration from the cities increased once more. In the meantime, some of the growth centers have acquired a much more negative image than they had initially. Within the context of the metropolitan housing market, these residental environments have slipped into a similar position as the least-favored neighborhoods of the large cities. The central cities no longer have a monopoly on social problems. In general, the growth centers have become increasingly similar to the big cities (Kruythoff 1989; Jobse et al. 1991).

In comparison to American and some British cities, the social problems in the large Dutch cities and the growth centers are relatively modest. This corresponds to the fact that the big Dutch cities had not developed such a one-sided 'Fordist' industrial profile as, for instance, the British cities in the West-Midlands and the northwestern regions. The transition to a 'post-Fordist' economy has therefore not led to a similar spectacular decline (for the British cities, see e.g., Martin 1988). In addition, the levels of, and especially access to social services were considerably higher in the Netherlands, and until now these have not been decreased as much. Also, the changes in the social structure have been less fundamental. In comparison with the American 'underclass', the conditions of the low-income groups in the Netherlands remain considerably more favorable (Engbersen 1990). In recent years, the general socioeconomic level of the large cities even seems to be improving (Rohde & Bertholet 1990; Musterd & Ostendorf 1991). Anderiesen & Reijndorp (1989) state that the comparison of some of the poorest Dutch neighborhoods with the conditions in American ghettos is therefore completely unfounded. In the big Dutch cities, the further decline of the social structure can still

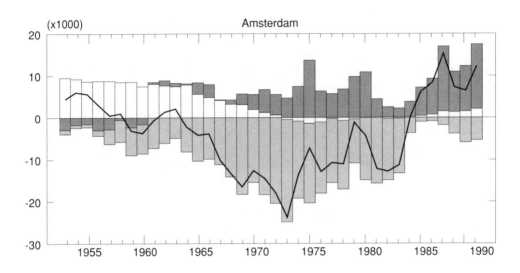

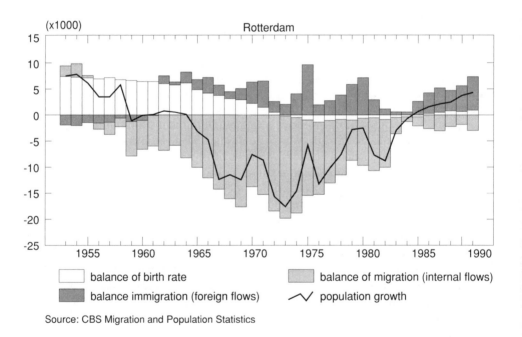

Figure 3.1   *Components of the population growth of the three biggest cities, 1953-1990*
(continued on next page)

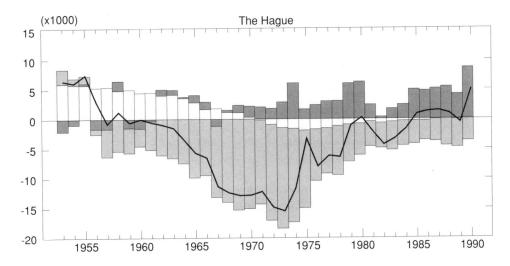

Figure 3.1   (continued)

be stopped by an effective prevention policy. Some neighborhoods in American and English cities are already beyond this stage (WRR 1990).

Section 3.3 deals in more detail with the impact of policy on the housing situation as it developed. Section 3.4 elaborates on the population developments outlined above.

3.3   The housing situation

The population size of the big cities has changed substantially during the past few decades. For twenty years, the number of inhabitants decreased continuously. Between 1965 and 1985, the large cities together lost 543,000 people, which meant a population decline that ranged from 22 to 24 percent in each of the four cities. In addition, the image of the big cities deteriorated.

More recently, because of the increase in residential construction activity in the cities and the simultaneous decrease in the growth centers and the suburbs, a slight increase has been recorded, or at least a stabilization of the population size (Jobse & Musterd 1989).

Figure 3.2 shows that during the 1970s, the housing production rate of the large cities was far below the national rate; at that time, the overall production peaked. The national growth of the housing stock ranged from two to four percent annually. In the large cities, new construction accounted for an annual increase of less than one percent, and the net effect of this was even substantially lower due to the high replacement

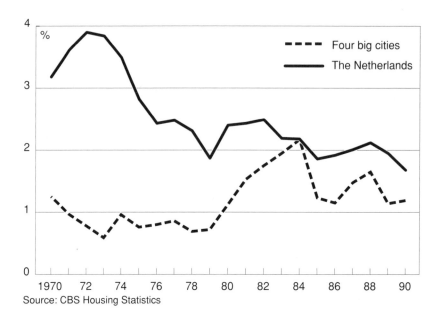

Source: CBS Housing Statistics

Figure 3.2   *Residential construction in percentages of the housing stock in the Nether-*
lands as a whole and in the four big cities, 1970-1990

factor. The housing stock of Utrecht and The Hague hardly expanded at all during
the 1970s. Their total net growth was less than four percent over the ten-year period.
The production in Amsterdam and Rotterdam was one to two percent higher.

This low output had nothing to do with the demand for housing; the demand was
large enough, as can easily be inferred from the long waiting lists of people in need
of housing. The fluctuations in productivity, and the ways in which the supply side
of the market reacted to the demand, were linked to the changing role of the private
sector. They were also tied to political ideas on where the expansion of the housing
stock could best be realized, as well as to local policies concerning the target groups
for new housing.

The extensive regulation of the housing market, low yields on investment, and a
growing range of alternative investment opportunities were the negative factors that
guided the private sector away from housing. Although the social housing sector
expanded after 1950 like never before, this could only partially compensate for the
decline of private-sector activities. New construction was also hindered by the shortage
of available construction sites.

During the 1970s, the production figures of new housing in the big cities dropped
to record lows. The main reasons for this were, on the one hand, the opinion that

the big cities had reached the limits of their expansion (Derde Nota 1976) - which was proved to be wrong afterwards - and the preoccupation with urban renewal. The shift towards the social sector also had major repercussions on the composition of the urban housing stock in the long run. The private rental sector lost its once dominant position, while the share of the social rental sector increased threefold. The owner-occupier sector did grow somewhat in most cities, but by Dutch standards - and certainly by international standards - it remained small in size. Residential construction for the higher-income groups remained a low priority for a long time, and therefore many opportunities to construct more differentiated residential environments were missed. Consequently, the differences between the big cities, on the one side, and their adjacent municipalities, on the other, increased sharply (WRR 1990).

By 1980, the big cities of the Randstad accelerated their housing production in an attempt to overcome their disadvantage. Slowly but steadily, they are paying more attention to the owner-occupier sector. They are being pressured by the decline of the economic base of many of their services and facilities. The population loss became too large, and the demand for housing by middle- and higher-income groups grew too excessive to resist. They withdrew their initial support for the growth-center policy because they realized that the expansion of the growth centers undercut their viability. The production of housing was stepped up, but the cities proved to be unable to keep building the high volume of new housing they produced in the mid-1980s (Figure 3.2). Still, the average production figures remain clearly above the - very low - level of the 1970s.

The preoccupation with social housing diminished during the 1980s. However, the construction of more expensive dwellings still needs to be made politically palatable by including social housing in new, expensive complexes. For decades, Amsterdam in particular maintained a policy that has been distinctly unfriendly towards owner-occupiers. Consequently, the ownership sector accounts for only ten percent of the stock at this time. In comparable West European cities, the equivalent sector commonly accounts for a multiple of this.

The small number of more expensive dwellings deters the upward filtering of more affluent households. Thus, many households with a somewhat higher income live in relatively inexpensive dwellings (Nota Volkshuisvesting 1988; Van Kempen & Teule 1990). Of the pre-war inexpensive rental sector, 33 percent of the dwellings are occupied by households with an above-modal income. In the post-war inexpensive sector, this percentage is as high as 41 percent (Van Kempen & Teule 1990). Although this situation is far from ideal from the point of view of a fair distribution of housing, it does have the advantage that the emergence of concentrations of poverty and the stigmatizion of residential areas is being prevented.

A special contribution to the population development and the residential construction processes is made by the administrative fragmentation of the metropolitan areas in the Netherlands. Dutch municipalities have a high degree of autonomy in comparison to other countries. Since many 'markets', such as the housing market and the labor market, have become regional entities, the need to adapt the administrative jurisdictions is increasingly felt. The consolidation of administrative jurisdictions is therefore a frequently recurring item on the political agenda in the Netherlands (e.g. Van der Wusten 1991). So far, this has not resulted in any significant changes. The situation that municipalities have the authority to set their own goals, by means of their construction policy and housing allocation policy, persists. And in many cases these policies overtly conflict with those of an adjacent municipality.

The recent halt of the population loss is not really a good indicator of an increased appeal of the big city. Both the pessimism of the 1970s ('the urban crisis') and the more recent optimism about the appeal of the large cities ('the new vitality') may not be entirely unfounded, but seen from some distance, both appear to have been somewhat exaggerated.

The 1960s and 1970s were indeed characterized by a rapid decline in the population of the big cities. Especially the higher- and the middle-income groups dwindled. Some have argued that this decrease occurred because these groups no longer considered the big cities attractive. But from the evidence presented above, one may also conclude that the poorly functioning housing market was party to the change, itself a result of the failure of public policy. The quantitative and qualitative shortages of the housing market limited the choice in the urban housing markets and stimulated suburbanization. Many of the outmigrants did not make a positive choice for suburban living. In many cases, they were forced to move (Van Geenhuizen et al. 1981; Elekan & Van der Heijden 1981). The aging of the housing stock, the bias in the construction program towards building for the lower-income groups, and the supply of housing that consisted predominantly of units that did not meet the preferences of the higher-income groups were strong incentives for the process of 'filtering down' (Musterd 1991). All developments that could have helped to compensate these trends were hindered. This applied especially to the urban renewal policy, which aimed - largely successfully - at maintaining the improved neighborhoods as areas for lower-income groups. The renewal of the working-class neighborhoods, originally built in the late 19th century, has therefore hardly generated an influx of higher-income groups for a long time (Ruimtelijke Verkenningen 1987).

The urban policy-makers showed themselves to be true sorceror's apprentices who only much later recognized the effects of their actions. Both the volume and the selective character of the migration was underestimated because of their initially over-optimistic perception of the competitive position of the big cities.

In the meantime the situation has changed. The recent population increase shows the impact of new (also foreign) demand for housing, of adaptations of policies, and of demographic processes (e.g. the growth of the number of small households). In addition, the economic recession of the early 1980s has left its mark. The outmigration of potential suburbanites to owner-occupier dwellings outside the cities slowed down. For that reason, the recent population growth has not to be welcomed too enthusiastically. In contrast to some foreign cities, the impact of gentrification processes in the big Dutch cities is in general still quite modest. This is because there are few suitable residential areas. Moreover, it is because the conversion of rental units into owner-occupier dwellings has been hindered in order to protect the inexpensive rental sector in the big cities.

3.4 Population developments

The exodus from the large cities caused not only a substantial decline in the size of the population, but also a drastic change in its composition. When the modal-income groups and the households with an income above that level left, the cities weakened socioeconomically. And the family households lost their once-dominant position, in spite of the influx of large numbers of foreign - especially Turkish and Moroccan - families.

Socioeconomic trends
During the 1960s and 1970s, the big cities developed into ever more complex mosaics of minorities. It is not so much the question of whether or not the cities favored the socioeconomically weaker groups in their policy. Rather, they found themselves more or less forced to house the poorest households. They assumed the responsibility for social housing; they later shared this task with the growth centers. Suburban communities frequently managed to ignore the housing needs of the weakest socioeconomic groups in their residential construction programs (Ostendorf 1989).

Economic restructuring has also had a major impact on the social composition of the big cities. The erosion of traditional industries in the large cities, and the economic recession of around 1980, brought on extensive unemployment. High unemployment rates prevailed among the lowest-income groups and those with limited education and training. The growth of modern firms and the recovery of the economy during the second half of the 1980s have not yet led to a substantial decrease in the unemployment figures. The fact that the 'new economy' creates not only jobs for the well-educated but also many low-paid jobs - also for those with limited training - (Sassen-Koob 1986) has not yet eased the problem. The weak socioeconomic profile of the cities is further accentuated by the continued influx of foreign immigrants.

One of the empirical indicators of the economic plight of the cities is the percentage of the labor force that is currently inactive. In 1989, this applied to 17 percent of the labor force in Amsterdam and Rotterdam, compared to ten percent nationally. The scores of suburban regions, on the other hand, are commonly below the national average (De Smidt 1991).

Demographic trends
In recent years, a new type of household has gained the upper hand in the population structure, namely the one-person household. In 1981, only 18 percent of the Dutch

households belonged to this type. By 1990, this percentage had increased to 23 percent. The number of married couples decreased by approximately 13 percent in the large cities between 1981 and 1985. In large parts of these cities, the singles have become the dominant population group (Jobse 1991). The single person has become the cornerstone of metropolitan society, displacing the family (Brunt 1990, p. 21).

Although this demographic change is most clear in the inner cities and the adjacent 19th century working-class areas, it is not limited to these neighborhoods. Like other demographic changes that started in the central parts of the cities, this one has spread like a wave from the center to the peripheral housing estates, and beyond into the suburbs (Table 3.1 and Figure 3.3)

The single persons were predominantly concentrated in the pre-war areas of the big cities during the 1960s. Now they make up 25 to over 40 percent of the households in the more recently built neighborhoods and in some of the suburbs. When we consider the entire 1980-1989 period for the three metropolitan areas together, it becomes clear that the highest rate of growth has been recorded in the growth centers. This is partly due to supply-side factors. In many of the older neighborhoods, singles households are already in the majority. A further relative increase is therefore becoming more difficult to attain. But the outmigration of singles to more recent neighborhoods is not only, and presumably not even mainly, caused by various forms of pressure. Also among the category of single persons, there is a wide variety of residential preferences. Even the young adults among them do not all consider the central city as the 'promised land' (Beaujon & Wöltgens 1984). In many cases, the migration of young people to the big cities does not express a deliberate choice for these residential environments. It can also be the result of a restrictive construction and allocation policy in some suburban municipalities (Ostendorf 1985).

Table 3.1   *The development of the number of singles in sub-areas of the urban regions of Amsterdam, Rotterdam, and The Hague (percentages)*

| | Amsterdam | | Rotterdam | | The Hague | |
	1981	1989	1981	1989	1981	1989
Inner city	62	79	41	43	48	72
1870-1905	49	64	32	49	44	48
1906-1944	33	53	34	46	33	43
1945-1959	30	45	31	44	34	36
1960-present	28	36	21	33	29	44
Suburbs	23	32	20	24	23	33
Growth centers	17	27	14	23	9	23
Total	32	44	26	34	30	39

Source: WBO-CBS, data processed by Stedelijke Netwerken

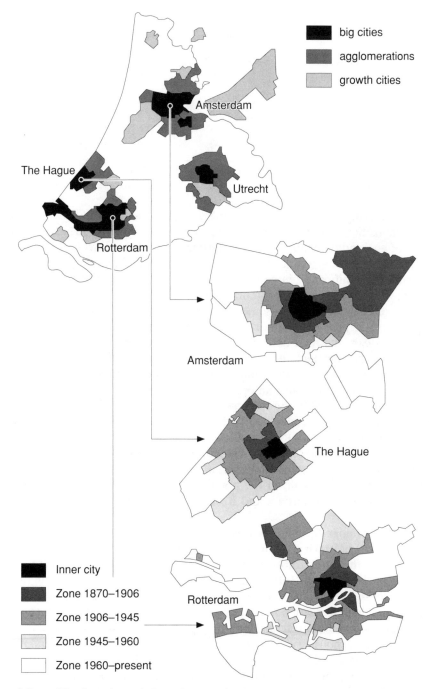

Figure 3.3   The location of the sub-areas in the metropolitan regions

Table 3.2   *Growth and decline (-) of national inmigration and outmigration, percentages*

	1989 vs 1985		1985 vs 1980		1980 vs 1975	
	in	out	in	out	in	out
Amsterdam	- 5	12	35	-20	-17	-21
Rotterdam	1	1	16	- 8	- 5	-32
The Hague	5	10	- 1	- 7	6	-29
Utrecht	2	11	4	-19	-10	-21

Source: CBS Migratiestatistiek; data processed by Stedelijke Netwerken

The exodus of young families during the 1960s and 1970s has also fundamentally altered the age composition of the big cities. Young adults (20-39 years old) and the elderly (60 years of age and older) are relatively strongly represented, while the number of children (0-14 years of age) and the number of middle-aged people (40-59 years old) have decreased significantly in comparison to the national average. In addition, in the latter two groups, the ethnic minorities of foreign descent are over-represented. Although foreigners account for some 15 to 20 percent of the overall population of the large cities, the proportion among school age children is as high as 35-40 percent.

During the 1980s, the dual developments of de-greening and graying of the large cities reversed, and now the middle-aged population is expanding (Hoogvliet & Jobse 1989). An important factor in this trend is that the post-war baby-boom cohort is now reaching middle age. It remains an open question, however, to what extent this is a permanent change. In 1989, the national migration balance of the cities - with the exception of Rotterdam - suddenly shifted, showing an increasingly negative outcome (Table 3.2). Even the continuous trend of a rapidly diminishing outmigration since 1975 seems to have shifted direction. The economic recovery in the late 1980s seems to provide a renewed stimulus for suburbanization, while the decreasing urban residential construction seems to slow down the population influx, which was of considerable volume, especially in Amsterdam and Rotterdam, around 1985.

The development under discussion proves to be age-specific, although it does not support the trend towards bolstering the middle-aged population groups in the city (Figure 3.4). In all cities, the outmigration of people in the 30 to 49 age cohort increases very rapidly. But in the cities of Rotterdam, The Hague, and Utrecht the inmigration of young adults (15-29 years old) is increasing faster than the outmigration of this group. It is remarkable that this was not the case in Amsterdam - although the city is considered to harbor an uncommon attraction for young people. This cannot be blamed solely on deficiencies in the housing construction, since Amsterdam's production output during the 1980s has been consistently above the average for the four largest cities.

Although the group of people 15 to 29 years old has always been the largest single age group among the migrants, and large enough to fully compensate for the loss of

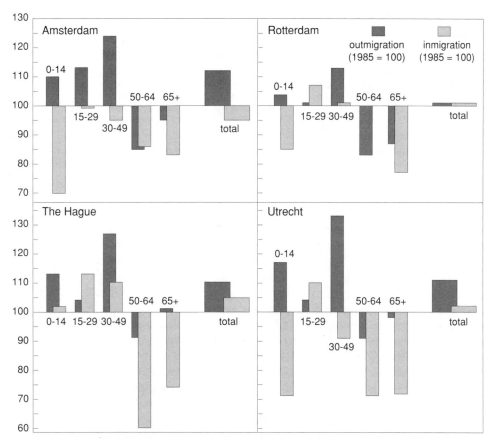

Source: CBS Migration Statistics, data processed by Stedelijke Netwerken

Figure 3.4   *Inmigration and outmigration in 1989 as ratios of 1985, in each of the four big cities, by age category*

people 30 to 49 years old, this situation has changed (Table 3.3). If only these two age groups are considered - they jointly account for between 81 percent (Rotterdam) and 92 percent (Utrecht) of all inmigrants, and between 71 percent (the three biggest cities) and 78 percent (Utrecht) of all outmigrants - it becomes clear how large the shift really is. The absolute volume of net outmigration of people 30 to 49 years old has almost doubled in each of the four cities.

Table 3.3   *Migration balance (intranational migration) of population aged 15-29 and 30-49, and both age groups together, by city in 1985 and 1989*

| | 15-29 years | | 30-49 years | | 15-49 years | |
	1985	1989	1985	1989	1985	1989
Amsterdam	5850	4275	-2315	-4330	3535	- 55
Rotterdam	1010	1590	- 695	-1215	315	375
The Hague	- 260	405	-1360	-2190	-1620	-1785
Utrecht	1515	2025	-1065	-2115	450	- 90

Source: CBS Migratiestatistiek; data processed by Stedelijke Netwerken

Ethnic immigration trends

A third significant change in the housing function of the large cities is the remarkably rapid increase in the number of households arriving from abroad; these people may or may not have the Dutch nationality. A disproportionately large part of this group moved to the big cities (Figure 3.1). Some 20 percent of the population of the big cities currently consists of foreigners. In contrast to the United States, for instance, there are hardly any expressions of extreme segregation in Dutch cities. In the United States, it is no exception to find neighborhoods where 70 to 100 percent of the population consists of immigrants (Clark 1986). This does not imply, however, that in other respects there are no sharp dividing lines in Dutch cities, for instance with respect to the choice of schools (Clark & Dieleman 1990).

Between 1970 and 1982, the size of the foreign population increased explosively because of family unification and the massive wave of immigration that preceded the independence of Surinam. After 1982, the immigration from Third World countries decreased sharply. This eventually proved to be a temporary relapse, partly because of the downturn of the economy. During the second half of the 1980s, the immigration increased once more, and peaked in 1990. Apart from migrants from the more traditional sources of immigrants, such as Turkey, Morocco, and Surinam, there is a rapidly growing number of refugees from countries with deep economic and political problems. Although it is attempted to disperse these immigrants, a substantial number of them find their way - legally or illegally - to the big cities.

The increase in the foreign population is not only the direct consequence of immigration but is largely due to natural increase. The very large second generation of foreigners has in the meantime reached the age of family formation. And although the fertility levels of the foreign population have substantially decreased, their score is still way above that of the Dutch population (Nusselder et al. 1990).

Also the distribution of the Turkish and Moroccan households within the big cities shows a wave-like pattern, starting from the center. At the moment there is a rapid growth in the number of foreigners living in the least expensive parts of the post-war housing stock. But a massive migration to the suburban zone surrounding the large cities has not yet occurred. For the time being, most of the foreign population seems to remain tied to the big cities with their relatively inexpensive housing stock because of their low incomes. For the same reason, they are focused on those growth centers that have become relatively unattractive, like Lelystad. Of all the people moving to Lelystad in 1989, some 15 percent came from abroad. At the same time, of all those moving to Almere, which enjoys a stronger socioeconomic position, only five percent originated abroad. In 1988, the figures were much the same. Given the limited demand for unskilled labor in the cities, and in the peripheral growth centers as well, this is a classic example of a 'housing trap'. The rapid growth in the foreign population, combined with their orientation to the residential environments listed above, will clearly mark their demographic and socioeconomic development over the next few decades. Amsterdam, for instance, expects that the foreign population will increase to 34 percent of the total population by the year 2010.

3.5   Developments in residential areas

The differentiation of the metropolitan population expresses itself spatially in a different pattern than before. Until the early 1970s, the lowest socioeconomic classes had been concentrated in the private rental sector in the inner cities and the 19th century neighborhoods. Contrary to what might have been expected, these groups were underrepresented in the sizeable post-war social housing sector. This sector was relatively expensive in spite of deep subsidies; the quality is good, and the units were built when construction costs were high. Consequently, for a long time this sector was dominated by a skilled-working class population and the people in the low to middle eschelons of the service industries.

This situation changed gradually after 1970. Private urban renewal in the inner cities, public urban renewal in the 19th century neighborhoods and in some of the early 20th century areas, as well as new construction on the periphery of the city and in the suburban zone changed their relative positions. This also altered the residential function of the older and of the relatively recent residential areas. In the big cities, these changes brought about by the housing policy led more frequently to downward filtering than to filtering up.

The most remarkable exception to this general trend was the development of the inner cities and some adjacent areas. Uncertainty about the future function of these areas, at the time mostly commercial functions or a mixture of commercial and residential uses, had resulted in widespread planning blight. When it became clear during the 1970s that the areas were destined for both residential and commercial functions, they revitalized. Housing turned from a 'loser' into a 'winner' sector (Den Draak 1985). Except for policy changes, evolving locational preferences also played a role. These resulted in a spatial dispersal of economic activities to the urban periphery and suburban areas (Jobse & Needham 1987; Hessels 1988) and thereby diminished the pressure on inner-city areas.

Change was especially pronounced in the very large inner city of Amsterdam, which combines a wide array of economic and cultural activities with its historic heritage. Because of private and public urban renewal it became a very popular residential area among the well-educated, albeit not always high-income singles and two-person households between 20 and 40 years of age. The increasing quality of the area coincides with a gradual increase in the number of financially better-off households (Musterd et al. 1988)

Hoffschulte & Musterd (1989) concluded that in Amsterdam the inner city and a few prestigious residential neighborhoods were among the few areas able to capture the middle- and higher-income groups. But this is not true of the great majority of Amsterdam's neighborhoods. They fulfill a very limited role for higher-income groups as an area of transition; in most cases these households reside there only temporarily. In this respect, the new urban vitality seems to have a narrow base with respect to housing.

It is remarkable that more recently built residential areas, which could be expected to occupy a relatively high position in the hierarchy of neighborhoods, have apparently little to offer the affluent households. Patijn et al. (1978) noted earlier that also peripheral housing areas in Rotterdam also functioned as transitional areas.

Although the 19th century and early 20th century neighborhoods have been the sites of extensive urban renewal operations, their effects have been completely different than in inner-city areas. Outside the inner city, urban renewal was carried out almost exclusively by the public sector, which aimed to provide affordable housing for the current population. In this respect the policy was successful. Due to deep subsidies, in combination with reconstruction and renovation activities, the areas remained fairly accessible to lower-income groups.

Nevertheless, the effects of intervention are diverse, and often deviate substantially from the policy goals. In most of the neighborhoods, physical improvement has not succeeded in making them more attractive to the original population, that is, Dutch families with a modal income or less. The number of families has declined sharply, in spite of urban renewal. Families form a minority among the households in the area, and in addition, most of them have an ethnic background.

Especially in Amsterdam, the 19th century neighborhoods house only a small proportion of families. With respect to the share of the single-person households, these areas now look very much alike the inner city. The situation is still different in The Hague; there a substantial number of families still live in renewed 19th century areas. But when the long-term trend is considered, there is a clear convergence tendency; with respect to the increase in non-family households, the urban renewal areas are becoming like the inner-city neighborhoods.

The influx of small households along with the decrease in families of Dutch descent in the older neighborhoods caused fierce controversy until the early 1980s. The authorities initially believed that this development had to be stopped or even reversed. The inflow of new population groups was assumed to undermine existing facilities. That, in turn, was feared to have negative social effects, leading to less safe neighborhoods, social conflict, and disintegration (Kok 1982). But the policy that aimed to achieve a balanced population structure was rarely successful. As so often, social developments proved to be stronger than policy. But it is doubtful whether this ought to be regretted. Even after the completion of the urban renewal operations, most 19th century neighborhoods are hardly suitable for families with children. The situation is quite different for other types of households (Van Engelsdorp Gastelaars & Vijgen 1990).

The 19th century working-class areas, which were still functioning as such in the 1950s, have gradually developed into the residential areas for those small households who appreciate the heterogeneity and anonymity they offer (Anderiesen & Reijndorp 1989). Thus the development that initially leads through a period of disintegration may eventually result in a new social balance.

Although the 19th century neighborhoods as a whole are dominated by low-income groups, some prove to offer a - temporary - attractive residential environment to households with an above-modal income (Anderiesen & Reijndorp 1989). The socioeconomic decline of the urban renewal areas seems to have passed its low point. The proportion of the households with a relatively low income is decreasing and the number of households with a very high income is rising (Rohde & Bertholet 1990; Musterd & Ostendorf 1991). This is more likely to be an expression of incumbent upgrading than of gentrification.

During the past few years, it has become increasingly clear that the major drawbacks of older neighborhoods are not their physical deficiencies but primarily their social problems. Relationships among neighbors are often determined by mutual feelings of fear and insecurity (Van der Pennen 1990; Wuertz 1990). The lack of social cohesion causes indifference with respect to the residential environment, in itself one of the causes of the total deterioration of the areas (Geurts & Gramberg 1989; Weerts 1990). With respect to this, Van Engelsdorp Gastelaars introduced the concept of the neighborhood with a dominant lifestyle. According to him, the construction policy should promote the function of neighborhoods for people with compatible lifestyles. More recently, such ideas have also been propounded in political circles and in the world of housing specialists.

The indirect effects of neighborhood decline and urban renewal on the development of the post-war areas should not be underestimated. Due to a long period of rent control, the rents in the earlier post-war neighborhoods have become relatively low, which has substantially improved the price-quality ratio in these areas. These neighborhoods were initially inaccessible to the lowest-income groups, but slowly they have come within their reach. Since the second half of the 1970s, neighborhoods built during the 1950s have attracted people from urban renewal areas, ethnic minorities, and other vulnerable population groups. The originally rather homogeneous population composition - predominantly people with a modal or an above-modal income - has been substantially changed; however, the actual extent of the change differs widely among neighborhoods.

A more heterogeneous population implies a range of lifestyles and residential behavior. Sometimes this enriches an area, and sometimes it leads to conflicts and social problems. On the basis of her research in Amsterdam, Van Kempen (1987, pp. 36) concludes that heterogeneity and instability have become the normal conditions in the post-war neighborhoods. She assumes that this is a permanent 'problem'.

In spite of their evident problems, the first generation of post-war neighborhoods seems to have good potential for a controlled functional change. Their favorable price-quality ratio could turn them into attractive and stable neighborhoods for low-income groups. The precondition for this is careful urban management (Dieleman & Jobse 1991).

The high-rise areas built in the 1960s and 1970s reveal a variety of problems. The situation is, however, not as bad as would seem from the abundant publicity about a number of individual problem complexes, among which Amsterdam's Bijlmermeer has become the most notorious. From these stories, many have gleaned the impression the high-rise is synonymous with problems. This is clearly not realistic (Hoekveld & Kersloot 1986; Van Kempen & Musterd 1991). Many high-rise neighborhoods prove to be viable areas. For instance, Omoord, Rotterdam's equivalent of the Bijlmermeer, is even in relatively great demand. But high-rise neighborhoods are particularly vulnerable, and an attentive and adequate management policy is very important to keep them problem-free.

Apart from the quality of management, there are several other relevant factors that determine the viability of high-rise areas: e.g., the price-quality ratio, the availability of single-family homes, and the quality of construction. The attempts to achieve a better quality than that typical of the preceding generation of dwellings usually resulted in relatively expensive housing. Often the price was only marginally below that of single-family homes in suburban communities or growth centers. During the peak of the 1970s, the emphasis of residential construction clearly shifted towards the single-family home; approximately one million of these were built within ten years. Contrary to what at least some of the planners had expected, even the high-quality multi-family structures could hardly compete with the single-family homes. The great majority of families prefer to live in a single-family home.

In areas with a generous supply of single-family homes, the high-rises never got a fair chance to prove their quality. For some complexes it was hard to find tenants from the minute they were completed. Others were rented but suffered from a high turnover rate. Some of the high-rise complexes of the 1960s and 1970s have such a weak position in the housing market that they can be labeled 'waiting rooms' or 'reservations' for groups with a temporarily or permanently weak housing-market position. Tenants who (still) lack opportunities to move elsewhere move into these complexes, but (often) only for a short time (Briene et al. 1989).

The fact that some of the high-rise complexes do not cater to the needs of those for whom they were originally intended, however, should not been taken too seriously. The long-lasting and one-sided orientation toward the housing needs of family-type households, and the consequent neglect of the needs of other types of households, has caused tensions in the urban housing markets. For many singles and other non-family households, the high-rise complexes offered the prospect of good housing for the first time. Also a substantial segment of the rapidly growing group of foreign immigrants found solace in this sector. In fact, the high-rise sector provided them with an alternative to the private rental sector, where the groups with a relatively weak housing market position had traditionally satisfied their housing needs. The rapid decline in the private rental sector seemed to endanger this function. The high-rise sector has provided the necessary compensation.

In the most recently built residential areas (on the urban periphery and in centrally located urban renewal areas), an increasing proportion of new construction is now being developed as owner-occupier housing or as expensive rental units; especially the national government has been promoting this shift. But because the new construction remains marginal in comparison to the present stock, the prevalence of inexpensive rental housing will hardly diminish.

The suburbs are the logical extension of the peripheral neighborhoods, in the sense that the proportion of owner-occupier units has traditionally been larger there. Most suburbs deliberately tried to remain somewhat exclusive by building a high proportion of owner-occupier dwellings.

The relationship between the population development of an area and the proportion of owner-occupier dwellings links it intimately with the performance of the national economy. This is clearly reflected in the fluctuating rates of in- and outmigration. A significantly greater proportion of the increased number of migrants from the cities settled in the remainder of the Randstad and the rest of the country. When the people who move with other household members are taken into account, the big cities show a net migration loss of almost 3,000 persons (up 67 percent from 1985) to the rest of the country outside the Randstad. The net loss to the remainder of the Randstad amounts to over 18,000 persons (up 23 percent compared with 1985). There is also an increase of persons migrating alone to the remainder of the Randstad. In 1985, the migration balance of the big cities in relation to the remainder of the Randstad was still positive for this group. In that year the cities gained almost 2,500 single migrants. By 1989 this had turned into a small negative net balance of 275 persons.

Because the outgrowth of most suburbs has been more gradual than that of the growth centers, many consider the suburbs to be of a superior quality. In spite of the decline of the typical suburban household - the family -, the demand for housing in such communities remains many time greater than what is available. This causes the house prices to increase, which further supports their 'prestige' image. Quality differences are certainly a factor in the explanation of the overspill of households from the growth centers to suburbs. The growth centers, originally intended to stop the migration from the cities to the suburbs, which the planners saw as a negative development, prove to be merely a way station on the road to the suburbs (cf. Jansen & Van Noortwijk 1987). The individual households still reach their favored destination, albeit in a roundabout way.

The growth centers that are linked to the large cities are far from a homogeneous type. In general, however, these settlements have experienced rapid shifts in their functions. Initially, their population largely consisted of families who were better off than the lowest-income households. But a number of these growth centers (e.g. Lelystad,

Capelle aan de IJssel) rapidly reached the limits of their expansion. Among the migrants to such municipalities, households and individuals with a weak social position, form an increasing share. Their social situation typifies not only their housing-market options (because of their limited financial means, and because of their low priority rating in the housing allocation system), but also their labor-market position. The proportion of handicapped persons drawing workmen's compensation benefits and the share of the unemployed among the migrants to the growth centers are very large. The function of these growth centers is shifting in the direction of an environment for starters in the housing market.

The literature suggests the existence of a rather strong relationship between the type of household and the preferred residential environment. Vijgen & Van Engelsdorp Gastelaars (1991) differentiate among urban, suburban, and ambivalent households. But they also suggest that the orientation is multi-dimensional. A high degree of labor-market participation as well as the absence of a partner both lead to a strong urban orientation; the presence of children in a household coincides with a preference for a suburban location. Because these dimensions are not mutually exclusive, there is room for ambivalent behavior. Some types of households can be positioned easily. Single persons, for instance, are urban in orientation. Traditional families and those seniors who (still) work are typical suburbanites. But single-parent families and households with two wage earners are much more ambivalent.

An understanding of such relationships is crucial to be able to come to grips with the changing functions of residential environments in metropolitan areas. Still, it remains difficult to make predictions on the basis of this knowledge.

The big city seems to be in a favorable position with respect to the current demographic and socio-cultural developments. These still lead to an increase of the share of small households, especially of singles. But the growth of the single-person households has already peaked. The increase in the share of these households in the Netherlands amounted to 19 percent between 1981 and 1985, but the growth rate declined to 5 percent between 1985 and 1990.

A second reason why predictions are difficult to make is that the concept of 'urban living' is dynamic. In some respects, some suburbs are becoming increasingly urban. This applies, for instance, to the availability and accessibility of services, such as shops with late business hours, child care, restaurants, etc. Also important, especially with regard to households with two wage earners, is the increased individual mobility. Often such households own two cars. Then, living outside but near big cities forms no significant obstacle to using the metropolitan facilities and services.

A further increase in the number of households with two wage earners should be expected, because despite its recent growth, the female labor market participation rate remains relatively low. But as the category expands, this type of household can become much more diversified and thereby demonstrate preferences for a much wider range of residential environments. The presence of children will be an important factor in the pattern of preferences, but it need not become the central explanatory variable.

3.6   Concluding discussion

Since the 1960s, the big cities of the Randstad have been undergoing a transformation that has altered their economic and social outlook. With respect to housing, the function of the cities has changed fundamentally as a result of general social developments as well as the housing policy of the cities and their surrounding municipalities. The most important change of the past thirty years was the acute rise in demand for housing by singles, single-parent families, and ethnic minorities. These groups comprise relatively many deprived households. Along with the advent of new types of households, and partly as a consequence of this, a spatial differentiation of the various types of households occurred.

The cities developed into residential environments where young adults, the elderly, singles, ethnic minorities, and low-income groups were overrepresented. At the same time, the population of the suburbs became increasingly dominated by families with a median income or above. It remains to be seen whether this contrast will be temporary or develop into a permanent characteristic of the metropolitan areas.

The revitalization of the large cities during the 1980s and the concurrent population growth (especially because of foreign immigration), is currently being threatened by renewed suburbanization. The significantly different household composition (brought about by the increase in the share of households with an urban orientation) seems to prevent a new wave of suburbanization similar to that of 1965-1975. There are also other reasons to expect that the contrast between central city and suburbs will decrease rather than increase. For instance, it seems that the growth in the number of singles is approaching its peak. In addition, the number of singles is now also rising in suburban communities. In general, the population of the municipalities adjacent to the cities, which often went through a period of explosive population growth, is becoming more balanced.

In comparison with the migration pattern of the 1960s and 1970s, the present one is more complex. The traditional pattern, whereby (young) singles move to the big cities while families go to the suburbs and growth centers, seems to have been expanded by a number of other variants. The preference for urban or suburban living is less clearly differentiated by household characteristics than before, while at the same time the impact of lifestyle has increased. In balance, the patterns correspond less to the stereotypes. For instance, the flow of migrants to the growth centers has become much more diverse over the past few years. Families still form the main component, but they are accompanied to a much larger extent than in the 1970s by the elderly, singles, and ethnic minorities.

Some tendencies resemble the development of American suburbs since the 1960s, which were characterized by Masotti & Hadden (1973) as the urbanization of the suburbs. One of the characteristic trends is an increasing heterogeneity of the suburban population. The suburb is no longer 'a green ghetto dedicated to the elite' (Mumford 1966, pp. 561), and not even 'just a family place' (Masotti 1973, pp. 19).

Not only the suburbs are experiencing changes that reduce the contrasts between the cities and their surrounding areas; the same is true of the big cities. The changes there apply to housing policy and the approach to urban renewal. In addition to the continuation of social housing construction and urban renewal for low-income groups, the development of high-quality housing for high-income groups has been put back on the agenda. Partly due to this change, and in part because of the improving economy, the socioeconomic level of the big cities seems to have increased.

Although the developments outlined above have slowed down the strong segmentation processes, the contrasts between the big cities and their adjacent areas will not rapidly disappear. The current differences in the quality of housing and residential environments are so large that it will take a long time before the convergence tendencies (or the weakening divergence) that have been going on since the mid-1980s will yield significant effects. That also applies to the change in size of the households. Although the share of singles in the total population has increased in the areas outside the big cities, the differences between the two types of areas remain considerable in this respect. In addition, extreme differences persist between the big cities and the suburbs in terms of housing stock, residential environment, and the services and facilities provided. This implies that the discrepancies in attractiveness and accessibility will probably remain. That will reinforce the spatial segmentation of the various population groups.

The changing residential construction policy and urban renewal approaches will have no more than a marginal impact on the residential function of the large cities. In spite of the boom in residential construction in the 1980s, its volume in the large cities remains modest (an addition of one to two percent of the existing stock per year). Therefore, even a major shift in the differentiation of new housing toward owner-occupier and single-family homes could only have an impact of any significance in the long term. Even so, no such spectacular change should be expected, given the local political balances and the nature of the available construction sites.

The question remains whether or not the reduction of the contrasts in housing situations between the large cities and their adjacent areas should be a policy goal. One of the most remarkable changes in housing demand during the past few decades, has been its increased differentiation. Seen in that light, the wide variety of housing environments in the metropolitan regions is an asset rather than a problem.

References

Anderiesen, G. & A. Reijndorp (1989), Rondkomen of vooruitkomen: Ghetto's in Nederland? In: F. Bovenkerk en L. Brunt (eds), De andere stad: Achter de façade van de nieuwe stedelijke vitaliteit. Werkstukken Stedelijke Netwerken 16, pp. 159-186. Amsterdam: Stedelijke Netwerken.
Atlas van Nederland (1984), Deel 1: Bevolking. 's-Gravenhage: SDU-Uitgeverij.
Beaujon, E. & E. Wöltgens (1984), Raakt de suburb haar kinderen kwijt. Amsterdam: Instituut voor Sociale Geografie, Universiteit van Amsterdam.

Berg, A. van den, Th. van Eijk & P. Misdorp (1988), Non-activiteit in de grootstedelijke gebieden in kaart gebracht. Wetenschappelijke Raad voor het Regeringsbeleid. 's-Gravenhage: SDU-Uitgeverij.

Briene, M.F.M., F.M. Dieleman, R.B. Jobse & J.Floor (1989), Beheer en verhuurbaarheid: Een empirische studie van een aantal naoorlogse woningcomplexen. Rotterdam/Utrecht: IOP-Bouw/Instituut voor Ruimtelijk Onderzoek.

Brunt, L. (1990), Stedelijk wonen. In: Vernieuwde Volkshuisvesting, pp. 19-24. Zoetermeer: Raad voor de Volkshuisvesting.

Clark, W.A.V. (1986), Residential segregation in American cities: a review and interpretation. Population Research and Population Review 5, pp. 95-127.

Clark, W.A.V. & F.M. Dieleman (1990), 'Zwarte' en 'witte' scholen in Nederland gezien vanuit Amerikaanse ervaringen. Geografisch Tijdschrift 24, pp. 139-147.

Den Draak, J. (1985), Binnensteden in Nederland: Beleidsopties en recente ontwikkelingen. In: J.P. Burgers & P. Stoppelenburg (eds), Het stedelijk woonerf, pp. 58-74. Tilburg: Instituut voor Arbeidsvraagstukken.

De Smidt, M. (1991), Bedrijfsprofiel van de Randstad; winnende en verliezende milieus. In: P. Hooimeijer, S. Musterd & P. Schröder (eds), De Randstad: balans van winst en verlies, deel 1, Stedelijke Netwerken, pp. 17-34. Utrecht: Stedelijke Netwerken.

Dieleman F.M. & R.B. Jobse (1991), Multi-family housing in the social rental sector and the changing Dutch housing market. Housing Studies 6, pp. 193-205.

Dienst Ruimtelijke Ordening Amsterdam (1990), Ontwerp Structuurplan 1990 Amsterdam: Deel II, De Toelichting. Amsterdam: Dienst Ruimtelijke Ordening.

Elekan W.G. & W.A. van der Heijden (1981), Waarom woont een Rotterdammer niet in Rotterdam? Migratiemotievenonderzoek. Rotterdam: Dienst Volkshuisvesting.

Engbersen, G. (1990), Cultural differentiation in a low income neighbourhood. In: L. Deben, W. Heinemeijer & D. van der Vaart (eds), Residential Differentiation, pp. 224-234. Amsterdam: Centrum voor Grootstedelijk Onderzoek.

Engelsdorp Gastelaars, R. van (1987), Van bouwen voor de buurt naar wijken met een overwegende leefstijl. Woningraad 21, pp. 7-11.

Engelsdorp Gastelaars, R. van & J. Vijgen (1990), Residential differentiation in the Netherlands: the rise of new urban households. In: L. Deben, W. Heinemeijer & D. van der Vaart (eds), Residential Differentiation, pp. 136-163. Amsterdam: Centrum voor Grootstedelijk Onderzoek.

Engelsdorp Gastelaars, R. van & W.F. Heinemeijer (1985), Stedelijk beleid en stedelijke organisatie van stadsgewesten: Het geval Amsterdam. Geografisch Tijdschrift 14, pp. 95-104.

Faludi, A. & A.J. van der Valk (1990), De groeikernen als hoekstenen van de Nederlandse ruimtelijke planningdoctrine. Assen/Maastricht: Van Gorcum.

Geenhuizen, M.S. van, et al. (1981), Volkshuisvesting in groeikernen: Een beleid sevaluatie. Utrechtse Geografische Studies 23. Utrecht: Geografisch Instituut, Rijksuniversiteit Utrecht.

Geurts, F. & J. Gramberg (1989), 's-Gravenhage met de rug tegen de duinen. In: F.M. Dieleman, R. van Kempen en J. van Weesep (eds), Met nieuw elan: De herontwikkeling van het stedelijk wonen, pp. 113-127. Delft: Delftse Universitaire Pers.

Hessels, M. (1988), Intermediaire diensten in stadsgewesten: (de)concentratie en (de)centralisatie. STEPRO-rapport 76. Utrecht: Geografisch Instituut, Rijksuniversiteit Utrecht.

Hoekveld, G.A. & J.M. Kersloot (1986), Hoe problematisch is de hoogbouw? Stedebouw & Volkshuisvesting 67, pp. 99-108.

Hoffschulte, C. & S. Musterd (1989), De wervingskracht van Amsterdamse woonmilieus. In: F.M. Dieleman, R. van Kempen en J. van Weesep (eds), Met nieuw elan: De herontwikkeling van het stedelijk wonen, pp. 71-82. Delft: Delftse Universitaire Pers.

Hoogvliet, A. & R.B. Jobse (1989), Naar een evenwichtiger opbouw van de bevolking. Bouw 44 9, pp. 35-37.

Jansen, A. & L. van Noortwijk (1987), Suburbs, jongeren en verhuisgedrag. In: Planologische Diskussiebijdragen I, pp. 377-386. Delft: Delftse Uitgeversmaatschappij.

Jobse, R.B. (1986), Bevolkingsontwikkelingen in de drie grote steden: Het ontstaan van leeftijdsspecifieke woongebieden. In: F.M. Dieleman, A.W.P. Jansen en M. de Smidt (eds), Metamorfose van de stad: Recente tendensen van wonen en werken in Nederlandse steden, pp. 77-91. Amsterdam/Utrecht: KNAG/Geografisch Instituut, Rijksuniversiteit Utrecht.

Jobse, R.B. (1988), De Amsterdamse bevolking in beweging: Demografische ontwikkelingen op wijkniveau, 1920-1985. STEPROrapport 67. Utrecht: Geografisch Instituut, Rijksuniversiteit Utrecht.

Jobse, R.B. (1991), Eenpersoonshuishoudens in de drie grote steden: Een nieuw dominant huishoudenstype? In: R. van Kempen, S. Musterd & W. Ostendorf (eds), Maatschappelijke verandering en stedelijke dynamiek. Volkshuisvesting in Theorie en Praktijk 30, pp. 43-58. Delft: Delftse Universitaire Pers.

Jobse, R.B. & S. Musterd (1989), Woningbouw in de Randstad: De gevolgen van een trendbreuk. Geografisch Tijdschrift 23, pp. 181-191.

Jobse, R.B. & B. Needham (1987), The economic future of the Randstad Holland. Urban Studies 25, pp. 282-296.

Jobse, R.B., H.M. Kruythoff & S. Musterd (1991), Groeikernen in een veranderend ruimtelijk en demografisch krachtenveld. Geografisch Tijdschrift 25, pp. 148-160.

Kempen, E. van (1987), De stadsbuurt in een veranderende samenleving: Idee en werkelijkheid. Geografisch Tijdschrift 21, pp. 27-37.

Kempen, E. van & S. Musterd (1991), High-rise housing reconsidered: Some research and policy implications. Housing Studies 6, pp. 83-95.

Kempen, R. van & R. Teule, (1990), Lage inkomens in de grote stad: Concentratie of juist niet? Geografenkrant, 9-90, pp. 10.

Kempen, R. van & R.B.J. Teule (1989), In de klem tussen stedelijke woningmarkt en ardeidsmarkt: Kansarmen in de Randstad. Deelrapport 2: De woonsituatie en funktie van de woningvoorraad. Werkstukken Stedelijke Netwerken 18. 's-Gravenhage: Stedelijke Netwerken.

Kok, J.B. (1982), Sleutelen aan de stedelijke bevolkingssamenstelling. Verkenningen in planologie en demografie. Amsterdam: Planologisch Demografisch Instituut, Universiteit van Amsterdam.

Kruythoff, H.M. (1989), Homogenisering en diversificatie in de Randstad: Ontwikkelingen in woonmilieus 1981-1986. Werkstukken Stedelijke Netwerken 15. Zoetermeer: Ministerie van Onderwijs en Wetenschappen.

Martin, R. (1988), Industrial capitalism in transition: the contemporary reorganization of the British space-economy. In: D. Massey & J. Allen (eds), Uneven Redevelopment: Cities and Regions in Transition, pp. 202-231. London: Hoddes & Stoughton.

Masotti, L.H. (1973), Prologue: Suburbia reconsidered: Myth and counter-myth. In: L.H. Masotti & J.K. Hadden (eds), The Urbanization of the Suburbs. Beverly Hills/London: Sage Publications.

Masotti, L.H. & J.K. Hadden (1973) (eds), The Urbanization of the Suburbs. Beverly Hills/London: Sage Publications.

Ministerie van Volkshuisvesting, Ruimtelijke Ordening en Milieubeheer (1976), Derde Nota over de Ruimtelijke Ordening. Deel 2: Verstedelijkingsnota. 's-Gravenhage: SDU-Uitgeverij.

Ministerie van Volkshuisvesting, Ruimtelijke Ordenening en Milieubeheer (1988), Nota Volkshuisvesting in de jaren negentig: Van bouwen naar wonen. 's-Gravenhage: SDU-Uitgeverij.

Mumford, L. (1966), The City in History: Its Origins, its Transformations and its Prospects. Harmondsworth: Penguin Books Ltd.

Musterd, S. (1991), Neighbourhood change in Amsterdam. Tijdschrift voor Economische en Sociale Geografie 82, pp. 30-39.

Musterd, S., R.B. Jobse & H. Priemus (1988), Bevolkingssegregatie in de Randstad: Enkele te verwachten ontwikkelingen. Stedebouw en Volkshuisvesting 7/8, pp. 293-301.

Musterd, S. & W. Ostendorf (1991), Inkomensontwikkeling en tweetoppigheid binnen de Randstad. In: R. van Kempen, S. Musterd & W. Ostendorf (eds), Maatschappelijke verandering en stedelijke dynamiek. Volkshuisvesting in Theorie en Praktijk 30, pp. 59-75. Delft: Delftse Universitaire Pers.

Musterd, S., R.B. Jobse & H.M. Kruythoff (1991), Residential mobility and urban change in the Randstad: some (dis)similarities between Amsterdam, Rotterdam and The Hague. Netherlands Journal of Housing and the Built Environment 6, pp. 101-113.

Nusselder, W.J., J.J. Schoorl & J.F.M. Berkien (1990), Bevolkingsvooruitberekening allochtonen in Nederland naar nationaliteit, 1989-1999: Bevolkingsgroepen met de Turkse, Marokkaanse en EG of overige niet-Nederlandse nationaliteit. NIDI-rapport 16. 's-Gravenhage: NIDI.

Ostendorf, W. (1985), Gemeentelijk woningmarktbeleid in het stadsgewest Amsterdam. Geografisch Tijdschrift 14, pp. 333-345.

Ostendorf, W. (1989), Het sociaal profiel van de gemeente; woonmilieudifferentiatie en de vorming van het stadsgewest Amsterdam. Nederlandse Geografische Studies 75. Amsterdam: KNAG.

Patijn, W., B. Sondermeijer & F. ter Welle (1978), Nota woningbehoefte Rotterdam tot 1987. Rotterdam: Dienst van Volkshuisvesting/Dienst Stadsontwikkeling.

Pennen, T. van der (1990), Wonen in een oude stadswijk. In: Stadsvernieuwing: Nu en straks, ontwerp en beheer, pp. 7-22. Rotterdam: Gemeentelijk Woningbedrijf.

Rohde, W. & P. Bertholet (1990), Stadsvernieuwing in cijfers; het voortgangsrapport Belstato. Amsterdam: RIGO.

Rijks Planologische Dienst (1987), Ruimtelijke Verkenningen 1987: Jaarboek Rijks Planologische Dienst. 's-Gravenhage: SDU-Uitgeverij.

Sassen-Koob, S. (1986), New York City: Economic restructuring and immigration. In: Development and Change 17, pp. 85-119. London: SAGE.

Schouw, R.J. & J. den Draak (1986), Stedelijke bevolkingsdynamiek en voorzieningen. In: F.M.Dieleman, A.W.P.Jansen en M.de Smidt (eds), Metamorfose van de stad: Recente tendensen van wonen en werken in Nederlandse steden, pp. 66-76. Amsterdam/Utrecht: KNAG/Geografisch Instituut, Rijksuniversiteit Utrecht.

Urban Europe (1982), A Study of Growth and Decline. Oxford: Pergamon Press.

Vijgen, J. & R. van Engelsdorp Gastelaars (1991), Een gevarieerd bestaan; het gebruik van tijd en ruimte in het dagelijks leven van enkele 'oude' en 'nieuwe' groepen binnen de Nederlandse bevolking. Werkstukken Stedelijke Netwerken 28. Amsterdam: Stedelijke Netwerken.

Weerts, F. (1990), Wijken en buurten verliezen snel kwaliteit ondanks renovaties en welzijnsmaatregelen. Binnenlands Bestuur 16-2-1990, pp. 10-11.

Wusten, H. van der (1991), Bestuurlijke winnaars en verliezers. In: P. Hooimeijer, S. Musterd & P. Schröder (eds), De Randstad: balans van winst en verlies, deel 1, Stedelijke Netwerken, pp. 57-70. Utrecht: Stedelijke Netwerken.

WRR (Wetenschappelijke Raad voor het Regeringsbeleid) (1990), Van de stad en de rand. 's-Gravenhage: SDU-Uitgeverij.

Wuertz, K. (1990), Het onherbergzame wonen: Sociaal-ruimtelijke symboliek en de beleving van onveiligheid. Leiden: DSWO-Press.

Drs. R.B. Jobse
Faculty of Geographical Sciences
University of Utrecht
P.O. Box 80.115
3508 TC Utrecht
The Netherlands

Dr. S. Musterd
Faculty of Environmental Sciences
University of Amsterdam
Nieuwe Prinsengracht 130
1018 VZ Amsterdam
The Netherlands

4. HOUSING AND PHYSICAL PLANNING

F.M. Dieleman & R. van Engelsdorp Gastelaars

4.1 The link between housing and physical planning

The Dutch housing policy that has been in effect since the early 20th century has influenced the spatial organization of the country in a variety of ways (cf. Faludi & Van der Wusten in Chapter 2 of this volume). Partly, this concerns deliberate spatial effects, intended by the authorities in question. For a long time, the national government and local authorities have used the production and allocation of housing as a means to reach two types of goals: a) to improve the quality of the housing stock in specific parts of the country, in urban regions, selected settlements, or parts of the cities; and b) to achieve an optimal location of new housing with respect to the existing housing stock or to other types of land use. The selection of residential construction sites can be used to protect 'weaker' types of land use, such as nature preserves, recreation areas, or open space.

It proved to be possible to influence the spatial structure of the Randstad through the control exerted by the national and local authorities over the residential construction process and urban renewal programs. The public sector had mainly three nstruments at its disposal to influence the spatial structure by way of residential development and urban renewal: a) brick-and-mortar subsidies for new construction and renovation of existing dwellings; b) quotas in the allocation of these subsidies; and c) the municipal land policy.

There is a wide array of brick-and-mortar subsidies for new residential construction and renovation of existing dwellings in the Netherlands. They cover not only the social rental sector but also the private rental and the owner-occupier sectors. For many years, the lion's share of residential construction qualified for such subsidies. In 1988, 1.9 percent of the Gross National Product was spent for this. In this respect, the Netherlands is clearly ahead of other Western European countries (Boelhouwer et al. 1991). Consequently, the social rental sector was able to expand greatly: to 40 percent of the housing stock in the Netherlands as a whole, and to over 50 percent of the stock in the big cities (Dieleman & Jobse 1991). This compares to 27, 24, and 16 percent in France, England, and Germany, respectively (MVROM 1991a).

In addition, the volume of new construction in the Netherlands has been higher than in the surrounding countries in relative terms during the past two decades, predominantly

F. M. Dieleman and S. Musterd (eds.), The Randstad: A Research and Policy Laboratory, 65–95.

because its population expanded much more rapidly. The number of households increased by 49 percent between 1970 and 1987. France has the second-highest rate of growth in Western Europe, but that is only 29 percent (MVROM 1991a).

The deep financial involvement of the government in residential construction, and its high volume, provided the authorities with a powerful tool to influence the growth of settlements and the reconstruction of old residential areas. This tool has been used abundantly; the financial instruments to plan the residential construction and the renovations were augmented by a spatial planning system (Adriaansens & Fortgens 1990). This spatial planning system worked predominantly through the quota system for residential construction and the municipal land policy.

During the 1950s and 1960s, the minister determined the volume and composition of the residential construction program and also allocated shares to each of the provinces. The provincial authorities then determined the shares of each of the municipalities, thereby bringing to bear spatial planning principles. Even the construction of private housing without subsidies was subject to this regime. If, for instance, a municipality allowed the construction of many social rental units, few private owner-occupier dwellings could be built, and vice versa (Van der Schaar & Hereijgers 1991). After 1970, the municipalities and provinces were able to exert more influence on the volume and composition of the new construction. The system was adjusted as follows: the municipal authorities adopt a multi-year plan for residential construction and renovations; the provinces advise the minister with respect to the allocation of the quota, considering their spatial planning goals; and the minister decides on the allocation of the quotas. Since the introduction of this system, the owner-occupier dwellings built without subsidies are no longer part of the quota system.

Through their land policy, the municipalities can exert considerable influence on residential construction, as well as on physical planning in general. Dutch municipalities tend to play a dominant role in the preparation of construction sites. They buy up the land, if necessary by exercising the principle of eminent domain. They arrange for the provision of sewers, greenery, roads, etc.; plot the subdivision; and provide the construction permits for each of the lots. This gives the municipalities a large measure of influence on the differentiation of the new construction by sector, on the land costs, and on the form of the extension of cities and villages. In urban renewal areas, the municipality has similar means to determine the process of reconstruction (Adriaansens & Fortgens 1990; Van der Schaar & Hereijgers 1991; MVROM 1991b).

Therefore, the influence of the public sector in the new construction of housing and in urban renewal is not only visible directly in the large share of social rental housing in the Randstad, but also in the spatial structure of this region. The separation of urban and agricultural land use is unusually pronounced and immediately obvious to anyone. This also applies to the compact housing pattern in the Randstad. Vandermotten (1991) demonstrates that the population density in Rotterdam and Amsterdam is very high compared to other Western European cities of similar size. He points out that in the Netherlands, a much higher proportion of the inhabitants live in the compact centrally located parts of the agglomerations. In comparison to Brussels and Antwerp, the population of the Randstad is very densely packed.

In the remainder of this chapter, we elaborate on the spatial effects that were the targets of the housing policy of the national government as far as the Randstad was concerned. Even a cursory inspection shows that during the past 45 years, three spatial objectives have continuously surfaced:
1) The goal to attain and maintain the highest possible housing quality, which has been reiterated time and again since 1945.
2) The thirty-year-old goal to concentrate new residential construction in a limited number of locations. These are either within or adjacent to the big cities or (in as far as the limitation to these cities appears to be unattainable) in a limited number of growth centers at a short distance from these cities.
3) The increasingly important goal to improve the housing quality in neighborhoods and areas with a relatively aging and dilapidated housing stock by means of urban renewal.

This discussion focuses on the extent to which these policies have been successful. Therefore, a more elaborate overview of the housing and spatial planning policies as they evolved over the past 45 years in the Randstad is presented first. Subsequently, an attempt is made to establish the extent to which specific aspects of these spatial development objectives have actually been attained. This leads to some comments on the conformity of the plans contained in the housing and spatial planning policies and the actions of the many parties involved in the residential development process.

4.2   Forty-five years of housing and spatial planning

1945-1960; Housing in the context of reconstruction
World War II caused a considerable destruction of capital in the Netherlands. More than half of the national production capacity was destroyed or had been disassembled and removed. The public transportation system was in shambles, partly because most of the rolling stock had been moved to Germany, and partly because many bridges, railroad yards, and overpasses had been damaged in war action. Over 20 percent of the more than two million dwellings inhabited in 1940 had been destroyed or damaged by the end of the war (Van der Cammen & De Klerk 1986). The repair of war damage was therefore given the highest priority after 1945. And the reconstruction remained the most important policy objective throughout the country, until well into the 1950s (Van der Schaar 1987).

Within the context of this reconstruction, the completion of a colossal residential construction program became a central element, also because the continuous economic and demographic growth during that period provided an extra incentive for the demand for housing. This challenge was felt in all parts of the country. Spatial planning

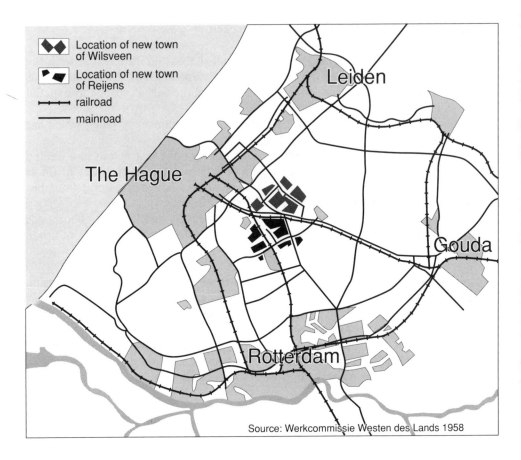

Figure 4.1   Location of new towns of Reijens and Wilsveen. Not realized

considerations and the balancing of construction quota among the various parts of
the country became in practice less influential for the siting of new dwellings than
the availability of sufficient local construction capacity. But during this period, the
threat of congestion in the western part of the country did become a matter of debate.
Such congestion could result from the obvious tendency among the thousands of people
in search of jobs from the agricultural regions in the north, the northeast, and the
southwest to migrate to this center of economic expansion. Several reports and articles
advocated promoting the outward growth of the Randstad into adjacent rural regions
as well as toward the remote parts of the country (Vermooten 1949; Nota 1960; Faludi
& Van der Valk 1990). But as we pointed out above, this growing consensus did not
yet lead to concrete measures with regard to the spatial distribution of the population
among the various regions on the basis of spatial planning considerations (Van der

Cammen & De Klerk 1986; Faludi & Van der Valk 1990).

There was also a clear difference between the planning debate of that period and the actual housing and spatial planning policy for the cities of the Randstad and their adjacent areas. The debate showed a growing consensus about the disadvantages of unchecked urbanization within and around the Randstad cities. There was also a growing agreement about the danger that an uncoordinated suburbanization could choke the 'Green Heart', and about the inability to accommodate the expansion of the cities by means of concentric extensions of their urban fabric (Figure 4.1). Consequently, a broad recognition of the need to establish new growth centers on the periphery of the Randstad emerged (Werkcommissie 1958).

In reality, the new housing developments of the big cities of the Randstad were largely built in the form of estates on their edges or just beyond the city limits, just like in the years prior to World War II. Such neighborhoods as Pendrecht in Rotterdam, Mariahoeve in The Hague, Schalkwijk in Haarlem, and Geuzeveld and Slotervaart in Amsterdam, provide good examples.

Finally, during this period there was little concern with management of the existing housing stock because of the prevailing housing shortage and the consequent emphasis on new construction. Slum clearance and urban renewal remained incidental and of limited scope. Such projects were predominantly implemented in the old inner cities to create room for city formation and to facilitate traffic circulation (Van der Cammen & De Klerk 1986; Evaluatienota 1990).

1960-1972; Housing in the context of concentrated dispersal
In many respects, the 1960 Memorandum on spatial planning in the Netherlands (which became later known as the First Memorandum) was already outdated from the moment it was released (compare Chapter 2 of this volume). The growth of the economy, of affluence, and of the population accelerated around that time, and the boom kept up into the 1970s. The cities of the Randstad could hardly deal with the growing demand. Consequently, nearby small towns and villages expanded ever more rapidly. Spatial planning became consequently synonymous with planning for urban expansion, for increasing mobility, and for expanding use of space during the 1960s. These principles found their expression in the Second Memorandum on spatial planning in the Netherlands, which was released in 1966 (Nota 1960; Tweede Nota 1966; Steigenga 1968).

The Second Memorandum assumed that the population of the Netherlands would eventually grow to 20 million people. That would be an increase of 7.5 million over the number in 1966. In addition, the planners counted on a rapid expansion of urban employment opportunities (the service sector and industries linked to the ports, such as oil refinery and the petrochemical sector) and a further decline of agricultural jobs. In short, the already existing concentration of people and jobs in the West and the South would tend to grow very substantially, according to the authors of the Memorandum. This would have a strong negative impact on the quality of life in those regions (for instance, because of the resulting pollution of the air and the water, as well as the diminishing of the remaining green space). Consequently, a policy of dispersal was proposed. This dispersal would have to be aimed at four regions: the remote regions in the North and Northeast of the country; the northern part of the province of North Holland, directly adjacent to the Randstad; the southern portion of the IJsselmeerpolders - then being reclaimed - which borders on the Randstad to the east; and the province of Zeeland, immediately to the south of the Randstad. The population dispersal would have to be achieved through the stimulation of economic activities, especially in Zeeland and the remote northern regions. Seaport activities were considered to be the appropriate sector to attain this goal. Yet even such a dispersal policy would not prevent a considerable growth of urban land use from occurring in and near the Randstad itself. In other words, in and around the cities of Amsterdam, The Hague, Rotterdam, and Utrecht space would have to be found in order to execute a substantial construction program (Tweede Nota 1966; Van der Cammen & De Klerk 1986; Van der Schaar 1987; Faludi & Van der Valk 1990).

At the scale of the individual agglomerations, the concept of 'metropolitan region' was introduced. This was understood to consist of an open constellation of one or more large urban centers (cities or agglomerations) together with their surrounding satellite settlements. This constellation functions as a single entity because of the many mutual links; what used to be a single compact city has developed into a metropolitan region that covers a much larger area (Tweede Nota 1966). A metropolitan region contained therefore not only the crucial urban functions, but it also comprised suburban residential environments and concentrations of employment. In addition, much open space was incorporated: recreation areas as well as nature preserves and farmland. The metropolitan region as a planning concept was intended to deal with two contradictory claims on space. On the one hand, the planners feared the consequences of uncontrolled suburbanization. This would make it impossible to provide an adequate system of public (rail) transportation, and such a form of dispersal would also undercut the economic base of all kinds of facilities and services. On the other hand, the planners were sensitive to the housing needs of the inhabitants of the metropolitan regions. A growing majority of these inhabitants desired a single-family (row) house with a garden in a small-scale environment with a good measure of greenery. Such environments were not available in the old cities. The metropolitan region was therefore introduced to make a compromise between dream and reality. Those city dwellers interested in the single-family house in a more rural setting would have to be accommodated in a pattern of 'concentrated deconcentration', which means a limited number of large growth centers within the sphere of influence of the large cities. This would enable the planners to provide them with an adequate level of services and facilities, the desired infrastructure for traffic and transportation, and an appealing residential environment that still contains elements of 'rural' living (Tweede Nota 1966). Small cities like Alkmaar, Purmerend, Zoetermeer, Hellevoetsluis, Dordrecht, Lelystad, and later also Almere, which at that time had not yet reached the planning stage, were named as the destinations for this overspill population from this cities (Figure 2.4).

Consequently, further residential construction in the West of the country would need to be concentrated in these growth centers (Tweede Nota 1966; Faludi & Van der Valk 1990). In addition, at the level of the cities and neighborhoods, the need to promote 'urban reconstruction' (renewal of city centers, slum clearance, renovation, facilities for traffic and transportation) was argued, especially with respect to the central areas of big and medium-sized cities. Obviously, at that time the authorities destined the inner city areas primarily for economic functions, not for residential use. In addition, they foresaw a change of residential qualities in the old neighborhoods that were slated for urban renewal, as well as a different population than the present one. These areas were to provide housing in low densities, with more greenery, for middle-class families. By the end of the 1960s, there was a spate of such plans in a wide range of cities (Van der Cammen & De Klerk 1986).

1972-1980; Housing in growth centers and urban renewal areas
By the end of the 1960s, the responsible authorities were again starting to question the desirability of the spatial developments that were unfolding in the country at that time. This doubt, especially in regard to the Randstad, concerned two distinct developments.

In the first place, they were increasingly worried about the continuing decentralization of the urban functions. The permanent economic expansion and growth of affluence steadily increased the amount of space used by firms and households. This caused these functions to expand into areas that were still rural. As far as the regions were concerned, the urban land use grew especially in the South and the East of the country, partly in response to migration from the Randstad. With respect to the population, the migration balance of the West of the country could only remain even because the Randstad itself become increasingly the destination of foreign immigrants during the 1960s (a rising proportion of whom were foreign guest workers from Mediterranean countries). Within the metropolitan regions, the suburbanization grew dramatically. Ever growing-numbers of urbanites exchanged their apartment for a single-family house outside the city, preferably for one in a small settlement within the Green Heart of the Randstad or in a suburb located in the attractive sandy areas near the big cities of the Randstad. The policy of concentrated deconcentration was a complete failure during the 1960s.

Secondly, there was increasing concern about the quality of the residential climate in the big cities themselves. The deconcentration of inhabitants and of businesses affected the economic and social structure of the cities of the Randstad in a numerical and qualitative sense. The quantitative change brought about by the deconcentration was the decline of the number of inhabitants and the number of jobs in the big cities. The firms and the households leaving the city were on average larger (by the number of jobs per firm and the number of people per household) than those that moved into the premises they left behind. And also in a qualitative sense, this deconcentration undermined the structure of the big cities. The people and functions that left the city were on the whole financially stronger than those that took their places.

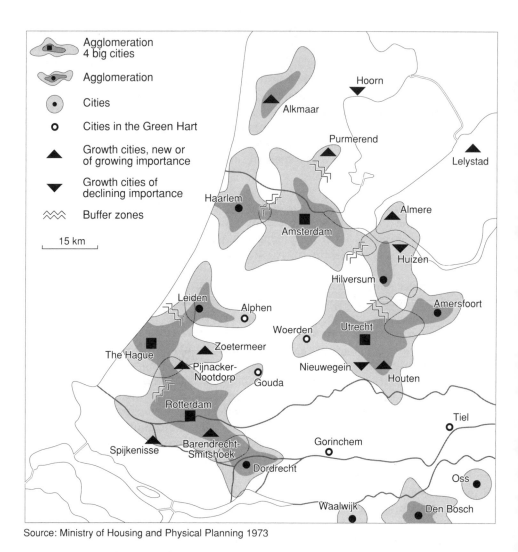

Source: Ministry of Housing and Physical Planning 1973

Figure 4.2   *Map with the growth cities and growth nuclei in the Third National Physical*
              Planning Report

The growing doubts about these developments spawned two types of reaction: a
substantial and a procedural one. The substantial reaction was a result of rethinking
the optimistic view of continuous growth, the viewpoint on which the spatial planning
principles of the 1960s had been based. The procedural reaction showed up in the

increasing need for an adequate set of instruments to transform the spatial planning goals into reality. With respect to the substantial reaction, the stock-taking Memorandum on spatial planning (Orienteringsnota 1973) marks the transition to the new stage in planning. As far as the procedural reaction is concerned, the new era was ushered in by a Memorandum on housing policy in 1972 (Nota Volkshuisvesting 1972; Orienteringsnota 1973; Witsen & Leeflang 1977; Van der Cammen & De Klerk 1986).

With respect to the regional developments, the migration of people from the Randstad to other provinces (especially to the province of Gelderland in the East and to Brabant in the South) became a source of increasing worry. This concern was fanned by the impression that the migration reflected increasing dissatisfaction with the quality of residential areas in the Randstad. It was clear that especially the big cities of the Randstad still had to cope with a shortage of housing and a lack of opportunities for open-air recreation. In addition, the volume and quality of employment opportunities and of services and facilities were being threatened. This led directly to the formulation of a policy to improve the quality of life in the western part of the country, especially by upgrading the residential environments in the metropolitan areas. Yet a certain measure of overspill of inhabitants and jobs to other parts of the country would still be condoned (Derde Nota 1976).

At the level of the metropolitan region, the need for a policy of concentrated deconcentration was once more underscored. This entailed a combination of two goals. One projects the improvement of the residential climate in the big cities by concentrated new housing developments, or by housing renovation (in the four big cities in densities of up to 100 dwellings per hectare). The other goal entails the creation of new residential areas towards the edge of the Randstad, sited along existing or newly built railroads within a range of a maximum of 25 to 35 minutes (inclusive of the transportation to the stations) from the big cities. These developments were built with a net density of 35 to 45 dwellings per hectare (Figure 4.2).

The growth centers concerned included Alkmaar, Hoorn, and Purmerend (to the north of Amsterdam), Lelystad and Almere (to the east, situated in the new IJsselmeer-polders), Huizen (east of Amsterdam), Houten and Nieuwegein (south of Utrecht), Zoetermeer (to the east of The Hague), and Spijkenisse and Hellevoetsluis (to the southwest of Rotterdam) (Nota Volkshuisvesting 1972; see also the Derde Nota 1976, for an outline of the policy).

At the level of the neighborhoods of the cities, the importance of urban renewal was increasingly emphasized during this period. The specifics of the strategy changed simultaneously. The process of city forming came to a halt during this period. On the one hand, this was because increasing numbers of offices and other businesses moved from the inner cities to locations at the edge of the city or to the suburbs. On the other hand, this was a result of the economic downturn of the 1970s. Partly in reaction to this reversal, housing policy considerations gained increased weight in urban renewal policy.

This provides at least a partial explanation for the authorities' acceptance of citizen participation. During this period, the principle of urban renewal to the benefit of the local inhabitants was increasingly adopted. This policy contained two typical elements. One was the retention of the original population (by building affordable housing). The other was the maintenance of the original urban physical structure, both with respect to the dwellings (more emphasis on housing improvements) and the form (the subdivision of the area and the pattern of streets). Obviously, these developments served one principal goal: to limit the overspill of the population from the big cities (Evaluatienota 1990; Van der Schaar & Hereijgers 1991).

1980-1986; Housing in compact cities
The authorities in the big cities of the western part of the country were obviously dissatisfied with the spatial developments in and around the Randstad. They had many reasons for this. The expansion of the Dutch economy during this period was increasingly concentrated in places outside the Randstad proper, for instance in the central part of the province of Gelderland (Ede, Wageningen, Arnhem), and in the belt of cities in Brabant (Roosendaal, Breda, Tilburg, Eindhoven). In the big cities, there was an acceleration in the rate of decline (in as far as this term may be used to describe the decrease of the number of inhabitants and of the local average income). To these authorities, the national spatial policy for the Randstad - as defined in the Third Memorandum on spatial planning - was too dualistic, in spite of the increased emphasis on the importance of the metropolitan environment. On the one hand, the national government had expressed its concern about the development of the big cities. 'The government wishes to guarantee the blossoming of the existing urban structures, and to stop the decline of the city. Its urban renewal policy gives priority to the improvement of the conditions of the population of the old neighborhoods. Such a policy can help slow down the depopulation of the (big) city, to strengthen the social structure, and to diminish the decline of the urban economic base. Also by other means, the growth of the urban population will be promoted' (Derde Nota 1976, p.7). But on the other hand, the same government strongly supported attempts to increase the effectiveness of the growth-center policy at the same time these words were being printed in the Third Memorandum (Bloemberg & Van Zeijl 1986; Faludi & Van der Valk 1990).

Increasingly, the city authorities advertised their own opinions concerning the desired policy for the big cities during this period. A notable example of this is the Master Plan for Rotterdam of 1978 (Structuurplan Rotterdam 1978). This plan draws attention to the endangered state of the big city as a place of residence (rather than as an economic center, etc.). It poses that the regional, national, and international functions of the big city become of lesser importance if they undermine the very existence of the city. The creation of high-quality residential environments within the city to help the city compete with its suburbs, became the focus of policy. Important points of action were identified: housing renovation in urban renewal areas; residential construction on sites abandoned by port functions and manufacturing complexes; and additional housing on vacant lots in the inner city and the green spaces in more recently built areas towards the edge of the city. Clearly, the authors of this plan wanted to stop, once and for all, the ever-increasing spatial deconcentration of households, businesses, and services and facilities. They envisioned a 'compact city' (Structuurplan Rotterdam 1978). Other cities followed suit. In another preliminary Memorandum in preparation of a major policy document on spatial planning (Structuurschets Stedelijke Gebieden 1983), the national government eventually also voices its support for the big cities. These local and national policy documents laid the groundwork for spatial policy in the years after 1983.

More than during the preceding plan periods, the existence of a strongly urbanized Randstad and the consequent imbalances among the regions is accepted as a basis for the national policy. The existing regional distribution of the population is thereby also acceptable, rather than an issue that needs to be redressed. Each region needs to take care of its own economic and spatial qualities and problems. As far as the Randstad is concerned, this implies that extra care needs to be given to the quality of the urban environment, especially in the metropolitan areas of the four big cities. In addition, this region needs to develop a so-called 'green structure' to safeguard its rural areas (especially that of the central Green Heart).

The metropolitan region remains an important concept. Its spatial extent, however, has diminished in this national policy document. The maximum distance between a growth center and its central city is established at eight kilometers. Only the metropolitan regions of the four big cities are allowed to be larger. In those cases, the maximum distance between the central city and potential major new residential developments can be as large as 12 kilometers. For the sake of comparison, in previous plans, a maximum distance of 15 kilometers between central city and growth centers was acceptable. This condensation is typical of the new vision espoused by the new policy. Construction sites within the existing cities are given a clear priority in the Memorandum. If not enough space can be created in this way, then locations on the edges of the existing urban areas will be approved for new development. And only then may locations at some distance from the cities be considered, but preferably these need to be attached to nearby existing (growth) centers. In other words, the existing policy of concentrated deconcentration is now being replaced by a policy to promote 'compact cities'. The growth center is no longer a central element of spatial policy, but is being reduced to a - in some cases - indispensable subsidiary element. Alkmaar, Hoorn, Lelystad, and Hellevoetsluis thereby lost their status as growth centers, because they are situated outside the redefined limits of the metropolitan regions.

As far as urban renewal is concerned, the importance of the residential function and of retaining the existing population in the old neighborhoods is reiterated. But renewal in high densities is given even higher priority than in previous policy. Densities of up to 110 dwellings per hectare are now considered acceptable in the urban renewal areas of the big cities (Structuurschets Stedelijke Gebieden 1983; Van der Cammen & De Klerk 1986).

4.3   Measurement of success: plan conformity and goal conformity

Within the context of the spatial policy for the Randstad, housing had to meet three different requirements during the entire period from 1945 and 1985. First, it had to contribute to the improvement of, or at least the maintenance of an adequate standard of living throughout the Randstad. The abatement of the housing shortage, for instance, was an important goal. Secondly, it was used to control the process of urbanization in and around the large agglomerations of the Randstad, whereby the protection of the Green Heart was an important goal. The concentration of housing development in a limited number of locations adjacent to or near the agglomerations was an important strategy to reach this goal. And finally, it had to help improve the quality of life in the aging neighborhoods, which had slipped into a state of deprivation because of the dilapidation of the housing stock. Housing renovation was an important strategy in this respect. The evaluation of the success of the Randstad policy between 1945 and 1985 can therefore be focused on these three policy lines. But before the results of the analysis are presented, the criteria for success should be spelled out.

In their study of the Dutch growth-center policy as one of the great achievements of spatial planning, Faludi & Van der Valk (1990) posit two approaches to the measurement of success: implementation research and evaluation research. The extent to which the policies of a planning organization determine the actions of executive organizations is the focus of implementation research. Like others before them, they call this 'plan conformity'. The core of this is formed by the question whether or not the projects have been carried out according to the plans. In addition, the effects of the planning measures on the behavior of the people and the organization of space can be investigated. This type of research can be defined as evaluation research. The conformity to the goals of the plan provides the measure of success in this respect. There is a difference between the two approaches: implementation research may, for instance, demonstrate that a project has been carried out in conformity to the plan, while evaluation research leads to the conclusion that the goals of the plan have not been met at all!

We propose to use this distinction in our evaluation of the housing policy in relation to the spatial planning of the Randstad. The effectiveness of the aforementioned policies has been evaluated several times from the point of view of plan conformity. In virtually all cases, the result was judged to be positive. This was clearly the case with respect to residential construction in the (western part of the) Netherlands during the period 1945-1985. Both by quantity and by quality, the production of housing appears to have been carried out according to plan (Van der Schaar 1987; Jobse & Musterd 1989a). The same applied to the growth-center policy. At least during the 1975-1985 period, the construction of new housing was largely concentrated in the official growth centers; this is certainly true for the segments that benefited from the various government subsidies. In addition, the numbers that had been planned were easily achieved (Bloemberg & Van Zeijl 1986).

The same conclusion applied to the compact-city policy, which followed the growth-center policy. Also this policy was successful when the shift of construction away from the growth centers towards the big cities since the early 1980s is considered. This conclusion is supported by the numbers of dwellings that have been built in the agglomerations since that date (Jobse & Musterd 1989a; 1989b). During the 1980s, urban renewal was largely carried out according to plan. The speed of the improvements has been evaluated as 'according to plan' or even as 'beyond expectations' (Rohde & Bertholet 1990; Evaluatienota Stadsvernieuwing 1990; Priemus et al. 1991). More than one hundred million guilders was invested in urban renewal projects between 1980 and 1990 (Beleid voor stadsvernieuwing 1991). One third of this amount was contributed from the national government's budget. And about 90 percent of the invested sum was spent on the renovation of dwellings and new construction in dilapidated areas of the cities.

Obviously, the three main dimensions of the housing policy from the point of view of spatial policy were realized in activities and products according to plan, at least during the period when they were identified as such. The investigation of plan conformity therefore needs no further attention in this discussion (compare Chapter 2 of the present volume).

Instead, we shall focus on the goal conformity of the implemented policy. The spatial planning and housing policies for the Randstad that were in effect between 1945 and 1985 will be judged by their effects on the quality of life; that is, by their contribution to the welfare and well-being of the inhabitants. This type of evaluation has rarely been carried out (nevertheless, compare Nozeman 1986; Arnold 1990; Priemus et al. 1991), even though the concepts of quality of life, welfare and well-being are frequently applied in the planning documents that were used for this review. Therefore, the following discussion focuses on the effects on quality of life of the residential construction program for the Randstad in general, and for the big cities and their metropolitan regions in particular. Subsequently, the evaluation of the housing and spatial planning policies shifts to the level of the newly built growth centers and of the urban renewal areas in the Randstad that were recently the scene of action.

4.4 Housing shortage, residential segregation, and filtering

The effects of policy on the quality of life are discussed in this section from two points of view: a) the number of dwellings completed in relation to the estimated and the real housing need; and b) the strong emphasis on the construction of social rental dwellings.

The target amount of new dwellings programmed to be built has actually been achieved over the past twenty years. Yet the serious housing shortage that persisted in the Randstad since World War II has not been resolved, in spite of the deep investments in housing by the government (cf. Section 4.1). The number of people on the waiting lists for social rental housing in the big cities remains extremely high. Often a young household has to wait for years before it can make a start in this sector.

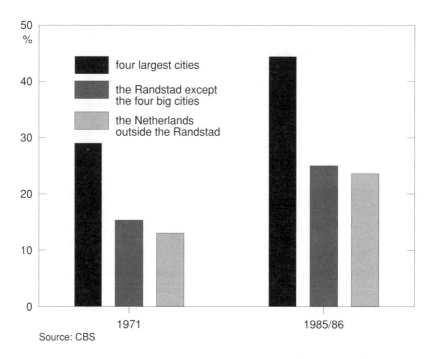

Figure 4.3   *Percentage one-person households in 1971 and 1985/1986*

The volume of new residential construction in the Netherlands depended strongly on the official estimates of housing need. But the housing needs in the Randstad were continuously underestimated. Therefore, the supply of new dwellings fell systematically short of the real need (Hooimeijer & Linde 1988). The low prognosis of housing need resulted from underestimating the process of the decline of household size during the past twenty years; especially in the big cities, this process proceeded very rapidly. Figure 4.3 illustrates that the small households have come to dominate the household structure in the big cities. Over the past two decades, the so-called second demographic transition took place in the Netherlands (Van der Kaa 1987). The concept of second demographic transition refers to a fundamental change in sexual behavior, the formation of relationships, and the number of children in a family. The transition started relatively late in the Netherlands compared to other European countries. By 1970, for instance, the average number of lifetime births per woman was still 2.6, while this number had already declined to 2.0 in countries like Sweden and Germany.

But after 1970, the development in the Netherlands became very rapid: the fertility rate declined to 1.5 in a very short time, the divorce rate tripled, and cohabitation became normal behavior (Dieleman & Schouw 1986). The effects of the high birth rate of the 1950s and 1960s, and the rapid transition from large families to small ones, caused a veritable explosion of demand for housing between 1970 and 1990. The total number of households in the Netherlands increased from 4.0 to 6.1 million.

This factor had not been taken into account in the planned volume of new residential construction. Especially in the Randstad, where the decline in family size was very rapid, this seriously affected the quality of life. The targets for residential construction were met, but the number was too small to eliminate the housing shortage (cf. Chapter 3 of the present volume). This brought about a rather paradoxical situation in the big cities. In spite of a large stock of affordable social rental dwellings (MVROM 1991a), access is difficult, especially for starting households and young migrants, who move to the city to study or work. By the end of the 1970s and the early 1980s, this housing shortage induced many young people to squat vacant housing. The housing allocation system was thereby thrown into disarray.

The housing shortage persists in the big agglomerations of the Randstad, in spite of the large quotas of new residential construction they have been given. But cities like The Hague and Utrecht have little room left within their borders for substantial construction programs (Gramberg 1989). Nearby rural places frequently object to large-scale extension plans of the cities. And because the municipalities determine their own land and construction policies, the needed residential construction can be stopped. Housing (and the households in search of it) then fall victim to the fact that residential construction is the most powerful instrument of spatial planning.

The strict control of the Dutch government over the housing market is also expressed in the tenure structure of the housing stock, as pointed out above. The private rental sector, which dominated the Dutch housing stock through the 1950s, diminished sharply thereafter (Dieleman & Jobse 1991). The tenure structure of the housing stock has undergone a revolutionary turn-around during the past twenty years (Table 4.1). For two decades, there was consensus on the promotion of social rental housing and the owner-occupier sector, at the expense of private rental housing. This was expressed through rent control in the existing stock, whereby the rents were kept low. Accordingly, existing private rental housing became unprofitable for individual landlords, and new investment was all but impossible. Consequently, large-scale deferred maintenance occurred in the older private rental sector, and many landlords decided to sell off their properties. At the same time, the social housing associations were enticed to construct new housing by deep subsidies. The stock of social housing went through a period of rapid expansion, and many low- and moderate-income households could be accommodated in adequate and inexpensive dwellings (Dieleman & Jobse 1991). Also the owner-occupier sector expanded in response to construction subsidies and tax incentives.

The development of the housing stock of the big cities followed the national trend closely, but with two exceptions (Table 4.1). First, the share of the private rental sector owned by individual landlords remained relatively large: Amsterdam and Rotterdam showed record highs in 1971. In that year, respectively 47 and 41 percent of the stock consisted of such housing (Table 4.1 also includes private rental housing owned by investment firms). In 1986, these shares had diminished to 26 and 13 percent, respectively. The spectacular decline in Rotterdam resulted from large-scale acquisition of the old private rental dwellings by the city. These houses were subsequently renovated and then added to the stock of social rental housing. Secondly, the big cities built few houses for sale to owner-occupiers, which implied that the social rental sector came to predominate, especially in Amsterdam (cf. Chapter 3).

The large social rental sector in the big cities, and in the Randstad as a whole, has improved the quality of life in the area in two ways. On the one hand, large groups of foreign immigrants, who move especially to the big cities, could be properly housed. Foreigners now account for up to 20 percent of the population of the big cities. During the 1970s, their housing situation had still been poor (Bovenkerk et al. 1985). But since they gained access to social housing during the 1980s, their housing situation has improved considerably (Van Praag 1989). The immigrants then spread throughout much of the housing market, which diminished residential segregation (Clark et al. 1992). On the other hand, the social rental sector met the housing needs of the households with a minimum income, a category that increased in number during the 1980s. As a consequence of the economic recession, their number swelled from 300,000 in 1981 to 800,000 in 1987. Many of them have found their way into social housing.

Much discussion has erupted during the past few years about the large size of the inexpensive social rental sector in the big cities (Dieleman & Musterd 1991). Many are convinced that this has increased the socioeconomic contrasts between the population of the big cities and the suburban communities. Musterd & Ostendorf (1991) show that the income differences between the cities and their surrounding area increased considerably between 1974 and 1984. Since then, the ratio has stabilized. But the concentration of deprived households in the large cities remains substantial, as Van Kempen et al. (1989) show. This concentration threatens the quality of life in the cities; services and facilities as well as some neighborhoods are deteriorating, which is also detrimental to the low-income groups.

Table 4.1   Tenure of the Dutch housing stock, 1971 and 1985/1986 (percentages)

| | 4 large cities | | The Netherlands | |
	1971	1985/86	1971	1985/86
Private rent	53.1	31.6	27.3	15.3
Social rent	37.4	50.8	37.3	41.5
Owner occupied	9.5	17.6	35.4	43.2
Total	100.0	100.0	100.0	100.0

Source: Census 1971 and CBS-WBO 1985/86

The impact of the composition of the housing stock on the filtering process in the big cities has also received much attention lately. Many households start their housing careers in the less expensive parts of the housing stock when they are young. They then filter up as their income position improves. But because of the one-sided composition of the stock in the big cities, many stay within the (inexpensive) social rental sector when their incomes grow, which leads to a bias in the use of housing. The national government has targeted this housing bias as the core of its housing policy (Volkshuisvesting in de jaren negentig 1990). The externalities of previous policy are now combatted with new policy: the tenants pay the bill by having to face major rent increases.

4.5   The bright and the dark sides of growth centers and urban renewal areas

Obviously it is possible to evaluate the rate of success of the spatial planning policy that has been in place since 1945 at the local level of individual neighborhoods and settlements. Certainly where the well-being of the inhabitants is used as the measuring rod for evaluation, the neighborhoods and the settlements, which comprise the territory of daily life, are the prime units for such a discussion. This observation has several implications. It is at this scale that the increasing heterogeneity of the population structure of the Randstad since the end of the 1960s is visible (cf. Chapter 3 of this volume). The households in this part of the country are increasingly diverse with respect to their livelihood and their participation in the labor process. There is also a greater diversity with respect to the possibilities for an internal division of labor and childcare. This leads to an increased diversity of lifestyles and the housing needs of the various types of households. And this, in turn, affects the spatial distribution of the households as they look for different residential environments within the Randstad. A brief discussion of these implications can be borrowed from Vijgen & Van Engelsdorp Gastelaars (1986; 1991).

Adults with a paid job are commonly tied to a fixed workplace - mostly outside the house - determined by their employer. In comparison to people without a job, their freedom of movement in time and space for other activities is limited. They devise strategies to increase their flexibility to protect the free time they have within the household. We can list three of these strategies. First, households with a relatively heavy workload, that is to say, households in which all adults have a job, tend to work in or close to their home. They also use nearby facilities and services. Secondly, the members of these households tend to combine their visits to the various places outside the home - places of work, shopping, etc. - into multi-purpose trips. And finally, they tend to hire people for various chores or frequently use specialized services to avoid having to do domestic tasks themselves. They employ domestic help, use cleaners, childcare, restaurants, and carry-out places to obtain their meals. Thereby these 'monetizing' households become more dependent than others on the facilities in their neighborhood (cf. Figure 4.4).

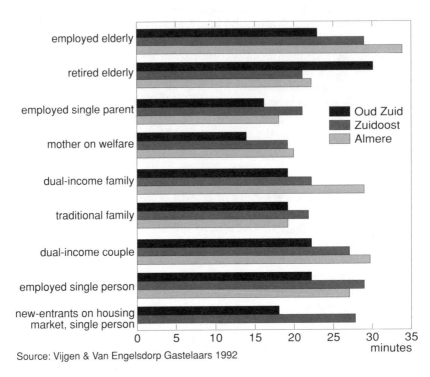

Source: Vijgen & Van Engelsdorp Gastelaars 1992

Figure 4.4   *Travel time to various destinations by location on weekdays (average number*
              of minutes)

The implications of these strategies are clear. In all these respects, compact, well-equipped neighborhoods near concentrations of employment provide the best residential environments. In other words, households with a heavy workload are oriented more than other households to urban neighborhoods in the inner city. But apartments without gardens and without hobby spaces are also acceptable.

The presence of more than one adult in a household affects the pattern of activities of the people concerned in two ways. First, the organization of the daily activities is much more simple than for single persons or for single-parent households. Households consisting of two wage earners are therefore less dependent on the environmental conditions listed above - the availability of plenty of jobs and services and facilities nearby - than working singles and single-parent families. They can better afford to have a residential location outside the city. The most extreme example of this, however, is the traditional family. This type of household has an extremely asymmetrical division of labor within the household. The woman takes care of all the domestic chores and thereby frees the man for time-consuming wage labor and commuting. Therefore, this type of household can function well in a real suburban environment.

The absence of a partner implies that there are fewer options to achieve by a division of labor within the household, which leads to stronger functional external links. It also implies an increased social dependency on the outside world. Singles are completely dependent on non-household members for their social life. Consequently, singles and single parents spend more of their free time in the company of outsiders and in places outside the home than members of other households do: in other people's homes, and in public places such as movie theaters and especially in bars (Vijgen & Van Engelsdorp Gastelaars 1991). This unavoidable social orientation toward the outside world is also translated into needs. To be able to maintain a social network of adequate quality and size, singles and single parents need a more or less central location among potential contacts. Proximity to a variety of public meeting places is also a requirement to be able to use them with a certain regularity. Both needs imply that single parents and certainly singles prefer an urban residential environment to a greater extent than other types of households. Cities offer the largest choice of bars, restaurants, and other public meeting places. In addition, cities are central places by definition, and they house more persons without a partner - that is, the important potential contacts for the social networks - than other places.

The presence of children in a household implies above all a clear restriction on the activities away from home for the parents. Their presence leads to less spendable income per person. For many activities, there is a charge for each individual. Thus, children lead to extra expenses and a further reduction of the spendable income per person. In addition, children tie the parents down. They cannot be taken along to all places, and leaving them at home requires baby sitting arrangements. Finally, the activities of the children fragment the spare time of the parents who do not work away from home. Altogether, the presence of children implies that the household is more oriented towards activities at home. Activities away from home need to be cheap or free of charge, while the children need in addition the well-known combination of quiet, safety, private garden, and other open-air playgrounds. All this predisposes family-type households for spacious single-family houses in suburban environments.

Because of these effects, the recent increase in the number of young, full-time employed singles and couples in the western part of the Netherlands causes a growing interest in neighborhoods in or near the urban core of the big Randstad agglomerations. And the steadily increasing labor participation rate among married women also leads to a reorientation of families on the housing market of the Randstad. These families may still prefer a house in a suburban environment, but the interest in peripheral rural areas has decreased significantly. There are more of these recent shifts in the preference patterns for housing and residential environments among the population of the Randstad. They are pertinent to our argument because they were not foreseen by the authorities. Still, they have had some unexpected effects on the success or failure of the various growth centers and urban renewal areas in the western part of the Netherlands, irrespective of their structure.

The foregoing argument implies that the growth centers in the western part of the country can best be described as social suburbs. They were built for people who needed social housing to meet their suburban housing preferences. Accordingly, the success of these growth centers depends primarily upon their relative quality as a suburban environment within the daily urban system - and by implication, the regional housing market to which they belong. Given the rapidly growing interest among married women and mothers in some (paid) role in the labor market, it may also be expected that growth centers with a favorable location with respect to concentrations of jobs and of facilities and services will be more successful than others. These locational aspects were, however, largely ignored by the planning authorities when they sited the growth centers. The jobs remain concentrated in the agglomerations of the big cities. They have also increased rapidly in the Green Heart, in the center of the ring of cities. Yet virtually all growth centers were sited in the rural periphery, towards the outer rim of the ring of cities: in the northern part of the province of North Holland and in the province of Flevoland, respectively to the north and the east of the city of Amsterdam, and on the islands to the south of Rotterdam. This choice of location, based on physical planning considerations, proved to be detrimental to the success of the growth centers, as was shown by the analyses by Bloemberg & Van Zeijl (1986) and Van Engelsdorp Gastelaars & Ostendorf (1991).

These analyses concerned the fate of all 13 growth centers that had at one time or another the official status in the national physical planning policy (see Table 4.2). The relative level of success is indicated by the level of unemployment in the growth center (Y1). In the debate on the growth centers this is usually considered to be a key indicator of its success or failure (Nozeman 1986; Bloemberg & Van Zeijl 1986). A second indicator for the ranking of growth centers by success rate consists of a combination of unemployment and housing vacancies (Y2).

These indicators are subsequently related to some measure of suburban character in the residential environment (X1), the location with respect to the centers of employment and of services and facilities in the Randstad (X2, proximity is considered to be a positive value), and the local presence of employment opportunities. The success rate of the growth centers, as indicated by Y1 and Y2, proves to be correlated mainly with X3, the relative location of the growth centers with respect to the big cities.

We posit that this provides sufficient evidence to support the claim that the growth center policy failed so far to account for the changing circumstances since the late 1960s. These changes refer to the increasing heterogeneity of the households, and consequently, the more pronounced spatial segregation of households by lifestyles. Increasingly, the migrants from the cities to the surrounding region comprise the 'suburbanites' (mainly existing families or households on their way to family formation). But more and more, the suburbanites stay away from the rural areas that are clearly

Table 4.2   *Growth centers by the quality of their residential environments and their success rate*

	X_1	X_2	X_3	Y_1	Y_2
Alkmaar	32	4	69	13	7.5
Almere	31	3	56	10	7.5
Capelle	24	2	36	11	12
Haarlemmermeer	44	2	70	6	4
Hellevoetsluis	32	4	34	11	11
Hoorn	44	4	66	13	10
Houten	64	2	47	5	2.5
Huizen	47	1	58	5	1
Lelystad	23	5	60	19	13
Nieuwegein	44	2	59	7	2.5
Purmerend	35	3	44	10	6
Spijkenisse	34	3	45	10	9
Zoetermeer	27	2	57	6	5
Rank correlation coefficient with Y_1 (Spearman)	+0.6	+0.9	-0.1		
Rank correlation coefficient with Y_2 (Spearman)	+0.7	+0.8	+0.2		

X_1 - Percent owner-occupier dwellings
X_2 - Rank of location relative to employment centers, 1986
X_3 - Number of local jobs as ratio to labor force (x 100), 1986
Y_1 - Percent unemployed
Y_2 - Rank of degree of success, 1985-86

peripheral with respect to the big cities. This is clearly a consequence of the growing labor market participation rate of the married women among the migrants from the city. At the same time, the 'urbanites' (including relatively many young single adults and singles of a somewhat older age cohort) deliberately choose the city as their place of residence. Only the growth centers located in the Green Heart of the Randstad can therefore be seen as successful, if this qualification relates to the quality of life for the inhabitants of these settlements.

The opinion that physical decline and social deprivation at the level of the neighborhood are related has motivated many authorities to start an urban renewal program. The use of urban renewal as an instrument to abate social deprivation in a neighborhood can therefore be seen as a fundamental aim of urban renewal policy in the Netherlands (Evaluatienota Stadsvernieuwing 1990; Rohde & Bertholet 1990; Priemus et al. 1991). Therefore we wish to measure the success of urban renewal in the agglomerations of the Randstad by the degree to which this policy has resulted in a higher welfare

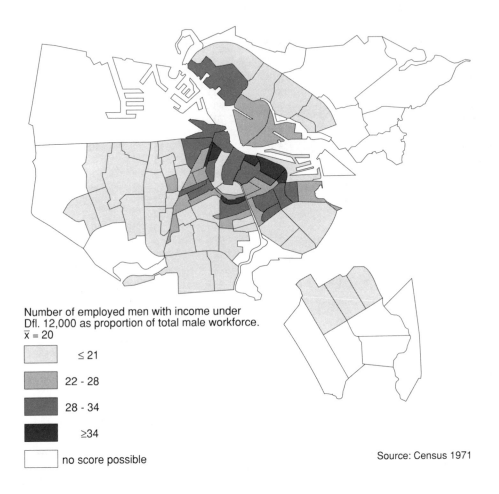

Number of employed men with income under
Dfl. 12,000 as proportion of total male workforce.
x̄ = 20

≤ 21

22 - 28

28 - 34

≥34

no score possible

Source: Census 1971

Figure 4.5   Income level of Amsterdam neighborhoods, 1971

attainment of the local population. However, this resolution cannot be carried out
without problems. For instance, there is no information concerning the level of well-being
in all the individual urban renewal areas of the four big Randstad agglomerations.
An analysis of the development of incomes in the Amsterdam statistical enumeration
districts will have to suffice. The development is traced for the period 1971 (the year
of the last Dutch census, and at the same time an adequate approximation of the start
of urban renewal) and 1990 (data from a survey on quality of life in various neighborhoods among the inhabitants of Amsterdam). Figures 4.5, 4.6, and 4.7 indicate the

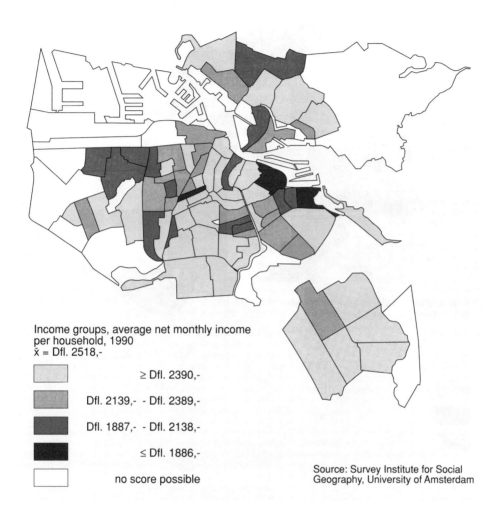

Income groups, average net monthly income per household, 1990
x̄ = Dfl. 2518,-

≥ Dfl. 2390,-

Dfl. 2139,- - Dfl. 2389,-

Dfl. 1887,- - Dfl. 2138,-

≤ Dfl. 1886,-

no score possible

Source: Survey Institute for Social Geography, University of Amsterdam

Figure 4.6   Income level of Amsterdam neighborhoods, 1990

shifts in the socioeconomic structure of the city between 1971 and 1990.

The picture is clear. Social upgrading has only taken place to any extent in the neighborhoods in or near the inner city, the historic core, which contains the most important centers of employment, retailing, and recreation. Six of the ten most upgraded neighborhoods are situated in the inner city, and three are located in the adjacent belt of neighborhoods developed at the end of the 19th century. Social downgrading, on the other hand, has been recorded especially on the periphery of Amsterdam.

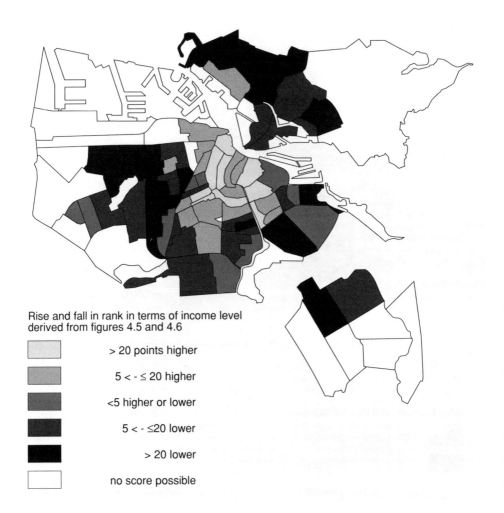

Rise and fall in rank in terms of income level
derived from figures 4.5 and 4.6

	> 20 points higher
	5 < - ≤ 20 higher
	<5 higher or lower
	5 < - ≤20 lower
	> 20 lower
	no score possible

Figure 4.7   Shift in relative income level of Amsterdam neighborhoods, 1971-1990

Virtually all the peripheral neighborhoods developed since 1945 underwent this process
to a major or minor extent (cf. Musterd & Ostendorf 1991).

At least one of the factors that have contributed to this turn-around has already been
touched upon above; this concerns the emergence of new types of households with
a preference for urban living. In Amsterdam, this proves to be a very significant factor.
Investigations have shown that these new households (predominantly the young and
somewhat older singles and couples with high educational qualifications) are intimately

tied in their daily activities to a relatively densely developed urban environment. Therefore, they dominate among the migrants to neighborhoods in and near the urban core. And finally, they account for an increasing share of the inhabitants of these centrally located neighborhoods (Vijgen et al. 1991; Buys & Cortie; Cortie et al. 1989; Van Engelsdorp Gastelaars et al. 1987). This process of social upgrading in central areas of cities has become known in the literature as gentrification. The inhabitants involved in the process are described as 'marginal gentrifiers' (young singles or cohabiting couples of students, artists, and young professionals setting out upon a career, all with a low income) (Rose 1984).

For our argument, it is important to know how much the urban renewal policy has contributed to the (relative) upgrading of the urban neighborhoods in or near the urban core. With the data at our disposal, this connection cannot adequately be shown to exist (Figures 4.7 and 4.8).

Irrespective of whether or not they were the scene of urban renewal, all inner-city neighborhoods of Amsterdam increasingly became the place of residence of households with a higher socioeconomic position between 1971 and 1990. In addition, the only inner-city neighborhood that has not yet felt the impact of upgrading (a peripheral harbor-related area on the east side) happens to be the one most intensively affected by urban renewal. Also in the belt of 19th century neighborhoods surrounding the inner city, the variations in upgrading (and downgrading) appear to be unconnected to the intensity of the urban renewal there. Hardly any urban renewal activities took place between 1971 and 1990 in the neighborhoods that show the clearest signs of upgrading. Conversely, the neighborhood that experienced the most severe degree of socioeconomic decline during this period (an old working-class neighborhood on the eastern edge of the city) underwent intensive urban renewal at the same time.

Obviously, the effect of urban renewal on social upgrading and downgrading in neighborhoods in or near the urban core of Amsterdam remains unclear. In the past, the goal of many urban renewal activities was to offer housing to the low-income people already residing in the area. But this goal is not manifest in the collected data. On the contrary, the general process seems to be one of social upgrading in the inner city. This leads to the displacement of low-income groups from these areas towards the belt of neighborhoods surrounding the inner city. Rather than being slowed down by urban renewal, this process seems to be stimulated by it.

If urban renewal is solely depicted in numbers of renovated dwellings, the shifts in the residential functions of the neighborhoods are lost from view. Because the city is increasingly the domain of young adults with a modest income who are just starting out on a housing career, there is some merit in adapting the urban renewal policies to accommodate these marginal gentrifiers. This would support the strategy to maintain an inexpensive stock of buildings where people can live and work. It would then be appropriate to leave room for the tenants to contribute to the renovation or alteration of the buildings. The present strategy of thorough renovation to achieve fully finished dwellings with a standard floor plan and a high rent does not suit the needs of the marginal gentrifiers as well.

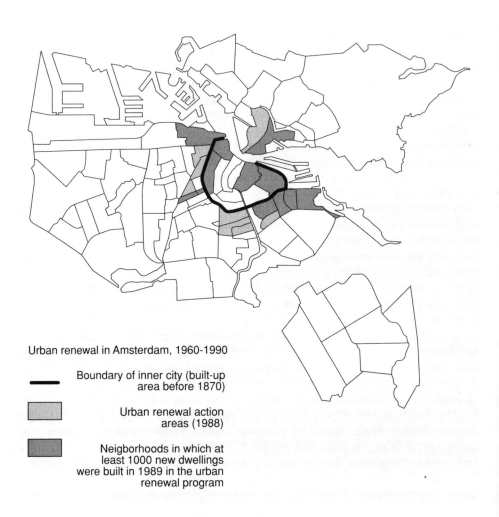

Urban renewal in Amsterdam, 1960-1990

Boundary of inner city (built-up
area before 1870)

Urban renewal action
areas (1988)

Neigborhoods in which at
least 1000 new dwellings
were built in 1989 in the urban
renewal program

Figure 4.8   *Urban renewal areas, Amsterdam*

4.6   Discussion

On the grounds of the above analysis, our conclusion can be straightforward. The spatial planning and housing policies with respect to the Randstad, carried out between 1945 and 1985, have not improved the quality of life in all cases in the affected regions, agglomerations, settlements, and neighborhoods. In many instances, they have not brought about an increase in the quality of life or in the well-being of the affected inhabitants. In other words: in terms of goal conformity (whereby the goal of the proposed spatial policy is to improve the well-being of the citizens involved, as explicitly stated in all the planning documents), this policy was not successful in all respects. We cannot explain this entirely. But undoubtedly, one of the factors is that all the planning authorities in this country have for decades supported the ideal of balanced development. This 'balance' applies to the social and functional structure of the regional and local residential environments, as well as to their physical structure. It is, for instance, also expressed in the often reiterated aim to balance the development of the West with that of the remainder of the country with respect to population size, congestion, the burden on the environment, employment opportunities, etc. in the policy that was in effect between 1945 and 1985 for the Randstad. In addition, it keeps resurfacing in the attempts to balance the importance of the various agglomerations within the Randstad. It also underlies the often repeated desire to limit the urbanization of the western part of the country and to protect the rural way of life in the regions and settlements under siege from the urbanization trends. And finally, it provided the incentive to deliver the slums of the large cities from their state of deprivation. The ideal of a balanced population (with respect to affluence as well as in sociodemographic and cultural terms) in the local and regional residential environments continuously inspired the planning authorities. From the perspective of the planning authorities, such a balance is an indication of a good quality of life, while a certain degree of specialization in the structure and provisions of these areas is considered to be a sign of one-sidedness and the accumulation of problems. Consequently, well into the 1980s, the spatial planning and housing policies with respect to the Randstad have systematically ignored the increasing diversity in the Netherlands with respect to social backgrounds and the lifestyles of the various population groups. This trend could have been observed since the 1960s. It has led to a steadily increasing diversity of claims with respect to residential environments. For too long, the policies have focused excessively on the lifestyle and housing needs of the traditional family. The policies were grounded in the image of the social organization of an undifferentiated society, consisting of a balanced structure of regional and local communities.

Since 1985, the point of reference for spatial policy has moved away from a balanced structure. All Memorandums that have since then been published, at the national as well as at the local level, contain policy principles that recognize the regional and local variations in potential in this country as legitimate. Suddenly, the utilization of the environmental and locational qualities of specific regions, agglomerations, and neighborhoods is emphasized in order to promote productivity or affluence. The rapidly increasing number of Public-Private Partnerships in this country, introduced to develop specific projects in specific locations, testifies to this structural change. For these constructions were designed to achieve spatial objectives in specific regions, cities, or neighborhoods by utilizing the methods of a market system.

A similar preference for market conformity in methods and solutions tailored to specific situations may be noted with respect to the spatial plans for the Randstad.

In 1988, the Randstad was unequivocally identified as the economic core of the Netherlands. Thereby it was designated as one of the core areas for investment. The other regions were more or less left to their own resources, using the slogan 'regions have comparative advantages'. Another change was that the special positions of Amsterdam and Rotterdam as the economic prime centers within the Randstad were recognized; consequently, the two mainports have been promised extra support. At the same time, such a large volume of new residential construction for the future inhabitants of the Randstad was announced that new construction in the Green Heart seems to be unavoidable. And for the first time in a long while, a recommendation has been made to implement a revitalization policy for the individual cities that is geared to the utilization of the qualities of the (potentially) attractive parts of the city, rather than being aimed at the resolution of the minimum-choice character of the neighborhoods. Consequently, there is a growing recognition of the variations in quality of segmented regions, cities, and neighborhoods, irrespective of their social, functional and physical diversity. (Notitie 1986; Vierde Nota deel a and d 1988; Volkshuisvesting 1990; Van Engelsdorp Gastelaars et al. 1987).

It remains to be seen whether or not this reversal in thinking about the spatial structure of regional and local residential environments will be sustained. As the new insights with respect to the spatial structure of the Randstad on the part of the national and urban authorities become more concrete, they seem to lose their slant towards market orientation and spatial specialization. In the subsequent volumes of the Fourth Memorandum on spatial planning, the regions outside the Randstad already receive more attention. Also the equality of the four big agglomerations of the Randstad has been re-introduced, and the Green Heart is once more forcefully protected. The spatial ideal of balance is still a strong principle in government circles. Only time will tell if this ideal will continue to block the perspective of the authorities on the increasing social and spatial differentiation in this country (Vierde Nota Extra 1991).

References

Adriaansens, C.A. & A.Ch. Fortgens (1990), Volkshuisvestingsrecht. Deventer: Kluwer.

Arnold, T.F. (ed) (1990), Stadsvernieuwing op weg naar de jaren negentig. Verslag van de studiedag Stadsvernieuwing 26-10-'89 's-Gravenhage. 's-Gravenhage: Ministerie van Volkshuisvesting, Ruimtelijke Ordening en Milieubeheer.

Beleid voor Stadsvernieuwing in de toekomst (1991), Ontwerpnota. 's Gravenhage: SDU-Uitgeverij.

Bloemberg, J.T.M. & J.B. van Zeijl (eds) (1986), De toekomst van de groeikernen. Een verkennende studie. 's-Gravenhage: Rijks Planologische Dienst.

Boelhouwer, P.J., H.M.H. van der Heijden & O.A. Papa (1991), Nederlands volkshuisvestingsbeleid in Europees perspektief. Delft: Onderzoeksinstituut voor Technische Bestuurskunde.

Bovenkerk, F., K. de Bruin, L. Brunt & H. Wouters (1985), Vreemd volk, gemengde gevoelens. Amsterdam: Boom.

Buys, A. & C. Cortie (1990), Tussenstop of eindstation? Een studie van wooncarrières in en om Amsterdam. Amsterdam: Instituut voor Sociale Geografie, Universiteit van Amsterdam.

Cammen, H. van der, & L. A. de Klerk (1986), Ruimtelijke ordening. Van plannen komen plannen. Utrecht/Antwerpen: Het Spectrum.

Clark, W.A.V., F.M. Dieleman & L. de Klerk (1992), School segregation: Managed integration or free choice. Environment and Planning C (forthcoming).

Cortie, C., B.Kruijt & S. Musterd (1989), Housing market change in Amsterdam: Some trends. Netherlands Journal of Housing and Environmental Research 4, pp. 217-233.

Derde nota over de ruimtelijke ordening. Deel 2: Verstedelijkingsnota. Deel 2a: Beleidsvoornemens over spreiding, verstedelijking en mobiliteit (1976). 's-Gravenhage: SDU-Uitgeverij.

Dieleman F.M. & R.J. Schouw (1986), Demographic impacts on the Netherlands' housing system. Looking toward and beyond the Year 2000. The Netherlands Journal of Housing and Environmental Research 1, pp. 69-82.

Dieleman F.M. & R.B. Jobse (1991), Multi-family housing in the social rental sector and the changing Dutch housing market. Housing Studies 6, pp. 193-206.

Dieleman F.M. & S. Musterd (1991), Maatschappelijke veranderingen en de herstructurering van de Randstad. Geografisch Tijdschrift 25, pp. 490-501.

Engelsdorp Gastelaars, R. van, R. Tooren & I. Westerterp (1987), Een woonbuurt in het Oostelijk Havengebied. Amsterdamse Sociaal Geografische Studies 11. Amsterdam: Instituut voor Sociale Geografie, Universiteit van Amsterdam.

Engelsdorp Gastelaars, R. van, & W. Ostendorf (1991), New Towns: the beginning and end of a new urban reality in the Netherlands. In: M.J. Bannon, L.S. Bourne & R. Sinclair (eds), Urbanization and Urban Development. Recent Trends in a Global Context. Dublin: University College.

Evaluatienota stadsvernieuwing jaren '80 (1990).'s Gravenhage: SDU-Uitgeverij.

Faludi, A. & A.J. van der Valk (1990), De groeikernen als hoeksteen van de Nederlandse ruimtelijke planningsdoctrine. Assen/Maastricht: Van Gorcum.

Gramberg, J. (1991), Segregatie, woning- en ruimtenood in Den Haag. In: R. van Kempen, S. Musterd & W. Ostendorf (eds), Maatschappelijke veranderingen en stedelijke dynamiek. Volkshuisvesting in Theorie en Praktijk 30, pp. 221-228. Delft: Delftse Universitaire Pers.

Hooimeijer, P. & M. Linde (1988), Vergrijzing, individualiseringen en de woningmarkt. (diss.). Utrecht: Faculteit der Ruimtelijke Wetenschappen, Rijksuniversiteit Utrecht.

Jobse, R.B. & S. Musterd (1989a), Dynamiek in de Randstad. Een analyse van woningbouw- en migratiestatistieken voor de periode 1970-1986. Werkstukken Stedelijke Netwerken 10. 's-Gravenhage: SDU-Uitgeverij.

Jobse, R.B. & S. Musterd (1989b). Changes in migration within the Netherlands 1975-1985. Tijdschrift voor Economische en Sociale Geografie 80, pp. 244-250.

Kaa, D.J. van der (1987), Europe's Second Demographic Transition. Washington DC: Population Reference Bureau Inc.

Kempen, R. van, R.B.J. Teule, W.J. Stam & J. van Weesep (1989), In de klem tussen woningmarkt en arbeidsmarkt. In: F.M. Dieleman, R. van Kempen & J. van Weesep (eds), Met nieuw elan. Volkshuisvesting in Theorie en Praktijk 23, pp. 19-36. Delft: Delftse Universitaire Pers.

Ministerie van Volkshuisvesting, Ruimtelijke Ordening en Milieubeheer (1991a), De ordening van de Nederlandse volkshuisvesting in europees perspectief. Achtergrondinformatie. 's-Gravenhage: Ministerie van Volkshuisvesting, Ruimtelijke Ordening en Milieubeheer.

Ministerie van Volkshuisvesting, Ruimtelijke Ordening en Milieubeheer (1991a), De ordening van de Nederlandse volkshuisvesting in europees perspectief. Verslag. 's-Gravenhage: Ministerie van Volkshuisvesting, Ruimtelijke Ordening en Milieubeheer.

Musterd, S. & W. Ostendorf (1991), Inkomensontwikkeling en tweetoppigheid binnen de Randstad. In: R. van Kempen, S. Musterd & W. Ostendorf (eds), Maatschappelijke verandering en stedelijke dynamiek. Volkshuisvesting in Theorie en Praktijk 30, pp. 59-75. Delft: Delftse Universitaire Pers.

Nota inzake de ruimtelijke ordening in Nederland (1960), 's-Gravenhage: SDU-Uitgeverij.

Nota Volkshuisvesting (1972). 's-Gravenhage: SDU-Uitgeverij.

Notitie ruimtelijke perspectieven; op weg naar een vierde Nota over de ruimtelijke ordening (1986) Rijks Planologische Dienst. 's-Gravenhage: SDU-Uitgeverij.

Nozeman, E.F. (1986), Nieuwe bouwlokaties in het licht van enkele doelstellingen van ruimtelijke ordening; een evaluatieonderzoek naar de bijdrage van nieuwbouw in het stadsgewest Utrecht aan overheidsintenties omtrent mobiliteit en bevolkingssamenstelling. Amsterdam: Planologisch Demografisch Instituut, Universiteit van Amsterdam.

Oriënteringsnota ruimtelijke ordening (1973), Achtergronden, uitgangspunten en beleidsvoornemens van de regering. 's-Gravenhage: SDU-Uitgeverij.

Praag, C.S. van (1989), De woonsituatie van etnische minderheden. Rijswijk: Sociaal en Cultureel Planbureau.

Rohde, W. & P. Bertholet (1990), Stadsvernieuwing in cijfers; het voortgangsrapport Belstato. Amsterdam: RIGO.

Rose, D. (1984), Rethinking gentrification: Beyond the uneven development of Marxist urban theory. Environment and Planning D 2, pp. 47-74.

Schaar, J. van der (1987), Groei en bloei van het Nederlandse volkshuisvestingsbeleid. Delft: Delftse Universitaire Pers.

Schaar, J. van der, m.m.v. A. Hereijgers (1991), Volkshuisvesting: een zaak van beleid. Utrecht: Het Spectrum.

Steigenga, W. (1968), Moderne planologie. Utrecht: Het Spectrum.

Structuurplan Rotterdam binnen de Ring (1978), Rotterdam: Gemeentedrukkerij.

Structuurschets voor de stedelijke gebieden, deel a: beleidsvoornemens (1983).'s-Gravenhage: SDU-Uitgeverij.

Tweede nota over de ruimtelijke ordening in Nederland (1966), 's-Gravenhage: SDU-Uitgeverij.

Vandermotten, C. (1991), Reflexions preliminaires sur une comparison des structures demographiques et socio-economiques de quelques villes Ouest-Europeennes. Bruxelles: Université Libre de Bruxelles.

Vermooten, W.H. (1949), Stad en land in Nederland en het probleem der industrialisatie. Een sociografische studie. Amsterdam: Universiteit van Amsterdam.

Vierde nota over de ruimtelijke ordening, deel a: beleidsvoornemens (1988),'s-Gravenhage: SDU-Uitgeverij.

Vierde nota over de ruimtelijke ordening, deel d: regeringsbeslissingen (1988), 's-Gravenhage: SDU-Uitgeverij.

Vierde nota over de ruimtelije ordening Extra, deel III: kabinetsstandpunt (1991), 's-Gravenhage: SDU-Uitgeverij.

Volkshuisvesting in de jaren negentig. Van bouwen naar wonen (1990). 's-Gravenhage: SDU-Uitgeverij.

Vijgen, J. & R. van Engelsdorp Gastelaars (1986), Stedelijke bevolkingskategorieën in opkomst. Nederlandse Geografische Studies 22. Amsterdam: KNAG/Instituut voor Sociale Geografie, Universiteit van Amsterdam.

Vijgen, J. & R. van Engelsdorp Gastelaars (1991), Een gevarieerd bestaan. Het gebruik van tijd en ruimte in het dagelijks leven van enkele 'oude' en 'nieuwe' groepen binnen de Nederlandse bevolking. Werkstukken Stedelijke Netwerken 28. Amsterdam: Stedelijke Netwerken.

Werkcommissie Westen des Lands (1956), Het Westen en overig Nederland. Ontwikkeling van de gebieden buiten het Westen des Lands. 's-Gravenhage: SDU-Uitgeverij.

Werkcommissie Westen des Lands (1958), De ontwikkeling van het Westen des Lands. Toelichting. 's-Gravenhage: SDU-Uitgeverij.

Witsen, J. & H. Leeflang (1977), Omtrent de Verstedelijksnota, Publicatie 77-2 's-Gravenhage: Rijks Planologische Dienst.

Prof.dr. F.M. Dieleman
Faculty of Geographical Sciences
University of Utrecht
P.O. Box 80.115
3508 TC Utrecht
The Netherlands

Prof.dr. R.E. van Engelsdorp Gastelaars
Faculty of Environmental Sciences
University of Amsterdam
Nieuwe Prinsengracht 130
1018 VZ Amsterdam
The Netherlands

5.   A WORLD CITY PARADOX - FIRMS AND THE URBAN FABRIC

M. de Smidt

5.1   Introduction

The urban system in the Netherlands differs from the general West European pattern in several respects. The Randstad Metropolis is a multi-nucleated urban system, quite unlike the primate cities of London and Paris. The intent of the Fourth Memorandum on Physical Planning is to meet the challenges set by the internationalization of the economy. The projected means to do so is by transforming inner-city renewal sites into locations for international head-offices and advanced business services. But this planning policy has to counteract the trend toward deconcentration of advanced office activities. That trend aggravates the threat to urban areas by hollowing out their economic base, thus concentrating the underprivileged segments of the population there. Part of the challenge is that the labor demand of advanced office activities does not correspond with the kind of labor supply available in the cities.

In addition to modeling itself on a world city, the Randstad wants to renew its longstanding position as a gateway. It seeks to provide access to the Single European Market. This goal can only be achieved if it is linked to the intent to internationalize the economy, as expressed in the Fourth Memorandum. New logistic systems operating within transnational corporations (TNCs) are increasing the flexibility of industry. New networks of suppliers and new locations for (sub)assembly are indicative of the presence of these logistic systems, which bring about a redistribution of transport nodes. Rotterdam is a major world seaport and Amsterdam airport is a hub for international airfreight and passenger traffic. As 'mainports', these two gateways are supposed to take advantage of the new logistic operations.

Some producer services could link these two goals. They could help the Randstad to become a true world city and to compete with other leading European 'mainports' as well. How to meet both challenges at the same time? How to cope with the deconcentration processes that are common to major urban regions? Which stage of postindustrial society has been reached? These are the key issues that will be addressed in this chapter.

F. M. Dieleman and S. Musterd (eds.), The Randstad: A Research and Policy Laboratory, 97–122.

5.2   Challenges of internationalization

Modernization of society is predicated upon industrialization. But it also entails the centralization of institutional power, starting with the concentration of bureaucracy in primate cities and the emergence of nation-states. The United Provinces of the (northern) Netherlands was a mere mercantile confederacy, dominated by cities in the province of Holland. From the sixteenth century onward, these cities were increasingly 'outward'-looking. The birth of the nation-state and the onset of in-dustrialization came rather late, whereas urbanization started early, particularly in the province of Holland (De Smidt 1987; Hoekveld 1990). Initially the international orientation did not focus upon the western rim of cities now known as the Randstad. The Hanseatic League, a federation of merchant cities, was mainly based in German and Scandinavian cities, including a range of IJssel cities in the eastern part of the Netherlands. In late medieval times some western cities linked the dominating ports of London and Bruges to the Hanseatic cities in the Baltic. At the time of the Westphalian Treaty (1648) the cities of Holland controlled three-quarters of the Baltic grain trade and of the Portuguese-French salt trade. They also controlled over half of the Baltic timber trade, as well as delivering half of the cloth to the Baltic cities (De Vries 1959). This means that the preindustrial economy was founded on a mercantile base.

From 1600 onward the Dutch penetrated the Mediterranean basin, connecting the Baltic and the Mediterranean trade routes. The international scope of Dutch business widened through colonial trade. This does not mean that the economy, though internatio-nalizing, was branching out worldwide. Neighboring countries dominated the scene in terms of trade. One-third of the international trade in 1780, was of a colonial nature which was more profitable than other kinds of trade. The western rim of cities, dominated by Amsterdam, surpassed Antwerp as a world trade center after 1585. The cities attracted the (qualified) immigrants they needed in order to have the workforce for a flourishing mercantile economy. Consequently, the province of Holland took the lead in all respects within the loosely organized federation of Dutch provinces. In the nineteenth century new manufacturing was established in the southern and eastern provinces earlier than in Holland and brought about some deconcentration (Keuning 1955). The era of the *belle époque*, a period when neighboring industrialized states were flourishing, gave new impetus to the dominance of the Randstad. However, the primate city of Amsterdam lost the international mercantile initiative to Rotterdam. As the port of the emergent Ruhr area, Rotterdam offered a major link between the leading British and German industrial complexes. During the same period, The Hague became the seat of a new bureaucracy. Utrecht evolved as a nodal point in the internal Dutch transport network, which developed with the emergence of the nation-state as vehicle of integration (Knippenberg & De Pater 1988).

From then on, internationalization was closely linked to a port economy. The emergence of TNCs and a strong export-led industrialization and agricultural upgrading provided a broader base for an 'outward'-looking economy. However, the thrust of

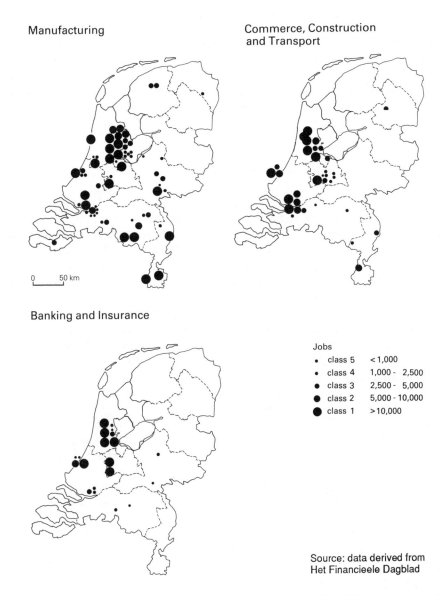

Manufacturing

Commerce, Construction
and Transport

Banking and Insurance

Jobs
- • class 5   < 1,000
- • class 4   1,000 - 2,500
- ● class 3   2,500 - 5,000
- ● class 2   5,000 - 10,000
- ● class 1   >10,000

Source: data derived from
Het Financieele Dagblad

Figure 5.1   *Location of head-offices according to strength of firm (number of jobs*
              controlled) 1988

internationalization was not centered in the Randstad (Figure 5.1). Some major
manufacturing companies have their main seat outside the Randstad: Philips

(Eindhoven), Akzo (Arnhem), and DSM (Heerlen in South Limburg). Traditionally, the main agriculture regions with a high export volume are located in the north of the Netherlands, although leading horticulture centers are concentrated in the Amsterdam region (Aalsmeer), West-Friesland, and the Rotterdam-The Hague area (Westland), being bound to their initial urban markets. The main elements of the specific Randstad-based international activities have made the Randstad both a management center, including head-offices and advanced business services, and a logistic center as well.

5.3   Playground of international business

Internationalization is an expression encompassing a wide variety of activities. Moreover, it is a process, not just coexisting phenomena, and this process supposes a number of interlinked developments. In describing an extremely open economy like that of the Netherlands, we have to narrow the concept of the process of internationalization. It should cover those processes governing (1) corporate international activities as well as (2) foreign-based activities, particularly of a non-EC nature, and (3) advanced business services connected with the international networks of these activities. This definition goes beyond the traditional description of the term management center, which comprises only head-offices. It would be better to employ the term transactional city. However, the connotation of that term includes all information-handling activities of a decisive nature and therefore purely domestic-oriented activities as well. The three basic elements of internationalization will be highlighted in the following overview of the Randstad as an international-oriented management center by domestic firms. The role of the top-100 companies will be assessed. This limitation to big companies means that a great number of internationally oriented small and medium-sized firms are excluded (De Smidt & Meyerink 1990; De Smidt & Wever 1990). Of the 47 large corporations in the Netherlands, each with more than 5,000 employees, 39 have their head-office in the composite metropolis known as Randstad Holland. However, the only available survey is limited to corporate headquarters of the top-100 companies according to the volume of sales. Among manufacturing firms, 40 of the 65 head-offices are located in this part of the Netherlands; among non-manufacturing firms, 29 of the 35 head-offices are present there (Van Rietbergen et al. 1990; De Smidt 1991b; cf. Ter Hart 1979). Taking the top-100 of banking and doing the same for insurance, it turns out that 16 out of 20 have their head-office in the Randstad; just a few medium-sized firms have their main office in the intermediate zone.

A classification of internationalization has been made in order to give a more detailed account of the stage of the internationalization process (Van Rietbergen et al. 1990; De Smidt 1990). Firms have been categorized according to the volume of sales and number of personnel abroad (Figure 5.2, Tables 5.1 and 5.2). The group of true 'internationals' is limited; for the most part these are manufacturing firms (15 of the 20) with two-thirds of the head-offices in the Randstad. More than half of both sales

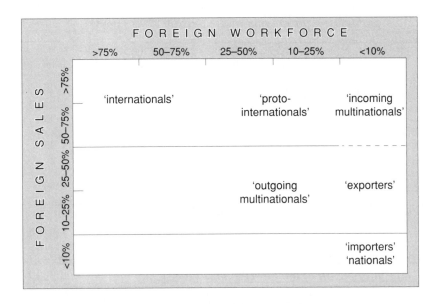

Figure 5.2   Degree of internationalization of firms: a typology

and jobs is located abroad. Runners-up are TNCs, which could be labeled as 'proto-internationals' and 'outgoing multinationals'. Both types are characterized by 10-50 percent of sales abroad. The former type is also strongly involved abroad as far as personnel is concerned, while the latter is more domestic-based in this respect. Mostly manufacturing firms of these categories have their headquarters outside the Randstad, whereas the non-manufacturing firms concentrate in this metropolis (cf. Tables 5.1 and 5.2). Corporate firms belonging to categories with a low proportion of personnel outside the Netherlands are by no means isolated from the internationalization process. There is a category of 'incoming multinationals' that is heavily engaged in exporting. These are mainly subsidiaries of large foreign companies, which are thus using the Netherlands as a gateway to Europe. They are mostly based in the Rotterdam port area (Loeve 1989). Sometimes domestic companies may be found in the same category. This is the case for the Dutch aircraft company Fokker and the dairy industry, the latter mainly located in peripheral areas. The category of 'importers' is also internationally active. These firms are located mainly at Rotterdam seaport, near Schiphol Amsterdam airport, or in the central areas of the country near Utrecht. There are just a few large 'national' firms, about five of the top-100! This demonstrates the extent to which Dutch-based companies are involved in the international economy.

The strong representation of internationally oriented firms in the Randstad has been illustrated by Van der Velde (1989). Of the 304 corporate organizations that have

Table 5.1   Degree of international orientation in terms of personnel and the regional and sectoral distribution of the top-100 firms (1988)

Zone	Personnel	>75% A	50-75% B	25-50% C	10-25% D	<10 E	Total
West	manufacturing	4	5	4	6	22	40
	other	-	4	8	2	15	29
Intermed.	manufacturing	1	2	1	3	5	12
cities	other	-	-	-	-	-	-
Rest of	manufacturing	-	2	2	1	8	13
the Neth.	other	-	2	-	-	4	6
Total		6	15	15	11	54	100

Source: Calculations based on data from Het Financiële Dagblad

Table 5.2   Degree of international orientation by sales and the regional and sectoral distribution of the top-100 firms (1988)

Zone	Sales	> 75% A	50-75% B	25-50% C	10-25% D	<10% E	Unknown	Total
West	manufacturing	18	12	4	2	3	1	40
	other	3	4	4	3	13	2	29
Intermed.	manufacturing	5	2	3	1	1	-	12
cities	other	-	-	-	-	-	-	-
Rest of	manufacturing	6	2	2	1	-	2	13
the Neth.	other	2	1	1	-	2	-	6
Total		34	21	14	7	19	5	100

Source: Calculations based on data from Het Financiële Dagblad

personnel abroad or generate foreign business, 67 are located in or around Amsterdam and Rotterdam. This figure includes foreign companies with subsidiaries in the Netherlands. These firms enhance the international significance of the Randstad as a management center. Their contribution should be considered in some detail here. For a long time, the Netherlands has been a major capital-exporting country. In the beginning of the 1980s, outgoing investments were twice as high as incoming investments in terms of stocks; by the end of the decade, this net balance had dropped to about 50 percent. After 1985 the stocks of foreign capital increased markedly. This was a sign of US, Japanese, and Scandinavian eagerness to participate in the Single European Market. At both sides of the balance of stocks of investments, the European Community gained importance due to ongoing integration effects. It is striking that services take a greater share of investments, increasing from 30 to 40 percent during the 1980s and comprising a wide variety of industries. US companies controlled 35 percent of the jobs provided by foreign firms in 1988. EC companies have more personnel (143,000, compared to US companies with 110,000) but are smaller in size (57 compared to 78 jobs on the average). EFTA countries and Japan have less impact (1988: 41,000 and 10,000 jobs respectively, compared to a total of 310,000 jobs) but their share is increasing due to anxiety about the imminent Fortress Europe 1992 (BCI 1990a).

The Randstad Metropolis is the exclusive seat of business services of foreign origin operating in the Netherlands. There is a clear-cut division of labor between the main urban agglomerations in this respect, comparable with the longstanding specialization of these cities. Amsterdam is a financial center and hosts airport-linked activities; Rotterdam is a transport center; and The Hague, as the government seat, has been preferred by consultancies. For distribution centers and related business services, the main ports of Amsterdam and Rotterdam are predominantly favored as a location. However, foreign business people have also discovered the advantages of some central locations in the Netherlands, the Utrecht region in particular, and the southern intermediate areas for easy access to the European market. Logistics plays an important role in considering whether to locate an operational headquarters in the Randstad. A consultancy report revealed that two kinds of head-offices were overrepresented in Amsterdam: small offices, because of new taxation laws (advantageous to holding companies); and large offices, including logistics control centers (KPMG 1988).

For about 20 years after the war, the Randstad also dominated the foreign manufacturing scene. Then deconcentration and restructuring changed this picture (De Smidt 1983; Loeve 1989). From the mid-1960s onward, a second economic core of the southern provinces became the preferred area for new foreign manufacturing establishments. They were looking for a less tight labor market, more space, and access to the European market, which was becoming more integrated.

This reflects a process of filtering down as well as a new geographical division of labor in the Netherlands. Southern provinces are favored for manufacturing, the Randstad for services. During the 1984-88 period of economic upheaval, 68 out of 81 new US service establishments, and all 29 new Japanese service establishments, chose a location in the Randstad. Likewise, 111 out of 144 new US sales offices and distribution centers located in the Randstad; for Japanese subsidiaries, this turned out to be 23 out of 26. Southern provinces offered 24 US and Japanese firms an alternative in this respect. For manufacturing, these provinces have been clearly preferred to the Randstad (BCI 1990b).

The Randstad has offered an operational base for internationally oriented domestic producer services for a long time. The profile of this sector has been changing under the influence of the dynamics in the financial world, as well as the professionalization of society and the externalization of specialized services. Producer services are now looking for decreasing transactional costs and limited information costs (Tordoir 1991). A process of cumulative causation has been set in action, involving downward filtering of routine activities to intermediate areas, taking advantage of telecommunication, and upward filtering of advanced office activities. Internationalization, informatization, and organizational change are interdependent processes. In this context two main issues will be dealt with, which express some major planning goals. The first is how to reach the target 'Amsterdam: Financial Gateway to Continental Europe'; the second is how to establish a control function in the networks of business services.

5.4   At the frontier of financial and business services

To evaluate the position of Amsterdam as a major financial center, several criteria can be used: (1) foreign banks and other financial institutions, (2) the international position of domestic banks, (3) the international role of the stock exchange, and (4) participation in the Eurovaluta market (Ter Hart 1987; Van Leeuwen 1989; Initiatiefgroep 1989).

Dealers in bonds are faced with the dilemma that their trade is no longer very sensitive to location, due to telecommunication and computer facilities, while they do have to know their business relations personally. Lead managers of banks in a syndicate find it absolutely necessary to have physical proximity to the client; this is not the case for the participants in the syndicate. Obtaining knowledge of the local market, establishing personal contact with clients, and supporting existing relations are crucial tactics if a foreign bank is to establish a subsidiary in a financial center. But these factors are not equally important to all forms of financial services. As Ter Hart and Piersma (1990) found, the determinants of physical proximity are the intensity of contacts, the balance between immediacy and intensity, the scale of the transaction, and the party one is dealing with (bank-customer and bank-investor transactions require physical presence more than interbank transactions). The criteria mentioned above will be now considered.

1. Foreign branches of banks start out doing import-export business. Later on, credit is provided to internationally operating firms, followed by a deeper penetration of the domestic economy (Fujita & Ishigaki 1986). Apart from the transactions just mentioned, foreign banks are participating in (Euro)valuta market transactions and in Eurobond issues (Advokaat 1986). In 1988, 43 out of 49 foreign banks were located in Amsterdam. During the 1980s there was a rise in the number of subsidiaries, while the number of branches stabilized and the number of participations and representative offices declined (Ter Hart & Piersma 1990). In Brussels these numbers are double, in Luxembourg threefold, in Paris quadruple (Van Leeuwen 1989). In London this figure is over 400, in New York over 300 (Daniels 1986).
2. The international position of Dutch banks is backed by their clients, such as major TNCs, and important institutional investment funds. It is also buttressed by a strong position in market segments such as venture capital, commercial credits, and trust funds, as pointed out by the initiative group 'Amsterdam International Financial Center'. The leading, recently merged ABN-AMRO bank can be compared with

the Deutsche Bank (now 18th in the world in terms of assets). ABN maintains a longstanding international tradition, even on the Pacific Rim, and is very active in international financial syndicates (Ter Hart 1987). Recently RABO, the Netherlands' second-largest bank, and ROBECO, Europe's second-largest investment fund, announced cooperation in investment banking. The third on the list, NMB, has been more active in international banking, in particular in the Americas, but merged recently with the domestic Postbank. New avenues will be pursued on the borderline of banking and insurance, as these two activities were recently separated by law. NMB-Postbank works together with Nationale Nederlanden, which is the country's largest insurance company and internationally the most active firm too.

However, there is some doubt about how internationally competitive Dutch banking really is. US- or UK-based mercantile banks are more aggressive, being supported by a merging corporate field. In Germany, France, and Belgium, connections between banks and giant firms are far more intensive.

3. The Amsterdam Stock Exchange takes fifth place in Europe and tenth worldwide according to sales volume. Relative to GNP, this institution ranks third, after that of Zurich and London. However, its expansion of activity lags behind that of Brussels, Paris, and London (Van Leeuwen 1989). The leading Dutch-based multinationals have been quoted on foreign stock exchanges too. It is said that Amsterdam lacks active intermediaries such as interdealer brokers.

4. Of increasing importance for financial centers is the Eurovaluta market. The Dutch share declined from 6 to 4.5 percent in the 1976-87 period, and the Belgian share increased from 5.6 to 9.1 percent in the same period. London is controlling half of that market (Van Leeuwen 1989). Some initiatives have been taken: for instance, the first Option Market in Europe was opened in 1978, and trading in financial futures has been developed. Three goals must be kept in mind when considering new initiatives: globalization of financial services, institutionalization of savings, and liberalization of financial transactions in the Single European Market. The target of making 'Amsterdam, Financial Gateway to Continental Europe' (1989) may sound overambitious in this respect. Although we cannot take its success for granted, it is a sign of increased vigor.

The major insurance companies are spread over the four main agglomerations. The European Single Market is inducing the top three companies (Nationale Nederlanden, Aegon, Amev) to expand their territory. Half of their volume of sales and half of their employees can be found abroad, albeit more in the US than in Europe. Jobs abroad have increased five fold compared to 15 years ago (Eppink & Van Rhijn 1988). Of course the single market is not the sole reason for these firms to expand outside the Netherlands. Economies of scale and distribution of risks as well as the decreasing attraction of a well-covered home market are also factors. Large foreign firms have penetrated the Dutch market; Prudential (UK) acquired a major Dutch firm (Delta Lloyd). Are advanced business services in the Randstad highly controlled, or could these activities be accommodated within a broader urban field? In this respect the 'information capital' hypothesis can be contrasted with the trickling down notion (Davelaar 1989; De Smidt et al. 1990). The computer sector fits the former concept. The starting point for software services was Utrecht; Amsterdam, dominated by foreign firms, was the initial location for computer hardware. The north wing (Amsterdam-Utrecht) is still dominant, whereas the south wing - in particular Rotterdam - is a runner up. There has been strong growth in the national market: in 1983 only 13 companies exceeded 3 million US dollars in net sales; in 1988, 51 companies sold over $ 3 million. The four Randstad metropolitan areas increased their share of head-offices and volume of net sales controlled by these offices (both over 60 percent in 1988), comprising half of the jobs. In the accounting sector spatial deconcentration occurred for market reasons. But head-offices did not deconcentrate; they have chosen new suburban loca-tions within the Randstad (Amstelveen, Rijswijk). The metropolitan areas of Amsterdam and Rotterdam control more than 80 percent of the volume of net sales as well as jobs. The most outspoken metropolitan activity is advertising, to a large extent American-owned and linked to the media sector of Amsterdam. For a long time, two-thirds of the annual sales volume was controlled by Amsterdam-based firms, followed by Rotterdam and The Hague (together they controlled 89 percent in 1988, up from 77 percent in 1983). The 'information capital' argument is relevant for the location of head-offices of all three business services. The 'innovation diffusion' or 'trickling down' hypothesis applies to the distribution of establishments as operational units, following the increasing market potentials. By locating all over the country and in major cities in intermediate areas, these establishments support the position of those places in these networks, stimulating a growth of the office sector (Van Dinteren 1987; Drenth 1990).

5.5   Mainports and logistics, Amsterdam and Rotterdam as hubs

Mainports are physical expressions of the international division of labor. Increasing internationalization of the economy is materialized in the major nodes providing a gateway to Europe. Moreover, they are becoming a crucial link in intercontinental traffic. Could Rotterdam (in sea traffic) or Amsterdam (in airfreight and passengers) be considered a turntable in this respect? The seaport of Rotterdam is Europe's biggest port for bulk goods as well as for containers. In general terms, the former category is not growing, although there is a shift from crude oil to transport of coal and ores. A new long wave of economic growth started with the introduction of containers with a higher value-to-weight ratio. Hinterlands are different for bulk goods; the Ruhr area is dominant in bulk traffic, whereas the southern regions of Germany are becoming more attractive for container traffic. Airfreight is also growing fast.

    Three-quarters of the container traffic is controlled by three major ports: Rotterdam (handling more than a third of all traffic), Antwerp, and Hamburg; the growth is stronger amond these two runners-up, particularly in high-value segments (Hornstra 1989). Rotterdam is a so-called 'load center', with feeder services to other, lower-ranking ports (Hayuth 1981). In container traffic a large part of the flow of goods between the US and the UK goes through the seaport of Rotterdam. Higher frequencies, bigger vessels or planes, and a higher rate of loading lead to economies of scale and scope.

In airfreight a comparable system of hub and spoke may be observed. The intercontinental orientation of Schiphol Airport increased, from the mid-1970s up to the mid-1980s. For passengers, the intercontinental proportion rose from a quarter to one-third; for airfreight, an increase from half to four-fifths in terms of weight was registered (De Smidt & Wever 1990). As a great deal of airfreight is transported by passenger planes, the significance of a home carrier is crucial. The position of KLM in the European processes of concentration and deregulation in airlines is uncertain. Special high-market segments are characterized by star-shaped networks, such as courier and express services through Zaventem, the airport of Brussels. This submarket is a good example of 'integrators', operating in an integrated transport system of air and ground traffic (Kramer 1990).

A competition is going on between major 'carriers' of seaborne or airborne traffic and overland transport companies. Both sides acquired a number of small, specialized firms and installed distribution and warehouse facilities all over Europe, connected with electronic data interchange systems for tracing and tracking goods. A multi-modal logistics system integrates transport based on water, rail, and trucks. For transport on inland waterways, Dutch firms control 40 percent of the EC market; for trucks 27 percent of border-crossing traffic is in their hands, the gross domestic product being just five percent of EC figures. The weakest link, however, is rail transport. The shift to the southern and eastern regions of the economic center of gravity in Germany, together with severe air pollution measures in effect there, will foster rail transport. In view of the likelihood of comparably strict rules for Alpine crossing traffic by trucks, this will be a great concern to Dutch transport firms. The Channel Tunnel, to be opened in 1993, will strengthen rail transport too. But the problems of crossing through the London region will support the roll-on/roll-off traffic through eastern UK seaports to the Benelux by truck. The opening of the Rhine-Donau link (September 1992) will offer new opportunities to vessels operating on the inland waterways, as Eastern European economies become integrated in a pan-European market.

Internationalization of the economy is expressed by the eagerness of US and Japanese corporate firms to establish a centralized European Distribution Center (EDC). Economies of scale, efficient control of smaller stocks, shorter completion schedules, and quick delivery times are basic ways to concentrate these efforts. ITT and IBM were among the first companies to select a few mainports: the seaport of Rotterdam and the airport of Amsterdam (De Smidt 1990). Adapting to the local market may be more difficult with centralized European distribution. Research by BCI (1990b) revealed that 2,000 American and 300 Japanese companies have a European distribution center. Of these, 15 percent (US), respectively 20 percent (Japan) have their EDC in the Netherlands, which is far higher than their share in manufacturing operations (7 percent; GNP 5 percent). Countries such as the UK, Germany, and Belgium have a comparable share in smaller American and Japanese EDCs, the UK and Germany being attractive for their home markets. Looking at large companies, the share of the Netherlands is much higher. Of *Fortune's* Top-500 American industrial companies, 175 out of 414 relevant firms (45 percent) already have an EDC in Europe, the Dutch share being 40 percent (about 70 EDCs). Of the *Tokyo Business Today's* Top-300 Japanese companies, 108 are engaged in these logistic operations, half of them in Europe. About 18 of these 50 companies have an EDC in the Netherlands. In other words, the Netherlands is a market leader in establishing EDCs of large non-EC companies. This gateway function - characterized by geographical location, distribution facilities, hinterland connections, and two mainports (sea and air) in close proximity - is strengthened by efficient customs facilities and language skills. On the other hand, the relatively small home market, high labor costs and social-security premiums, as well as traffic congestion are disincentives for operating an EDC in the Netherlands. Regarding logistics, Belgian ports are strong in material management supply, the Dutch ports being better in physical distribution, taking advantage of networks of multi-modal traffic (Bijlsma & Goossens 1989). In regard to major European transport mega-firms, 24 out of 36 sea- and airborne companies operate activities in the Netherlands, as do 30 out of 75 inland transport companies (Stam 1991).

It is intriguing to note that in the Netherlands, EDCs subcontract storage to logistics transport companies far more often than in other West European countries (39 percent compared to 23 percent according to the BCI 1990 study). This indicates the stronghold of the Dutch in distributive operations. Increasingly, other functions are being added to distribution activities after the establishment of an EDC, such as servicing, repair, assembly, R&D and even European headquarter activities. As already pointed out, many Amsterdam-based headquarters of non-EC firms include logistic operations (KPMG 1988).

The special Dutch position in logistics is not limited to the mainports of Rotterdam and Amsterdam. Of course, transhipment of goods takes place there. However, 40 percent of international trukking firms, according to carrying capacity, are located in the intermediate zone outside the Randstad (the provinces of North Brabant, Gelderland, and Limburg), a quarter operate out of Rotterdam seaport, and one-tenth are located in the Amsterdam agglomeration (ETIN 1987). These companies could have an establishment in the mainports and build their main distribution and storage facilities there. But they take the disadvantages of these mainports into consideration; these include high labor costs, inflexible labor market, expensive land costs, and infrastructural bottlenecks (Van der Loos & Harleman 1988). No wonder recent gross investments in assets in the (inland) transport sector were mainly directed outside the Randstad (Stam 1990).

5.6   International trade, contacts, and networks

Before the Industrial Revolution old industrial centers were based on the commercial links of these merchant cities of Holland. Textile manufacturing as well as the processing of foods and beverages were early industries; petrochemical industries are a modern example. The Rotterdam port offers a major break-point for transhipment of crude oil, which reaches the European market by a network of pipelines, inland waterways, trains, and trucks. Later on linkages emerged between participants, a so-called petrochemical complex. A highly developed export-oriented economy needs a large volume of imports. Within the Netherlands a division of labor has evolved: the southeastern manufacturing in the rim of medium-sized cities versus services in the Randstad. According to the Chambers of Commerce, the export centers of Amsterdam (24%) and Rotterdam (28.5%) do not export more than the national average (27%). This figure is much lower in the Hague (11) and Utrecht (13). Utrecht is an import center. Wholesaling activities are important in the main cities, and business services form a key sector of the urban economy. The large cities are growing faster in terms of the number of jobs (14%, national average 9.8%, 1987-1990). Investments are lower in the large cities (0.4% compared to 3.5%).

Networks could include physical links in transportation. However, logistics also need telematics to avoid being disconnected. New coupling constraints have to be faced (Poeth & Van Dongen 1985). The Holland International Distribution Council proposed the establishment of a logistics informatics frontier by a quick automation of customs data (Sagitta), cooperation of all transport-oriented information networks (Cargonaut for Amsterdam airport, Intis for Rotterdam seaport, Hermes for the railways, Tradicom for truck transport, and UTC for both inland waterway vessels and truck transport) and a national approach to teleports (Schaake 1989). Yet the establishment of these telematics systems is not the ultimate goal. There is a need for the delivery of services. It is currently being debated to what extent telematics systems are amenable to a sectoral approach. The basic idea of a teleport is being questioned. A teleport can be defined as 'an access facility to a satellite or other long haul telecommunications medium, incorporating a distribution network serving the greater regional community and associated with, including or within a comprehensive related real estate or other economic development' (Van der Niet 1989). A related concept is that of 'transpolis', focused on the transport sector and initiated near Schiphol, Amsterdam's airport. Teleports differ in functions to be dealt with. Logistics-oriented initiatives in Rotterdam, the Enschede region, and Bremen can be noted, as well as a media-oriented approach in Cologne, whereas the early Amsterdam initiative retains its broad aim. In France, industrial policies are dominant in this respect, revitalizing restructuring areas (Metz, Roubaix) and, at the same time, buttressing the (inter)national position of Paris. Modern telematics facilities could, however, be offered without teleport facilities, taking also into account that most large firms use specific computer configurations.

Contacts can be routinized. In a transactional economy face-to-face contacts are of crucial importance. Business services and corporate head-offices, or divisional head-offices, are seats of this type of contacts, facilitated by international or even intercontinental airports. Face-to-face contacts are also essential for international organizations and internationally oriented cultural and scientific institutions. As far as producer services are concerned, Dutch exports are lower than the EC average. This is also the case for Germany, whereas Paris and in particular London are leading centers. In the Netherlands, imports of producer services grow faster than exports of these services. For Germany, a better development has been noticed (Tordoir & De Haan 1987). As stated earlier, international producer services in the Randstad are controlled from abroad; the Randstad is the end of the line, not the starting point.

Looking at the orientation and range of external contacts, research on (divisional) head-offices and advanced business services showed that the Randstad definitely is a coherent metropolitan region, although there is a clear-out division of labor within a 'multi-tiered' system of cities (Dwarkasing et al. 1988, Tordoir 1991). International orientation is highest in the Amsterdam-Southeast subcenter, followed by The Hague-Southeast subcenter (Rijswijk) and Rotterdam city center. In the old city centers, international activities are underrepresented. In the last decade a strong deconcentration tendency of nearly all advanced business services occurred (Hessels & De Smidt 1991). Some recent initiatives to foster these activities in the inner cities may fuel the urban economic engine; these include the IJ Waterfront in Amsterdam, and the areas near the central railway stations in The Hague and Utrecht. Planning decisions, however, take a much longer time in those cities than in downtown Rotterdam. The inner ring of the Randstad, next to major express ways, is a highly desirable zone. Recent national government policies will limit the number and extension of these locations. As far as linkages are concerned, in most (sub)centers the workforce is drawn from the Randstad as whole. Only in Amsterdam, is there an 'internal' labor market as well. In this respect there is an integrated Randstad Metropolis.

5.7   Toward a global city

In recent years the term 'world city' has been frequently used, derived from the German 'Weltstadt'. According to Grimm Deutsches Wörterbuch, the word 'Weltstadt' was coined by Goethe in 1787 to express the cultural influence of cities (Gottmann & Harper 1990). The advantage of this expression is that it refers not just to the "slavery of great numbers" (Mumford 1966, p. 605) but also denotes networks. These include the external orbit as well as the clustering of interlinked activities, although internal networks lost importance in favor of external networks. Patrick Geddes introduced the term 'world city' to the English-speaking world to indicate very large urban systems with widespread networks (Hall 1966, p. 1). At present, world cities might be defined as 'control centers of the global economy' (Friedmann 1986). These are centers of information exchange with an enormous volume of transactional activities resulting from the linkages in the networks. These activities are carried by quaternary occupations, including managerial, research, and professional personnel (Gottmann 1983). Gottmann cites the cynical expression of the telecommunication specialist Arthur C. Clarke: "The purpose of life is information processing" (Gottmann & Harper 1990, p. 234). It can be stated that "as the global economy expands and manufacturing operations are rationalized at the global level, the demand for centralized knowledge-intensive activities and for the infrastructure necessary to support global operations increases" (Knight 1986, p. 396). Facilities could include a versatile labor market, expert consultation, meeting points, accessibility (airport), education, shopping, and other amenities (Gottmann & Harper 1990).

The original idea of a cultural meaning of world cities, as intended by Goethe, should not be forgotten, however. The cultural geography of the Netherlands has been influenced by a welfare-state-based distribution of cultural provisions. Nevertheless, Amsterdam has kept its position as a cultural 'primate city', the place where most cultural productions originate, cultural companies are established, and people of the cultural and media world are living (Van Kempen 1982; Van Beetz 1988; Borchert et al. 1988). The economic effects of professional artistic activities in Amsterdam are important; the employment in the arts comprises 12,000 jobs (Hietbrink et al. 1985). Amsterdam's cultural facilities can be compared with the 'nearby' German cities like Frankfurt, Düsseldorf, and Cologne and with Brussels in terms of quality, versatility, cultural heritage, and opportunities for experimentation (Van Beetz 1988). In Rotterdam, a blue-collar city, there is a strong desire to close the gap with The Hague and Utrecht. Architectural projects in the modern inner city express a willingness to create a metropolitan ambiance. German cities have also launched a cultural offensive (e.g. the development of Frankfurt's museum bank along the Main and Cologne's media park).

In geographical terms the conurbation of the Randstad is part of a megalopolis comprising - as in the original idea of Gottmann (Gottmann & Harper 1990) - the Amsterdam-Cologne-Lille triangle and a major portion of an even larger 'megistopolis', embracing the urbanized isthmus between Venice and the old English industrial districts - which Doxiades would call an ecumenopolis. It is striking that these expressions, dating from the 1960s, made a come-back during the upheaval of the economy during the late 1980s. What matters is that within a Single European Market, these cities and regions will be competing and complementary at the same time, although the transfer of national urban hierarchies to one European urban hierarchy will be questionable (Rodwin & Suzamani 1991). Hit-parades of European cities are compiled, the Reclus team taking the lead. Behind London and Paris, at a respectful distance, a number of cities follow, according to a number of criteria. The next rank includes Munich, Frankfurt, Brussels, and Amsterdam. Hamburg and Rotterdam are in a second league (Brunet 1989), followed by Utrecht and The Hague, as well as Düsseldorf. The Randstad Holland, taking its four leading cities together, is the third conurbation of Europe. The Reclus team discerned specializations as well, classifying Amsterdam and Rotterdam as international communication centers, The Hague as an international government center, and Utrecht as a center of technology and research.

A common indicator of management centers is how they perform as headquarters of companies operating worldwide. As the ECL survey demonstrates, the Randstad is less important than the combined performance of the four leading German centers together (Munich, Hamburg, Frankfurt, Düsseldorf). This is particularly the case for head-offices of manufacturing companies; for transportation the opposite is true. The

Randstad lags far behind London and Paris according to this criterion (Dwarkasing et al. 1989; De Smidt & Van der Mark 1991).

Two avenues of reasoning dominate the discussion of megalopolis. One is the comparison of competing world cities, which has been presented already. An alternative proposition concerns the idea of transport routes, linking complementary centers. The latter argument is axial oriented, whereas the former is nodal oriented. The Reclus team discerned a 'dorsale européenne', ranging from Merseyside to Venice and comprising half of all EC urban activities on 18 percent of its surface (Brunet 1989). In a recent study by a team from the Dutch National Physical Planning Agency (Verbaan et al. 1991), these two approaches of 'specialization and concentration' versus 'chains and zones' have been offered as two alternatives for a future European policy on urbanization. It can be questioned, however, if these concepts could be discerned in such a fundamental way, being complementary notions at the same time. For the Dutch case of the Randstad, metropolitan scenarios of a world city versus a logistic node are difficult to discern.

5.8   Deconcentration of the Randstad Metropolis and the North wing South wing divide

Already in 1963 Gottmann wrote: "Perhaps the planning of the Dutch government of the distribution of people and industries in Holland is the closest a policy of national control has come to successfully providing for the people's needs while preserving the esthetics of the landscape" (Gottmann & Harper 1990, pp. 108). A policy of deconcentration has also been carried out in other major West European metropolises. This policy has been successful insofar as a booming economy fostered an autonomous deconcentration of both economic activities and people. Government policies for deconcentration have been even more strictly enforced in the 1970s, a period of recession. The relocation of government services has been questioned (De Smidt 1985). Restructuring problems in the large cities, a successful growth center policy within the major metropolitan areas (excluding suburban developments), and a positive re-evaluation of economic policies of the large cities facing rising unemployment figures during the early 1980s: all these factors led the government to abandon the dispersal policies in 1983. The result was a Myrdal-type growth along the fringes of the Randstad, a selective deconcentration of Randstad metropolitan areas, and backlash effects on peripheral areas. However, it is very difficult to apply grand theories to the Dutch case. The limited size and the extreme openness of the country mean that grand theories such as that of Myrdal (1957) or Perroux (1955) are not applicable. Moreover, the integration of the Netherlands is a very recent phenomenon, indeed (Keuning 1955; Knippenberg & De Pater 1988). For middle-range theories, such as the trickling-down hypothesis of Thompson (1986), it is not clear which spatial level is relevant for the Netherlands. The hypothesis will be tested on a metropolitan level.

Taking a long-term perspective, the average annual growth figures shown in Table

Table 5.3   Average annual percentage growth of jobs, total and by region

	North wing	South wing	Randstad	Outer provinces	Netherlands
1963-83	0.8	0.3	0.5	0.9	0.7
1984-88	3.9	2.2	2.7	3.3	3.0

Source: CBS, De Smidt 1991a

Table 5.4   Division of jobs in percentages according to sectors, total and by region, 1989

	0-5 agriculture, manufacturing	6-7 trade, transport	8-9 services
Large cities			
- Amsterdam	15	26	59
- Rotterdam	22	31	47
- The Hague	15	23	62
- Utrecht	14	26	60
North wing	23	27	50
South wing	29	27	44
Randstad	25	27	48
Outer provinces	35	22	43
Netherlands	31	25	44

Source: CBS, De Smidt 1991a

5.3 indicate that growth in the Randstad as a whole is much lower than in the outer provinces. This is attributed to the low figures for the south wing of the Randstad in contrast to a nearly double national average of growth of jobs in two decades of prosperity and recession after the Dutch emancipation to a European level (1963). Figures for the period 1984-88, an era of economic upheaval, are even more striking. The north wing showed a high growth rate, far above the national average, whereas the south wing lags way behind. This illustrates the structural difference between both wings of the Randstad Metropolis (Knol & Manshanden 1990). As far as the main sectors of the economy are concerned, the north wing is less oriented toward manufacturing and more heavily involved in services than the south wing. The outer provinces are oriented more toward manufacturing and less toward transport and trade. The position of the four main cities (not agglomerative figures!) is more explicit (Table 5.4). Rotterdam is overrepresented in transport, the only city that is not underrepresented in manufacturing compared to its wing. The other cities are largely oriented toward services, Amsterdam and Utrecht being more commercially oriented than the government

Table 5.5   *Division of jobs in percentages according to occupations, total and by region, 1989*

	North wing	South wing	Randstad	Outer provinces	Netherlands
Qualified staff	31	29	30	26	28
Administrative	21	20	20	16	18
Commercial	11	10	11	11	11
Services	12	12	12	12	12
Manual labor	20	22	21	28	25
Other	5	7	6	7	6

Source: CBS, De Smidt 1991a

seat of The Hague. From a labor market point of view, the occupational structure is more relevant, though showing fewer differences on the level of wings (Table 5.5). The Randstad as a whole is more oriented toward highly educated staff as well as lower clerical jobs, laborers being underrepresented. Specific figures for the large cities are lacking. The Randstad is in many respects a transactional city, taking the organizational profiles of the top Dutch firms and non-profit institutions into account.

Inside this metropolis a division of regions can be made according to growth rate and type of activities:

a. The three large agglomerations in the province of Holland (Amsterdam, Rotterdam, The Hague), which are stabilizing their numbers of jobs on the long term (an annual growth rate of 0.1-0.2 percent). After a deep recession in the 1979-83 period, when 28,000 jobs were lost, particularly in manufacturing industries (shipbuilding), a period of revitalization began in the greater Amsterdam region (an annual increase of over 4 percent!) and the greater Rijnmond region (an annual increase of 2.2 percent, equal to that of the southern wing). This upswing is in stark contrast to the continued depression in the problematic region of The Hague. A restructuring process of manufacturing industries and the upheaval of the transport sector as well as of business services changed the functional economic structure tremendously (Knol & Manshanden 1990; Kramer 1990).

b. The frontier regions inside and outside of the Randstad Metropolis - which, according to the Hall-Klaassen urbanization cycle hypothesis, are zones of suburbanization - including planned growth centers and medium-sized towns in intermediate zones between major cities (Manshanden & De Smidt 1991). The preservation of the Green Heart has been a long-standing policy goal in Dutch physical planning for 35 years (cf. Chapter 2). Along the highways, although concentrated in a few medium-sized towns, the pressure for building offices combined with warehouse facilities is very strong. Outside of the Randstad Metropolis a comparable process of trickling-down is going on. This is not just an issue of relocation; it is a far more complicated process of reorganization of firms and the establishment of new foreign subsidiaries as well. In the Green Heart and the province of Utrecht the number of jobs in the period 1984-88 increased by 73,600 jobs (11.7 percent), which does not exceed the average Randstad job creation by much (11.2 percent!). In recent years agglomerations have offered opportunities, as will be discussed below. The new town in the polder (Almere) is also a growing fringe area.

c. The restructuring manufacturing zone at the northern fringe of the Randstad metropolis, including the specialized traditional manufacturing area of the Zaan (timber and food), the city of Haarlem (metals), and IJmond (the blast furnaces area of Hoogovens). This region is quite different from the flourishing high-tech towns of Leiden and Delft, which restructured their economy back in the 1950s and 1960s.

5.9   Subcenters challenging traditional inner-city CBDs

Theoretically it can be debated whether or not the Randstad economy is currently undergoing suburbanization. Old inner-city centers are losers and subcenters are winners. Of course this could be labeled suburbanization, but it is not a mere dispersal of economic activities. A deconcentration, oriented toward the subcenters, is taking place, and there is a recent trend toward locating along highways at the outskirts of metropolitan areas or even beyond.

All cities lost jobs in the 1970s and early 1980s, with Utrecht and Amsterdam at the forefront (Beumer et al. 1983; Zondag & Stijnenbosch 1989). The economic crisis hit all the major metropolitan areas, except the centrally located city of Utrecht.

Did revitalization of the urban economic engine from 1984 onward foster development in the inner cities or the subcenters? Looking just at offices in Amsterdam, the southeastern subcenter took a leading position during the 1980s. This was also the case for the southeastern subcenter near The Hague (Plaspoelpolder in the suburban town of Rijswijk) and for the Kanaleneiland subcenter at the border of the city of Utrecht near the national expressway interchange. However, the modern inner city of Rotterdam - where office construction is getting started again, after being prohi-bited by the city council during the 1970s - proves to be the prime location for offices in this metropolitan area. Even there some subcenters are growing, in particular for business services (Brainpark and Oosterhof at the eastern fringes of the city near the inner Randstad highway netwerk).

A recent survey on business services by Hessels (1991) demonstrated that some push factors are common to all environments. These include the need for expansion of office floorspace and accessibility. But pull factors, such as accessibility and representation, are more appealing in subcenters, in particular outside cities. Urban cores have a limited market range for offices, the local market being overrepresented and the national market being underrepresented (Table 5.6). Suburbs show the reverse in these respects. International office activities are distributed over several zones. In the 1977-88 period

Table 5.6   *Division of business services establishments according to market range and location in the four main Randstad metropolitan areas (percentages)*

Market range	Urban core	Other urban areas	Suburbs	Total
Local	28	44	28	100
Metropolitan area	17	35	48	100
Randstad	18	33	49	100
National (outside R.)	12	33	55	100
International	17	39	44	100
Total	18	36	46	100

Source: Hessels & De Smidt (1991)

Table 5.7   *Division of business services establishments according to subsectors and location in the four main Randstad metropolitan areas (percentages)*

	Urban core	Other urban areas	Suburbs	Total
Legal services	21	39	39	100
Accountants, etc.	5	40	55	100
Computer services	10	26	64	100
Engineering, architects	21	38	41	100
Advertising agencies	16	45	40	100
Economic consultants	27	34	39	100
News agencies	43	43	14	100
Employment agencies	54	43	14	100
Business services	9	52	39	100
Total	18	37	45	100

Source: Hessels & De Smidt (1991)

the three cities in the province of Holland lost over 10 percent of their business service establishments, whereas the suburbs increased theirs by 36 percent. Apparently, relocation is just a minor issue, while the location of new offices is of overriding importance. Looking at the sectoral profiles of the different milieus, the urban core has an overrepresentation of employment agencies (mostly accommodated in former shops), news agencies, and economic consultants. Suburbs became strongholds for computer services and accountants. These are the fastest growing business services and are sensitive to accessibility by car (Table 5.7).

The Fourth Memorandum on Physical Planning (1988) launched an offensive in favor of the inner cities, identifying specific urban-renewal districts as international environments to be financed by public-private partnerships. Later on a revised edition of the Memorandum (VINEX 1991) prohibited new investments at suburban locations not linked to rapid public transport systems (A locations being provided with intercity trains, B locations with rapid transit of other kinds). Very recently the national government has given higher priority to accommodating logistics operations at highway (C) locations to buttress the gateway position of the Netherlands. There is a firm commitment to back the waterfront projects of Amsterdam (IJ-Waterfront) and Rotterdam (Waterstad, Kop van Zuid) as well as the inner-city projects of The Hague (Bank, Spui) and Rotterdam (Weena), and the Utrecht City Project, although the Utrecht plan is not part of the offensive to attract international investments.

The combined policy of enforcing planning restrictions and offering opportunities at prime locations is a long-term strategy backed by private investment funds. They hope that the flat (in terms of prices) and overbuilt Dutch real-estate market will be confronted with scarcity and higher prices, at the same time causing a spatial gradient of prices in metropolitan areas similar to that in other European metropolises (Dwarkasing et al. 1989; Lie & Bongenaar 1990; De Smidt & Van der Mark 1991). However, B locations with good accessibility will be favored to A locations. One location-leader, the new head-office of the recently merged ABN-Amro Bank, will be located in a small subcenter at the southern edge of the city of Amsterdam, not at the IJ-Waterfront opposite the old inner city of Amsterdam, the traditional financial center. Some inner-city urban-renewal projects take too long to negotiate. Sometimes the proposed mix with social housing and accessibility measures for cars (including parking facilities) are questioned. In contrast to London and Paris, people who work at managerial and staff level in the Randstad cities are not accustomed to use public transport.

This deconcentration of business is the last stage in a broader deconcentration process, starting with wholesaling and manufacturing industries back in the 1960s. Together with offices, major urban provisions such as (university) hospitals and laboratories left the inner city and were located at the urban fringe (Doorn 1989; Nozeman 1986). The success of the growth centers, providing good housing for middle-class and working-class families, drained the city. The nearby growth centers attracted economic activities too. A complicated commuting pattern has developed in the main urban agglomerations. At the same time, long-distance commuting is increasing, because these agglomerations are confronted with severe housing shortages. The growth center policy has been exchanged for a compact city idea that, particularly in The Hague and Utrecht, requires either an agglomeration government or an extension of the territory of large cities (De Smidt 1990).

5.10   Evaluation

The Netherlands has a dual ambition: to be a principal gateway to Europe, and to transform the Randstad into a true world city. At the same time, the Green Heart is being preserved (Ottens 1990). The traditional dispersal policy, which was formulated to buttress regional development, has been abandoned, putting enormous pressure on physical planning in the Randstad. In the long run, however, deconcentration is continuing, both at the level of macro-regions and at the metropolitan level. International activities are no longer bound to the major inner cities of the Randstad. Locations inside the Randstad Metropolis oriented toward the network of highways are favored, particularly by rapidly growing business services like computer software and accountancy. The physical capacity of the major Randstad metropolitan regions is too limited to accommodate all logistics activities. The southern provinces offer a number of transport facilities leading to the heart of the Single European Market. In this respect a broader urban field has emerged. As far as high-ranking functions at non-manufacturing company level and advanced business services are concerned, the Randstad is in the lead. But for manufacturing, including high-tech activities, the intermediate cities of the province of North-Brabant and Gelderland are favored.

Physical planning tries to control the expansion caused by the economic boom that started in 1984. It offers inner-city renewal locations for international business, while restricting locations along the highways. As a compromise, business managers, prefer to locate in subcenters.

References

Advokaat, H.G. (1986), Amsterdam als financieel centrum. In: P.E. de Hen et al. (eds), Om het behoud van een explosieve stad. Werk en welvaart in en om Amsterdam, pp. 135-158. Muiderberg: Coutinho.

BCI (Buck Consultants International) (1990a), Nederland, de Randstad en buitenlandse investeerders. Nijmegen: BCI.

BCI (Buck Consultants International) (1990b), Centrale Europese distributie door Japanse en Amerikaanse bedrijven. Nijmegen: BCI.

Beetz, F.P. van (1988), Cultuur en steden. In: Rijks Planologische Dienst, Ruimtelijke Verkenningen, pp 12-38. 's-Gravenhage: Rijks Planologische Dienst.

Beumer, R.H.J., J.J. Harts & H.F.L. Ottens (1983), Ontwikkeling en ruimtelijke struktuur en ruimtelijke funktieverschuivingen in de vier grote stadsgewesten. Utrecht: Geografisch Instituut, Rijksuniversiteit Utrecht.

Bijlsma, E. & R.H. Goossens (1989), Logistieke organisatie van buitenlandse ondernemingen in Nederland. Utrecht: Geografisch Instituut, Rijksuniversiteit Utrecht.

Borchert, J.G., M.H. Stijnenbosch & F. de Nooij (1988), Atlas van Nederland, deel 6: Voorzieningen. 's-Gravenhage: SDU-Uitgeverij.

Brunet, R. (ed) (1989), Les villes 'européennes'. Rapport pour la DATAR. Paris: RECLUS.

Daniels, P.W. (1986), Foreign banks and metropolitan development: A comparison of London and New York. Tijdschrift voor Economische en Sociale Geografie 77, pp. 269-287.

Davelaar, E.J. (1989), Incubation and Innovation. A Spatial Perspective. Amsterdam: Free University.

Dinteren, J. van (1987), The role of business services in the economy of medium-sized Cities. Environment and Planning A 19, pp. 669-686.

Doorn, P.K. (1989), Sociale structuur en ruimtelijke mobiliteit. Utrecht: Geografisch Instituut, Rijksuniversiteit Utrecht.

Drenth, D.H. (1990), De informatica-sector in Nederland tussen rijp en groen. Nederlandse Geografische Studies 108. Amsterdam/Nijmegen: KNAG/Faculteit Beleidswetenschappen Katholieke Universiteit.

Dwarkasing, W., D. Hanemaayer, M. de Smidt & P.P. Tordoir (1988), Ruimte voor hoogwaardige kantoren. Nederlandse Geografische Studies 71. Amsterdam/Utrecht/Leiden/Delft: KNAG/ Geografisch Instituut, Rijksuniversiteit Utrecht/Research voor Beleid/INRO-TNO.

Dwarkasing, W., D. Hanemaayer, R. van der Mark & M. de Smidt (1989), Kantoren in metropolen. Internationaal vergelijkend onderzoek naar toplocaties voor de kantorensector. Leiden/Utrecht: Research voor Beleid/Geografisch Instituut, Rijksuniversiteit Utrecht.

Eppink, D.J. & A. van Rhijn (1988), The internationalization of Dutch insurance companies. Long Range Planning 21, pp. 54-60.

ETIN (1987), Effecten van de verschuiving van het economisch zwaartepunt in West-Duitsland voor een aantal werkgelegenheidssectoren in Gelderland, Noord-Brabant en Limburg. Tilburg: Economisch Technologisch Instituut.

Fourth Memorandum on Physical Planning (1988), On the Road to 2015. 's-Gravenhage: SDU-Uitgeverij.

Friedmann, J. (1986), The world city hypothesis. Development and Change 17, pp. 69-83.

Fujita, M. & K. Ishigaki (1986), The internationalisation of Japanese commercial banking. In: M. Taylor & N. Thrift (eds), Multinationals and the Restructuring of the World Economy, pp. 193-227. London: Croom Helm.

Gottmann, J. (1983), The Coming of the Transactional City. College Park, Maryland: Institute for Urban Studies.

Gottmann, J. & R.A. Harper (eds) (1990), Since Megalopolis. Baltimore: The Johns Hopkins University Press.

Hall, P. (1966), The World Cities. London: Weidenfeld & Nicholson.

Hart, H.W. ter (1979), Vestigingsplaatsaspecten van top-management. (diss. Amsterdam). Meppel: Krips Repro .

Hart, H.W. ter (1987), Amsterdam, het financiële hart van Nederland. In: H. van der Wusten (ed), Postmoderne aardrijkskunde, pp. 117-136. Muiderberg: Coutinho.

Hart, H.W. ter & J. Piersma (1990), Direct representation in international financial markets: The Case of foreign banks in Amsterdam. Tijdschrift voor Economische en Sociale Geografie 81, pp. 82-92.

Hayuth, Y. (1981), Containerization and the load center concept. Economic Geography 57, pp. 160-176.

Hessels, M. (1991), Zakelijke diensten: winnende en verliezende deelmilieus in de Randstad. In: S. Musterd & P. Hooimeijer (eds), De Randstad: balans van winst en verlies, deel 2, pp. 67-80. Amsterdam/Utrecht: Stedelijke Netwerken.

Hessels, M. & M. de Smidt (1991), Regrouping business service networks: deconcentration in the Randstad Holland. In: M. de Smidt & E. Wever, Complexes, Formations and Networks. Netherlands Geographical Studies 132. Utrecht/Nijmegen: KNAG/Geografisch Instituut, Rijksuniversiteit Utrecht/Faculteit Beleidswetenschappen Katholieke Universiteit.

Hietbrink, S., F. van Puffelen & J.A.M. Wesseling (1985), De economische betekenis van de professionele kunsten in Amsterdam. Amsterdam: Stichting Economisch Onderzoek.

Hoekveld, G.A. (1990), Nederland, deel van de wereld. In: B.C. de Pater, G.A. Hoekveld & J.A. van Ginkel (eds), Nederland in delen, een regionale geografie, deel 1, pp. 17-39. Houten: De Haan.

Hogenbirk, J. & A. Loggers (1989), Dynamiek van de commerciële vastgoedmarkt, 1983-1988. Utrecht: Zadelhoff.

Hornstra, T. (1989), Container- en roll-on/roll-off vervoer over de Noordzee. Utrecht: Geografisch Instituut, Rijksuniversiteit Utrecht.

Initiatiefgroep Amsterdam als internationaal financieel centrum (1989), Amsterdam: Financial Gateway to Continental Europe. Amsterdam.

Kempen, E. van (1982), Amsterdam als centrum van cultuurproduktie. Geografisch Tijdschrift 26, pp. 380-393.

Keuning, H.J. (1955), Mozaïek der functies. Den Haag: Leopold.

Knight, R. (1986), The advanced industrial metropolis: A new type of world city. In: The Future of the Metropolis, pp. 391-436. Berlin: Walter de Gruyter & Co.

Knippenberg, H. & B. de Pater (1988), De eenwording van Nederland. Schaalvergroting en integratie sinds 1815. Nijmegen: SUN.

Knol, H. & W. Manshanden (1990), Functionele samenhang in de Noordvleugel van de Randstad. Nederlandse Geografische Studies 109. Amsterdam/Utrecht: KNAG/Economisch-Geografisch Instituut Universiteit van Amsterdam/Geografisch Instituut Rijksuniversiteit Utrecht.

KPMG Klynveld (1988), The 1988 Survey of Foreign-based Companies with European Headquarters in the Amsterdam Area. Amsterdam: KPMG.

Kramer, J.H. (1990), Luchthavens en hun uitstraling. Nederlandse Geografische Studies 116. Amsterdam/Nijmegen: KNAG/Faculteit Beleidswetenschappen Katholieke Universiteit.

Leeuwen, M.J. van (1989), De rol van Amsterdam in de internationale financiële wereld. Amsterdam: Stichting Economisch Onderzoek.

Lie, R. & A. Bongenaar (1990), Toplocaties: produktiemilieu en investeringsmilieu. Nederland in internationaal perspectief. Amsterdam: SBV.

Loeve, A. (1989), Buitenlandse ondernemingen in regionaal perspectief. Vestigingsfactoren en regionale effecten van buitenlandse bedrijven in Nederland. Nederlandse Geografische Studies 84. Amsterdam/Utrecht: KNAG/Geografisch Instituut, Rijksuniversiteit Utrecht.

Loos, P. van der & H. Harleman (1988), Meer dan Rotterdam en Schiphol alleen.

Een kwalitatief onderzoek naar logistieke dienstverlening aan buitenlandse verladers door Nederlandse transport- en expeditiebedrijven. Utrecht: Geografisch Instituut, Rijksuniversiteit Utrecht.

Manshanden, W. & M. de Smidt (1991), North Wing of the Randstad; Suburbanization versus the city. Netherlands Journal of Housing and Environmental Research 6 (forthcoming).

Mumford, L. (1966), The City in History. Harmondsworth: Penguin Books.

Myrdal, A. (1957), Economic Theory and Underdeveloped Regions. London: Duckworth.

Niet, A. van der (1989), Teleport in a European Context. Amsterdam: World Teleport Association-Europe.

Nozeman, E.F. (1986), Nieuwe bouwlocaties in het licht van enkele doelstellingen van ruimtelijke ordening. Amsterdam: Planologisch en Demografisch Instituut, Universiteit van Amsterdam.

Ottens, H.F.L. (1990), An interpretation of recent trends in urbanization in the Netherlands. Netherlands Journal of Housing and Environmental Research 5, pp. 49-64.

Perroux, F. (1955), Note sur la notion de pôle de croissance. Economie appliquée, pp. 307-320.

Poeth, G.G.J.M. & H.J. van Dongen (1985), Rotterdam of de noodzaak van een infrastructuur voor informatie. Rotterdam: Erasmus Universiteit.

Rietbergen, T. van, J. Bosman & M. de Smidt (1990), Internationalisering en diensten. Geografie van de zakelijke en financiële diensten. Muiderberg: Coutinho.

Rodwin, L. & H. Suzamani (1991), Industrial Change and Regional Economic Transformation. London: Harper Collins Academic.

Schaake, F.E. (1989), Telematica en de concurrentiekracht van Nederland als distributieland. Den Haag: SC&M/NDL.

Smidt, M. de (1983), Regional locational cycles and the stage of locating foreign manufacturing plants. The Case of the Netherlands. Tijdschrift voor Economische en Sociale Geografie 74, pp. 1-11.

Smidt, M. de (1985), Relocation of government services in the Netherlands. Tijdschrift voor Economische en Sociale Geografie 76, pp. 232-236.

Smidt, M. de (1987), In pursuit of deconcentration: the evolution of the Dutch urban system from an organizational perspective. Geografiska Annaler 69B, pp. 133-143.

Smidt, M. de (1990), The new business logistics and the Netherlands Randstad. In: M. Hebbert & J.C. Hansen (eds), Unfamiliar Territory. The Reshaping of European Geography, pp. 73-84. Aldershot: Avebury.

Smidt, M. de (1991a), Bedrijfsprofiel van de Randstad. In: P. Hooimeijer, S. Musterd & P. Schröder (eds), De Randstad: balans van winst en verlies, deel 1, pp. 17-34. Utrecht: Stedelijke Netwerken.

Smidt, M. de (1991b), Management centers and internationalization of firms in the Netherlands. Tijdschrift voor Economische en Sociale Geografie 82, pp. 148-154.

Smidt, M. de, D. Kluyver, C.L. Mes & M.C. Conijn (1990), Internationalization, informatization and organizational change: a profile of banking and business services in the Netherlands. Netherlands Journal of Housing and Environmental Research

5, pp. 323-337.

Smidt, M. de & R. van der Mark (1991), European metropolises in competition for offices. GeoJournal 24, pp. 247-256.

Smidt, M. de & G. Meyerink (1990), The internationalization of a Dutch corporation: The case of AKZO. Tijdschrift voor Economische en Sociale Geografie 81, pp. 225-232.

Smidt, M. de & E. Wever (1990), An Industrial Geography of the Netherlands. London: Routledge.

Stam, W.J. (1990), De transportsector in beweging. In: Werkstukken Stedelijke Netwerken 23. Delft: Stedelijke Netwerken.

Stam, W.J. (1991), Enkele aspecten van de Randstad als logistiek knooppunt. Delft: Delft University Press.

Thompson, W.R. (1968), Internal and external factors in the development of urban economics. In: H.J. Perloff & L. Wingo (eds), Issues in Urban Economics, pp. 43-62. Baltimore: The Johns Hopkins Press.

Tordoir, P.P. (1991), Advanced office activities in the Randstad-Holland metropolitan region: location, complex formation and international orientation. In: P.W. Daniels (ed), Services and Metropolitan Development, pp. 226-244. London: Routledge.

Tordoir, P.P. & M.A. de Haan (1987), De economische en ruimtelijke ontwikkeling van internationaal georiënteerde kantooractiviteiten. Delft: INRO-TNO.

Velde, B.M.R. van der (1989), Internationalisatie van de andere kant bekeken. In: P.J.M. van Steen & P.R.A. Terpstra (eds), Met beide benen op de grond. Regiologie, van theorie tot praktijk, pp. 129-138. Groningen: Rijksuniversiteit.

Verbaan, A.A. (ed) (1990), Ruimtelijke perspectieven in Europa. Den Haag: SDU-Uitgeverij

Vinex (1991), Vierde Nota over de ruimtelijke ordening extra. Den Haag: SDU-Uitgeverij

Vries, J. de (1959), De economische achteruitgang der Republiek. (diss. Leiden). Leiden, Universiteit van Leiden.

Zondag, H. & M.H. Stijnenbosch (1989), Struktuur van de werkgelegenheid en de bedrijvigheid in de vier Randstadgewesten. Werkstukken Stedelijke Netwerken 13. Utrecht: Stedelijke Netwerken.

Prof.dr. M. de Smidt
Faculty of Geographical Sciences
University of Utrecht
P.O. Box 80.115
3508 TC Utrecht
The Netherlands

6.   THE RANDSTAD - A WELFARE REGION?

R.C. Kloosterman & J.G. Lambooy

6.1   Introduction

The Dutch welfare state at present seems to be in dire straits. The costs of maintaining a very extensive system of social benefits rose very fast in the 1980s and have become an almost unbearable (or should we say intolerable?) burden. An increasing number of persons called upon the state for financial help in that decade. Especially the number of unemployed or disabled persons rose to unprecedented heights. The number of recipients of unemployment benefits rose from 230,000 in 1980 to 575,000 in 1989. In the same period the number of recipients of benefits for disability and illness increased from 886,000 to 1,093,000 (CBS 1991). Meanwhile, economic growth in the Netherlands had fallen to a postwar low; the average yearly growth per capita of gross domestic product for 1979-1988 was just 0.7 percent (OECD 1990). These two simultaneous developments made it increasingly difficult to sustain the existing welfare arrangements, let alone expand them in terms of benifits or eligibility. The Dutch welfare state had gone through a phase of 'hyperbolic expansion' (De Swaan 1988) between 1945 and 1974. Yet it was neither prepared nor designed for the new situation that arose after the first, and even more pronounced after the second oil crisis in 1979. Since then, all kinds of pressure groups have been able to mount stubborn, and in most cases effective, resistance against cuts in the welfare arrangements. The strain on the national budget due to the oilcrisis and the welfare lobby has led to recurrent national budget problems. Accordingly, the current national political debate is largely centered on the future of the welfare state.

However, the future of the national welfare state - although of obvious importance - is not our main concern in this chapter. Below, we will analyze, albeit briefly, the role of the welfare state from the angle of its effects on the Randstad Metropolis. Especially, the focus will be on the welfare state as a redistributor of income with respect to the Randstad - in money or kind. One reason for this is that redistributing is perhaps *the essential function* of the welfare state. Moreover, the redistributing of income has a strong spatial dimension in the Netherlands. The spatial distribution of recipients of welfare benefits, especially the unemployed, shows that a disproportionately large number of them live in the four largest cities of the Randstad (Amsterdam, Rotterdam, The Hague, and Utrecht). The impact of the welfare state as redistributor of income,

F. M. Dieleman and S. Musterd (eds.), The Randstad: A Research and Policy Laboratory, 123–139.
© 1992 *Kluwer Academic Publishers. Printed in the Netherlands.*

therefore, has a clear spatial dimension, which has to be taken into account when trying to assess the position of the Randstad. In addition, we will also take a brief look at other impacts of the welfare state on the Randstad as an important employer and as a provider of public services like transport and education. These aspects will help us to determine the position of the Randstad - or, better, of the four largest cities of the Randstad (viz. Amsterdam, Rotterdam, The Hague and Utrecht) - within the welfare system.

6.2   The Dutch welfare system

The welfare state as we now know it, "a vast conglomerate of nationwide, compulsory and collective arrangements to remedy and control the external effects of adversity and deficiency" (De Swaan 1988), is the result of many years of theoretical debates and social conflicts - in the Netherlands and elsewhere. The concept 'welfare state' was first used during World War II. It was coined specifically to bring out the contrast between a democratic type of government, which would take care of those who could not earn their own living, and the 'warfare state' of Nazi-Germany (cf. Schuyt 1991). The roots of the welfare state reach further back in time, however. In the nineteenth century, many countries saw the rise of national arrangements with respect to education, health care and disability insurance. A patchwork of all kinds of local and private welfare arrangements was replaced by nationally uniform, compulsory, and collectively financed eductional, health-care, insurance, and assistance systems in, among other countries, France, Germany, Great Britain, and the Netherlands (De Swaan 1988). After World War II, these national, compulsory, and collective systems were extended by including unemployment insurance and old-age pensions. Eventually, in the 1960s, an all-encompassing and relatively generous system of welfare arrangements was erected in the Netherlands (Van Zanden & Griffith 1989). However, even when intervention in the 'free market' came to be broadly accepted, there remained at least a difference between social democrats and liberals as to the extent of power the state should be endowed with.

The role of the state and, more explicitly, the rise of the welfare state, has attracted the attention not only of politicians and (potential) interested parties such as the unemployed and taxpayers, but also the social scientists. The goals of supporting the weak and the dispossessed originate from economic, social, political, and religious sources. These goals have found their way into the social sciences, for instance in the theories of Marx, Pareto, Beveridge, Keynes, and Erhard. Welfare theory attempted to define a common basis on which to measure the consequences of various goal systems. This theory was developed mainly within the economic tradition of the Neoclassical school of thought. It was based in particular on the assumption that an optimal allocation could be achieved, whereby all decisions about production and consumption would be made in such a way as to satisfy all people, given their preferences, their incomes, and their production possibilities. According to the criterion of Pareto optimality, one person could only be made better off - through a different allocation - if no others would be made worse off. Newer theories did allow for the deterioration of positions for some people, but only if other people gained more and if this fully compensated for the losses experienced by others in the relevant collectivity.

The assumptions of this theory were rather abstract. Consequently, the results could be expressed in general terms only. Some people, therefore, said that 'welfare economics' should be given a different name: 'farewell economics'. This theory was developed in a static world without spatial and dynamic dimensions. Cities and regions do not have a place in this theory. External effects are non-existent and all people are fully informed and act rationally.

Although this theory is abstract, some essential elements can be used to analyze social and economic problems in cities and regions, especially with regard to the possible trade-off between productivity and the redistribution of income. Newer developments, like the new political economics, focus on the process of decision-making. It is also possible to focus on the ways in which the goals of a certain society can be integrated with the economic processes. Moreover, the attention may be turned to the processes related to the distribution of economic positions. For instance, one could study the position of the unemployed or of those people who live on social benefits, as opposed to those having well-paid positions in the labor market (Lambooy 1972, 1980; Lambooy et al. 1983). The social goals are formulated by the politicians, in the political process leading to a 'social preference function'. Modern political economics (Buchanan & Tollison 1984; Van Winden 1988), however, contends that even politicians do not always act according to the rules for achieving general welfare, but more often than not act to further their own well-being. The conclusion of much recent research is that interest groups (like labor unions, employers, neighborhood groups, churches, and ethnic groups) do not act according to a social welfare function, but rather to the best of their own interests.

The Dutch welfare state is, of course, no exception in this respect (De Swaan 1988; Van Zanden & Griffith 1989). The initial phase of constructing the Dutch welfare state (1945-1960) was followed by a period of extending and refining the welfare system. All kinds of interest groups tried to extend eligibility for the benefits and to raise their levels of payment. Most of these efforts were successful. As full employment was considered to be more or less the normal state of the economy, the costs of the welfare system remained bearable.

This development of the Dutch welfare state was no isolated event. In his book The Three Worlds of Welfare Capitalism, Esping-Andersen (1990) firmly places the Netherlands in one group with France, Italy, Belgium, and Germany. This so-called continental cluster of welfare states is mainly characterized by a low rate of labor participation, in comparison with the United States and Sweden, for instance. This low rate of labor participation is partly the result of the built-in mechanisms for reducing the supply of labor in these particular welfare states. This tendency to reduce the labor supply is the result of several factors. On the one hand, it is relatively easy to exit from the labor force by means of accessible and generous unemployment, disability, and early retirement benefits. On the other hand, the entry of women into the (official) workforce is not encouraged, for instance by public programs for child care or fiscal arrangements for dual-earner households. Also the scope of labor market programs to reintegrate the jobless in the labor market is very limited in countries like Germany, France, Belgium and the Netherlands, especially in comparison to Sweden.

The combination of high unemployment benefits with easy access to these benefits has led to a massive exodus from the labor force, especially of older male blue-collar workers in the Netherlands. Their rate of exit is the highest of all OECD member countries (OECD 1990). The net rate of labor participation of all males in the Netherlands declined from 89.3 percent in 1970 to 75.0 percent in 1980, and to 68.8 percent in 1987 (Van Paridon 1990).

We might say that these policies put a premium on non-participation and have resulted in rather large numbers of people who do not have a (formal) job. A large proportion of them live on welfare, and their benefits are relatively high to international standards.

Currently, these characteristics have been losing some of their relevance to the Dutch situation (cf. Kloosterman & Elfring 1991). The ever-present fiscal and budgetary crisis has finally forced the government to take measures to reduce the number of welfare recipients, as well as to pursue an explicit policy of increasing the rate of labor participation (WRR 1990b). Moreover, after 1986, when the growth of the economy really picked up again, shortages became manifest in parts of the labor market. This has led to a paradoxical combination: a large number of vacancies on the one hand, and a large number of inactive members of the labor force on the other. In order to explain the situation that has arisen in the Randstad, we will refer to these characteristics of the Dutch welfare state as an employer and as a provider of benefits. Before we can turn our attention to these two aspects, however, we first have to put the Randstad and the large cities within the framework of the Dutch welfare state.

6.3   The welfare state and the Randstad

The welfare system: nationally financed, locally administered
There is a long tradition of strong local government in the Netherlands. This is one of the reasons why, already in the 19th century, city governments took responsibility for the provision of many kinds of care for the lowest income groups. Although primary responsibility lay with the churches and relatives, the city governments (of liberal and socialist coalitions) started special programs. The first problem they tackled was the medical situation, through providing medical care and better housing conditions. Other programs provided education, public infrastructure, and, of course, direct income transfers.

Gradually the contribution of the churches declined. The relatives could no longer carry the burden either. Therefore the role of municipalities became more important. In addition to the local welfare resources, a strong movement towards centralization emerged, seeking to decrease the regional differences between social security recipients.

In the 1920s, the system of tax collection and redistribution was centralized. From then on, the central government gradually assumed the principal responsibility for the provision of welfare. Still, the municipalities maintained many fields of action, particularly those connected with the provision of services.

The Netherlands has developed a unique model: a high degree of centralization of tax collection and social contributions combined with a high degree of decentralization of expenditure on welfare. This is based on the constitutionally strong position of the Dutch local government. Within this framework, municipalities and corporatistic local institutions (which are run by deputies of employees and employers) such as the Industrial Insurance Administration Offices ('GAK' and 'GMD') actually operate the welfare system. The municipalities administer the (government) welfare payments, whereas the local Industrial Insurance Administration Offices administer the social security, which is financed by (nationally fixed) contributions paid by both employers and employees.

In 1990 the total public expenditure in the Netherlands amounted to 274 billion guilders, or about 60 percent of GDP. Almost 40 percent, or 108.5 billion guilders, belonged to the category of social security expenditure. In 1989, the municipalities received 48 billion guilders (11 percent of GDP) to cover their expenditures. No less than 90 percent of this budget was funded by the central government; local taxes and other local sources accounted for the rest: a meager 10 percent (WRR 1990a).

With respect to paying the municipal welfare bill, the ratio between municipal and central contributions is legally set at one to nine. But the overhead costs of the welfare provision have to be footed by the municipality alone. This means that municipalities do have a stake in reducing the number of welfare recipients within their jurisdictions. However, since the central government pays the most of the costs of municipal welfare, and because the other part of the social security system is paid out of employer and employee contributions on a nationwide scale, the costs of the locally administered welfare system are mainly passed on to the national level. Consequently, cities with numerous welfare recipients within their municipal boundaries are generally certain of adequate funding. The other side of the coin, however, is a very limited scope for local policy.

The Dutch welfare state, therefore, is - generally speaking - locally administered, centrally determined, and nationally funded.

Polarization on a local level
Welfare recipients are not, of course, evenly distributed over the country. Before being able to enquire further into this matter, we have to provide more information about the Randstad as a whole and about the four big cities.

The Randstad is an urbanized *region*, with relatively strong internal relations. But this region cannot be considered as one *urban* agglomeration, although this is sometimes suggested (Hall 1966). Despite some overlap, the labor markets of the various cities function as separate entities, at least within the two 'wings': the *northern* wing, encompassing the area from Haarlem, via Amsterdam and the Gooi region, towards

Utrecht and Amersfoort; and the *southern* wing, consisting of the urban agglomerations of The Hague, Rotterdam (the 'Rijnmond region'), and Dordrecht. There is some evidence that these 'wings' are expanding towards the east. The southern wing also seems to be expanding to the southeast, into the neighboring province of Noord-Brabant. The national government, in its national development plan (the Fourth Report on Physical Planning), consequently developed the idea of the 'Central Ring of Cities', encompassing not only the four largest Randstad cities, but also the cities of Breda and, Eindhoven, as well as the Arnhem-Nijmegen agglomeration. As a matter of fact, apart from the four northern provinces, the entire country could be seen as one large 'urban field' or a multi-nucleated urban system.

Consequently, the spatial differentiation in a socioeconomic sense does not show up markedly at the level of the Randstad as opposed to the rest of the Netherlands. Even at a lower level of aggregation, that of the statistical units called COROP regions, the differentiation is not outspoken. However, if we descend further and look at the municipal level, wide discrepancies appear. Especially the four big cities and their surrounding suburban municipalities show sharp contrast (Atlas van Nederland, 1988; Van Engelsdorp Gastelaars & Vijgen 1990). An overrepresentation of old and young, foreign, employed, single, and lower-income people live in the cities. An overrepresentation of middle-aged families with children, Dutch, employed, and higher-income people are to be found in neighboring suburbia (see Figures 6.1 and 6.2).

This socioeconomic dichotomy is mainly the result of selective migration patterns that already surfaced in the early 1960s (Kloosterman 1991). Only after 1974 did the changes in the composition of the population of larger cities become strong enough to bring the average income per wage earner down below the national average (WRR 1990a). After that, the situation got steadily worse. Also a sharpening of the contrast could be observed between the core cities and the surrounding suburbs, where average incomes per wage earner are above the national average.

Recently, however, the situation in the large Dutch cities seems to have changed slightly. The gap in average income between the cities and the suburban surroundings is being narrowed. this is at least partly due to the influx of high-income residential households, like two-earner families (cf. Amsterdam: Musterd & Ostendorf 1991). The suburban areas, however seem to preserve their character of white family household residential environment' (Van Engelsdorp Gastelaars & Vijgen 1990). Also lower-income groups, with or without jobs, are more or less trapped in the larger cities. Therefore, the socioeconomic dichotomy between the Randstad cities and Randstad suburbs still seems to be relevant.

The principal variable in explaining this dichotomy is the spatial distribution of cheap housing. The four big cities have constructed an ample supply of cheap dwelling units. This choice was primarily based on political priorities. The housing supply exerted a strong attraction on weaker groups (in terms of labor market opportunities). The big cities contain a disproportionately large share of the cheap housing stock. These cities consequently function as a kind of gateway for households with low incomes (welfare recipients, pensioners, students, and immigrants). These households are more

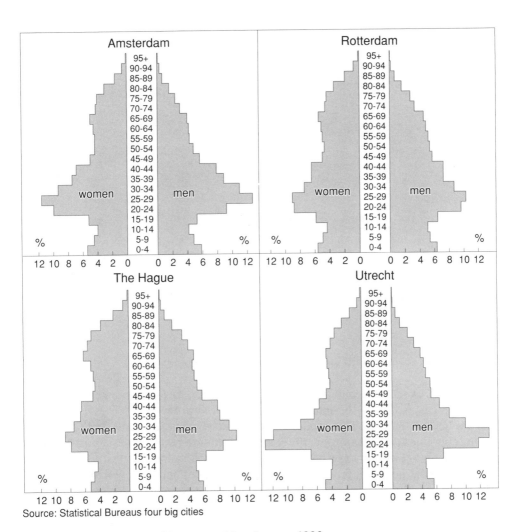

Source: Statistical Bureaus four big cities

Figure 6.1   Demographic composition by age, 1990

or less forced to live in the big cities. In fact, groups of people who have weak positions on the labor market and are thus likely to become dependent on some kind of welfare tend to be disproportionately located in the four big cities. In order to study the impact of the welfare system on the Randstad, we therefore have to focus on these four big cities.

The Netherlands

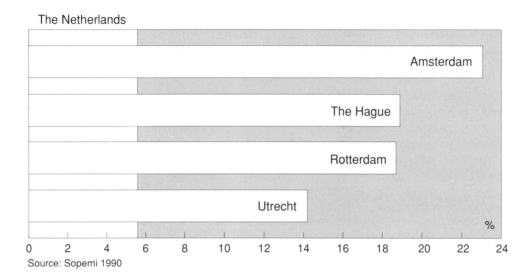

Source: Sopemi 1990

Figure 6.2   *Incidence of allochtones (ethnic minorities), 1988; percentages of the total*
              population

6.4   The welfare state as a (re)distributor of income

People most likely to receive some kind of welfare are overrepresented in the four big cities. This is due to the interaction between the process of selective migration and the housing market. This expectation is borne out by the figures in Table 6.1. In the four big cities of the Randstad, the number of welfare recipients is almost a quarter higher than in the country as a whole. If we take a look inside these cities themselves and focus upon the urban renewal areas, the differences become even more marked. The share of welfare recipients in these areas is more than one and a half times the national average. Especially the 19th-century neighborhoods have high numbers of unemployed and of people dependent on social security (Anderiesen & Reijndorp 1990). Since the 1970s, these neighborhoods have functioned as gateways for immigrants in the Netherlands. Many of these 19th-century have been subjected to extensive public programs of urban revitalization. As a result, the quality of the dwellings and of the neighborhoods themselves has been upgraded. While Dutch families, with a husband, a wife and children have become a minority there, 'new urbanites' (Dutch, young, and well-educated) are increasingly opting to live in these neighborhoods. Consequently, part of the gateway function is being taken over by neighborhoods dating from the interwar period (Hoogvliet 1991).

The share of ethnic minorities in the urban renewal areas, however, is still dispropor-

Table 6.1   *Total number of welfare recipients, 1987; percentage of total population in the age groups of 15-64 years**

Four big cities	13.5
Urban renewal areas in four big cities	16.0
The Netherlands as a whole	10.5

* Disablement benefits, unemployment benefits and general welfare (AAW, WAO, NWW, OIAW, TW, RWW and ABW).
Source: SCP (1990), p.166

tionately high; at the end of the 1980s nearly a quarter of the population in these areas belonged to this category. At that time, almost half of the total ethnic minority population of the Netherlands lived in urban renewal areas (SCP 1990).

The specific structure of the Dutch welfare state stimulates non-participation in the workforce. It combines relatively generous welfare benefits with easy access to the system. Therefore, the high rate of non-participation (as a result of unemployment, disability or other reasons) in the four cities does not have such a destructive impact on the social fabric as it does in American cities for instance (Soja 1991).

It is revealing to take a look at some data on the distribution of incomes in the four cities (Figure 6.3). The differences between the core cities and the national average seem small enough. The distribution in the urban renewal areas is obviously more skewed, but even there the deviation remains limited.

The Dutch welfare system seems to be satisfactory from the angle of spatial income distribution. Although there is a clear spatial pattern of welfare recipients, the spatial income distribution is much more blurred.

The cumulative dislocation that has occurred in the ghettos of cities like Chicago does not exist in Dutch cities. The so-called 'tangle of pathology' in American ghettos was triggered by a steep drop in average income in these neighborhoods. This drop was precipitated by declining participation rates, caused by the restructuring of the economy (the shift from manufacturing to service industries). At the same time, the outmigration of the middle classes, which was made possible by the lifting of discriminatory regulations, brought down the average income (Wilson 1987). This resulted in a concentration of poverty and, eventually, in the almost complete breakdown of the social fabric. Shops closed, schools deteriorated, and community-life disappeared.

The cities in the Netherlands are also confronted with the effects of economic restructuring and selective migration. The cumulative dislocation here seems to be effectively blocked by the Dutch welfare system. Specifically, that process is blocked by the level of and eligibility for the benefits, as well as by the fact that the system is funded nationally and administered locally. This does not mean, of course, that all is well within the Randstad cities. There are problems of unemployment, poverty, racism, social isolation, and deprivation. The Dutch welfare system, however, has prevented some neighborhoods from sliding into the abyss by keeping up the income level of the welfare

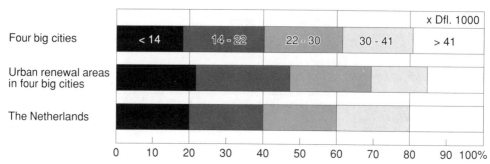

Figure 6.3   Distribution of net household income 1987; thousands of guilders

recipients. In some cases, the welfare system even created a stimulating environment for all kinds of informal activities (Engbersen 1990). Most of these activities are illegal as welfare recipients are not allowed to earn extra money, at least not above a certain amount. Nevertheless, they have been beneficial to the local economy.

6.5   The welfare state as an employer and a provider of services

The welfare state as an employer
The welfare state is not only a redistributor of income; it is also a major employer and a provider of various services. What is the impact of the welfare state on the four big cities in terms of jobs and services?

The contribution of the public sector in employment in the four big cities is only slightly higher than that in the country as a whole (Table 6.2). This is striking, since one of these four is The Hague, the center of national administration. Public sector employment in The Hague is definitely higher than the national average, but this is compensated to a large extent by the low share in Rotterdam. Amsterdam and Utrecht are more or less in line with the national average.

If we look at the levels of public sector employment in terms of gender bias, taking the four cities together, we find that the difference between these four cities and the national average is largely due to the employment of males. Therefore, the higher rate of female participation in the four big cities (Knol & Manshanden 1990) cannot be attributed to the public sector.

The share of public sector employment in the four big cities does not diverge much from the national average. It seems that the wage cuts in the public sector (Elfring & Kloosterman 1989; Kloosterman 1991), which led to a sharp increase in the number

Table 6.2   Public sector employment in the four big cities (agglomerations, COROP
             regions), September 1988; percentage of total number of jobs

	Male	Female	Total
Amsterdam	29.7	47.5	36.4
Rotterdam	19.2	49.2	29.5
The Hague	38.7	57.5	46.0
Utrecht	26.8	55.1	37.5
Four big cities	27.5	52.1	36.6
The Netherlands	23.5	52.1	33.7

Source: CBS, Employment Statistics

Table 6.3   Changes in number of jobs by wage class (gross hourly wages) and type
             of activity in the Greater-Rotterdam area. 1979-1987

Wage class:	Low	Middle	High	Total
Type of activity				
Manufacturing industry	- 3,500	-20,000	5,100	-18,400
Tertiary services	13,200	2,300	900	16,400
* Trade, hotel, catering	2,200	5,700	- 1,400	- 4,900
* Transportation	2,200	4,600	- 700	6,100
* Producer services	8,800	3,400	3,000	15,200
Non-market services	19,100	14,300	-10,600	22,800
Manufacturing and services	28,800	- 3,400	- 4,600	20,800

Source: Elfring & Kloosterman (1990)

of low-paid jobs, has not affected the four cities much more than it has the national
economy. Research has shown that the changes in the distribution of jobs according
to hourly wage-level in the public sector (non-market services) in Greater-Amsterdam
and Greater-Rotterdam had a considerable impact on overall wage distribution (see
Tables 6.3 and 6.4).

In both the Greater-Amsterdam and the Greater-Rotterdam area, the wage cuts affected
all pay scales. Besides inducing a rise in low-paid public-sector jobs, these wage cuts
have also led to a substantial decrease in the number of high-paid jobs in the public
sector. This decrease has more than offset the growth of high-salary positions in the

Table 6.4   Changes in number of jobs by wage class (gross hourly wages) and type
of activity in the Greater-Amsterdam area, 1979-1988

Wage class:	Low	Middle	High	Total
Types of activity				
Manufacturing industry	- 600	- 7,400	2,800	- 5,200
Tertiary services	14,000	10,300	9,100	33,400
* Trade, hotel, catering	6,700	- 7,500	2,100	1,400
* Transportation	1,700	14,300	- 600	15,400
* Producer services	5,600	3,500	7,600	16,700
Non-market services	11,600	22,300	-10,200	23,700
Manufacturing and services	25,000	25,200	1,700	51,900

Source: Kloosterman (1991)

private sector in the Greater-Rotterdam area. Meanwhile, the decrease in the Greater-Amsterdam area almost matched the increase in high-paid jobs in the private sector. Ironically, the deep wage cuts in the public sector were made more or less inevitable by the sharp rise in social security premiums, while the benefits from that system helped to cushion the impact of the restructuring of the Dutch economy (Kloosterman & Elfring 1991).

The welfare state as a provider of services
It would be a misunderstanding to perceive the welfare state only as income redistribution and employment provision. In fact, the entire structure of conditions confronting the urban population is influenced by the functioning of the welfare state. A strong indirect redistribution of income in kind, or rights to consume, is part of the modern welfare state. Education, public transport, medical care, care for children and for the elderly, and housing are examples of the fields where these effects can be observed. The modern city is a mixture of elements from both the free market and the subsidized and regulated structures. Basically the government can influence the decisions made by both producers and consumers by setting a legal framework and by (re)distributing income and user rights. In the latter case rights do not necessarily have to be based on actual income transfers. By setting low prices for housing, public transport, and education, even low income groups have access to these amenities. The extreme case is when cities provide services without demanding monetary compensation. In most cases, however, a fixed price is attached to the consumption of the services provided.

This part of the welfare system has an enormous impact on the 'quality of life' (QOL).

The great differences between European and American cities, as far as living conditions are concerned, reflect the indirect support of lower-income groups as much as direct income transfers. One of the most obvious examples is the Netherlands' relatively high (even for Europe) level of indirect transfers related with housing. The recipients of income support are not always aware that construction costs are subsidized as well, resulting in relatively low rents. The same holds true for other consumption goods, like transport and education. Primary and secondary education is almost completely free, and higher education is relatively cheap. Medical care is provided at fairly high standards to everyone with a lower than median income. Even for those with higher incomes, medical services are relatively cheap and well controlled by central agencies.

The 'QOL' resulting from all these cheaply provided rights-to-consume is very important, not only as amenities for today's consumers but also as an avenue for upward mobility for the children of the poor. Even if poor people live in more or less bad environments, their children are provided with good education and medical care. This is not a sure way to prevent people from having to stay in poor neighborhoods and bad environments. But they are not forced to remain in such areas and under such circumstances if they have enough personal drive to pursue a career.

The opposite side of the public provision of consumer rights to lower-income groups is the problem of financing in relation with the just distribution of the costs of the system. Many people in the Netherlands have voiced concern about how equitable and efficient this system actually is. It is often said that too many people are eligible for welfare benefits and that the prices set for consumer rights are too low. This system results in relatively high taxes and jeopardizes continuation of public services at the present high level. The financial base (from taxes and compensation) is considered to be weak, because of the high costs and the increasingly negative reactions from the general public.

The big cities in the Randstad contain a large proportion of the country's disadvantaged population, but the municipal authorities do not have sufficient means to take care of them. The municipal authorities become increasingly dependent on central government control, particularly because they are under pressure to work more efficiently in the provision of consumer rights. It seems that the welfare state has arrived at a stage where the structure of redistribution will have to be reassessed. Political measures to reduce the burden are met with severe opposition from interest groups.

In a theoretical vein, it is relevant to consider how a cut in welfare payments, along with downsizing of redistribution in kind, will affect the 'QOL' of the urban population. Will these measures influence the crime rate and generate other social problems? If that were the case, as many people predict, the effects of economizing on these costs may give rise to (higher) costs in other parts of the social system. On the other hand, the effects could be beneficial. These cutbacks might stimulate people to start taking care of themselves by accepting lower-paid jobs and re-entering the workforce. There is no easy answer to this dilemma. Both solutions may be either right or wrong. The only way to find out is by experimenting with the levels of redistribution. Comparisons between the countries in continental Northern Europe and the Anglo Saxon countries would suggest that the former have a higher 'QOL' but much depends on how it is measured.

An interesting question concerns urban size. The following hypothesis could be advanced: 'The integration of lower-income groups and ethnic minorities into the social fabric is easier in countries with a polycentric urban structure than it is in countries with a strong dominant primate city'. This hypothesis is based on the observation that large cities are places where minorities can be 'stored away' out of the sight until it is too late to formulate policies for integration. Real ghettos develop, often too large to be controlled by local government. In a polycentric structure, in contrast, the minorities are 'visible' much earlier, and policies can be devised to integrate them into the urban social fabric.

6.6   Conclusion

It has been argued that the Dutch welfare state is extremely generous towards people - whether employed or unemployed - who have weak positions in the economy. The welfare system is not based on direct income transfers only, but on indirect transfers as well. This has been the basis for a relatively high 'QOL' in Dutch cities, possibly one explanation for the absence of major social troubles. Many people (politicians and economists alike) regard this situation as costly and inefficient. There is some evidence of inefficieny of the welfare system in regard to the labor market. Yet a beneficial impact on the development of cities does exist in the sense that the unemployed - who are overrepresented in the large cities - are able to cope financially. The restructuring of the economy in the early 1980's and the resulting high unemployment in the cities brought grief in many individual cases. But it did not dramatically affect the social fabric of the urban societies. Seen from this angle, the specific Dutch characteristics of the welfare state are especially important for the structure of the labor and housing markets. The generosity of the system may be one of the reasons why social conflicts in the Dutch cities are fewer and less severe than in many other countries. Poverty does exist, of course, but it is less conspicuous here than in cities like New York, London, Paris, or Liverpool.

For (inner) cities and weak regions, the redistribution of income has been very beneficial. Unemployment and social disruption are not creating severe rifts in society, at least not on the scale common in many other countries. Besides, children are offered better prospects for development. In this respect, the Netherlands resembles Scandinavian countries.

Maintaining the system of social security, however, has put such pressure on the public financial basis that other functions, like employment and provider of services, have suffered. The increase in low-paid jobs in Greater-Amsterdam and Greater-Rotterdam can be attributed mainly to wage cuts in the public sector. Also the current problems in the public transport system, for example, reflect chronic underfunding of public services. These effects are, of course, not confined to the Randstad. But they can be related to the position of the Randstad as a 'welfare region': a part of the country where some areas (the big cities) rely heavily on government support.

The current debate about the Dutch welfare system is not focused on the necessity to support the weak. Instead, it concerns how to finance it and how to limit abuse. This is particularly important in relation to an increased flow of new immigrants. But a fundamental reconsideration of ways and means is necessary to determine the balance between the working and the non-working parts of the population.

Apart from discussions on how to cut the budgets for transfers in both money and kind, a debate has been developing about how to organize the system. In particular, it focuses on how to deal with the position of local governments and of the private sector. There is strong pressure to decentralize the implementation of central government policies. This task could be delegated to municipalities and the private sector, the latter meaning not only enterprises and investors, but relatives and charities as well. Then the state would no longer take primary responsibility; instead of the welfare state, something like a 'civic state' and 'civic economics' would have to be developed. New definitions of 'citizen' and 'social legitimacy' should be formulated. In these new entities, more parties than only the state would participate to cure the social ills of the present economy, in which 'natural' tendencies would seem to exist to split the population into some kind of 'duality' (Lambooy 1986).

Decentralization to the municipalities would provide a way to involve the private sector in the process of defining and solving problems. As yet, many initiatives, in the Netherlands and elsewhere, have been developed in the form of Public-Private Partnerships, for example to develop projects for urban renewal or for the creation of new jobs and enterprises. The results are not bad. Yet they are too limited for this kind of construct to be considered as a real alternative for the welfare state. Moreover, decentralization of the financing of social security would be a step backwards from the modern welfare state, implying a return to the situation of before the 19th century (De Swaan 1988). Competition of local communities against each other and a drastic shrinkage of the social security system would be inevitable. Urban developments in the near future will remain difficult, reflecting the growing tension between ever-larger population groups lacking means of their own. The welfare state has to be redefined, but it surely cannot be abandoned.

In Europe, the level of the urban QOL is still much higher than in the United States. The point of no return, which seems to have been reached in many American and in some British cities, is not yet in sight in the Netherlands (WRR 1990a)

References

Anderiesen, G. & A. Reijndorp (1990), The stabilization of heterogeneity. Urban renewal areas in Amsterdam and Rotterdam. In: L. Deben, W. Heinemeijer & D. van der Vaart (eds), Residential Differentiation, pp. 202-213. Amsterdam: Centrum voor

Grootstedelijk Onderzoek.

Atlas van Nederland (1988), Deel 3: Steden. 's Gravenhage: SDU-Uitgeverij.

Buchanan, I. & R. Tollison (eds) (1984), The Theory of Public Choice: II. Ann Arbor: University of Michigan Press.

CBS (1991), Statistisch Zakboek. Voorburg: CBS.

Elfring, T. & R.C. Kloosterman (1989), De Nederlandse Job Machine. EGI-Paper 38. Amsterdam: Economisch-Geografisch Instituut, Universiteit van Amsterdam.

Engbersen, G.B.M. (1990), Publieke bijstandsgeheimen; Het ontstaan van een onderklasse in Nederland. Leiden: Stenfert Kroese.

Engelsdorp Gastelaars, R. van & J. Vijgen (1990), Residential, differentiation in the Netherlands: the rise of new urban households. In: L. Deben, W. Heinemeijer & D. van der Vaart (eds), Residential Differentiation, pp. 136-163. Amsterdam: Centrum voor Grootstedelijk Onderzoek.

Esping-Andersen, G. (1990), The Three Worlds of Welfare Capitalism. Cambridge: Polity Press.

Hoogvliet, A. (1991), Winnende en verliezende woonmilieus in de vroeg-20ste-eeuwse zone. In: S. Musterd & P. Hooimeijer (eds), Randstad: balans van winst en verlies, deel 2, pp.119-132. Utrecht: Stedelijke Netwerken.

Kloosterman, R.C. (1991), A Capital City's Problem: The Rise of Unemployment in Amsterdam in the 1980s. Amsterdam: Research Memorandum Amsterdam, Faculty of Economics.

Kloosterman, R.C. & T. Elfring (1991), Werken in Nederland. Schoonhoven: Academic Service.

Knol, H. & W. Manshanden (1990), Functionele samenhang in de Noordvleugel van de Randstad. Nederlandse Geografische Studies 109. Amsterdam/Utrecht: KNAG/Economisch Geografisch Instituut, Universiteit van Amsterdam/Geografisch Instuut, Rijksuniversiteit Utrecht.

Musterd, S. & W. Ostendorf (1991), Inkomensontwikkeling en tweetoppigheid binnen de Randstad. In: R. van Kempen, S. Musterd & W. Ostendorf (eds), Maatschappelijke verandering en stedelijke dynamiek. Volkshuisvesting in Theorie en Praktijk, pp.59-75. Delft: Delftse Universitaire Pers.

Lambooy, J.G. (1972), Redelijke regionale politiek. In: L.H. Klaassen (ed), Regionale economie, pp. 323-356. Groningen.

Lambooy, J.G. (1980), Transfers Through the Tansport Sector. Paris: CEMT.

Lambooy, J.G., P.C.M. Huigsloot & R.E. van de Lustgraaf (1982), Stedelijke ontwikkeling en beïnvloedbaarheid. In: J.G. Lambooy, P.C.M. Huigsloot & R.E. van de Lustgraaf, Greep op de stad?, pp. 9-87. 's-Gravenhage: SDU-Uitgeverij.

Lambooy, J.G. (1986), Amsterdam Duaal; enkele beschouwingen over de relatie technische ontwikkeling en arbeidsmarkt. (Dies-rede 1986). Amsterdam: Universiteit van Amsterdam.

Paridon, C.W.A.M. van (1990), Arbeidsmartktparticipatie in Nederland; Plaatsbepaling in internationaal perpectief. 's Gravenhage: Wetenschappelijke Raad voor het Regeringsbeleid.

OECD (1990), Historical Statistics. Paris: OECD.

Soja, E.W. (1991), The Stimulus of a Little Confusion; A Contemporary Comparison of Amsterdam and Los Angeles. Amsterdam: Centrum voor Grootstedelijk Onderzoek.

Schuyt, C.J.M. (1991), Op zoek naar het hart van de verzorgingsstaat. Leiden: Stenfert Kroese.

SCP (Sociaal en Cultureel Planbureau) (1990), Sociaal en Cultureel Rapport. 's-Gravenhage: SDU-Uitgeverij.

Swaan, A. de (1988), In Care of the State. Cambridge: Polity Press.

Wilson, W.J. (1987), The Truly Disadvantaged; The Inner City, the Underclass, and Public Policy. Chicago: The University Press of Chicago.

Winden, F.A.A.M. van (1988), The economic theory of political decision-making: a survey and perspective. In: J. van den Broeck (ed), Public Choice, pp.9-43. Dordrecht: Kluwer Academic Press.

WRR (Wetenschappelijke Raad voor het Regeringsbeleid) (1990a), Van de stad en de rand. 's Gravenhage: SDU-Uitgeverij.

WRR (Wetenschappelijke Raad voor het Regeringsbeleid) (1990b), Een werkend perspectief; Arbeidsparticipatie in de jaren '90. 's Gravenhage: SDU-Uitgeverij.

Zanden, J.L. van & R.T. Griffith (1989), Economische geschiedenis van Nederland in de 20ste eeuw. Utrecht: Het Spectrum.

Dr. R.C. Kloosterman
Faculty of Economic Sciences
University of Amsterdam
Nieuwe Prinsengracht 130
1018 VZ Amsterdam
The Netherlands

Prof.dr. J.G. Lambooy
Faculty of Economic Sciences
University of Amsterdam
Nieuwe Prinsengracht 130
1018 VZ Amsterdam
The Netherlands

7. RANDSTAD INFRASTRUCTURE: ITS USE AND ITS DEFICIENCIES

P. Rietveld & W. Stam

7.1 Introduction

The Randstad is a metropolitan area with a high spatial density, both in terms of infrastructure and demand for transport. During the latter part of the 1980s, the demand for transport rose rapidly. The demand was induced by a booming economy in a period of slow expansion of infrastructure. As a result, the bottlenecks in the Randstad's transport system became a matter of public concern. This concern was heightened by the growing awareness of a rising threat to the position of the Randstad: changes taking place in freight transport were jeopardizing the role of the Randstad as an international distribution center. The transport sector, and especially the international arrival and removal of goods, is an important economic function of the Randstad. International competition in this field made it imperative to upgrade the transport infrastructure in the Randstad. At the same time, however, there was an increasing awareness of the negative environmental externalities caused by transport, especially in a region like the Randstad, which is so densely populated. The demand for transport was growing, particularly in relation to the international freight transport, which is so important to the Randstad. The conflict between that demand and the negative environmental externalities is one of the main issues addressed by research and policy in the Netherlands since the late 1980s.

Figure 7.1 serves as a frame of reference for this chapter. Economic development is undoubtedly one of the key factors governing urban spatial development. Location decisions of both households and firms depend on economic development as expressed by indicators such as household income and sectoral composition. In the Randstad, the postwar period was characterized by a high level of economic growth. This initiated the ongoing process of suburbanization around the large urban centers. In the same period, world trade grew by leaps and bounds. In terms of the international division of labor, the Randstad region specialized as a 'gateway to Europe'.

As depicted in Figure 7.1, infrastructure and transport play specific roles in the interaction between economic development and urban spatial form. The mass introduction of the car during the 1960s depolarized human settlement patterns which otherwise would not have been possible. In the international context, the position of

F. M. Dieleman and S. Musterd (eds.), The Randstad: A Research and Policy Laboratory, 141–163.

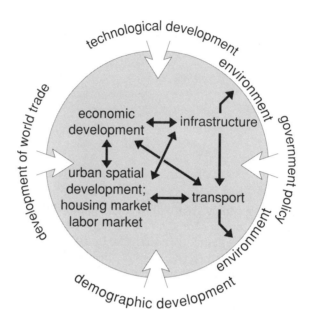

Figure 7.1   Conceptual scheme for the analysis of transport and urban development

urban regions as nodes in the urban system is to a large extent determined by their role in infrastructure and transport networks.

However, economic development does not automatically lead to a simultaneous growth of transport volume and infrastructure. In fact, if necessary provisions are made to balance the growth of these two elements, urban development might actually be hampered. For instance, transport volume in the Netherlands grew rapidly in the second half of the 1980s, while infrastructure investment remained rather modest. Among other reasons, this was due to budgetary problems of the national government.

The ensuing bottlenecks entail a certain degree of risk. Urban development in the Randstad may be negatively affected by these bottlenecks, since infrastructure and accessibility are crucial factors in the international competition between urban regions (Bruinsma & Rietveld 1991). And stagnation in the Randstad may in turn hamper economic development in the country as a whole. This example demonstrates that infrastructure and urban development can have major feedback effects on economic development.

Four factors mentioned in the conceptual scheme have a more or less autonomous influence: flow of world trade, technological innovation, demographic trends, and government policy. The government can influence urban development through physical planning and the supply of infrastructure. This does not mean that government is an exogenous factor. Recent studies (Ottens 1989; Musterd 1991) indicate that certain policy changes (for example, the compact city) are partly induced by economic developments. Thus, it is easy to overestimate the impact of government policies on urban development.

A factor exerting a major influence is technological innovation. The application of new transport technologies - like the introduction of trains and cars, the containerization of much of world trade (cf. Cheshire 1990), and the increase in size of airplanes - has shaped and altered the urban system in a decisive way. The third factor mentioned in Figure 7.1, the flow of world trade, has a strong influence on open economies, of which the Dutch economy is an example. The role of the Randstad region as a link in international transport networks is strongly influenced by this factor.

Using Figure 7.1 as a frame of reference, this chapter is organized as follows. Section 7.2 focuses on freight transport. The position of the Randstad as a node in international networks is explained, along with the economic implications of this position. Next, the changes in world trade and their likely consequences are dealt with. In order to assess the focus of infrastructure and transport policy in the Netherlands, it is essential to understand these shifts. The developments in domestic transport are not discussed here, as they play a less dominant role.

Passenger transport is the subject of Section 7.3. Here the focus is less on the international scale and more on interactions within the Randstad. Most traffic movements in the Randstad can be attributed to passenger transport, and especially to trips within the separate agglomerations. Passenger transport depends strongly on economic development, since ownership and use of cars is closely related to income (see Figure 7.1). Another factor influencing passenger transport is government policy. Physical planning is one of the tools, but it is doubtful whether it will be strong enough to counter the upward trend caused by economic and demographic developments (see Chapter 8). In regard to commuting, the Randstad has a polycentric form. This implies that it does not consist of one spatially well-integrated labor market. On the other hand, in terms of business-related passenger trips, the spatial interaction between the agglomerations in the Randstad is much higher.

Generalizing, the difference in scope between freight transport, commuting, and business-related passenger trips indicates different levels of spatial integration. In order to formulate policies to control the growth in mobility, it is essential to circumscribe the relevant spatial regions; it is also necessary to have a clear view of the changes in the spatial structure connected with the economic development. The relation between transport and infrastructure on the one hand and the spatial structure of the Randstad on the other is therefore the subject of Section 7.4.

Finally, Section 7.5 deals with the deficiencies of the Randstad's infrastructure in the context of the conceptual scheme of Figure 7.1. Accordingly, it deals with strategies to resolve a conflict of interest. One side of this conflict is the growth of mobility and the economic significance of transport. The other side consists of the environmental externalities caused by transport and infrastructure, and the need to upgrade the infrastructure.

7.2   Freight transport: growth and focus on value added

Introduction
As mentioned in section 7.1, international freight transport is an important economic activity for the Netherlands, and especially for the Randstad. As De Smidt shows in Chapter 5, international comparative studies conclude that the position of cities within the Randstad in the European hierarchy of cities is largely based on a strong position in 'international communication'. Compared with other Western European countries, the Netherlands conveys in transit a relatively large international flow of goods (Koopman 1990). In this section, we will confine ourselves to a discussion of international transport.

This international specialization, and the function of the Randstad as a node in European distribution networks, is to a large extent based on the strength of the 'mainports': Schiphol airport and Rotterdam harbor. The transit function means that a very large part of the goods handled have their origin or destination in the European hinterland. The Dutch home market is relatively small, and traditionally the Netherlands has fulfilled a function as 'gateway' to the European market, notably Germany. Measured in tons handled, Rotterdam has the largest harbor in the world, and Schiphol airport is among the top five European airports.

This means that freight transport in the Netherlands, especially in the Randstad, is very dependent on international trade developments. As a consequence, the worldwide economic stagnation of the late 1970s and early 1980s led to stagnation in tonnage handled. From 1984 onwards the international trade has recovered, and the volume of goods arriving in and removed from the Netherlands is rising once again, as Table 7.1 shows.

The port of Rotterdam handles more than 40 percent of the country's total arrival and removal of goods. Like most European ports, it experienced a serious decline in the early 1980s. In 1983 tonnages handled reached a lowest point of 234 mln. (in 1979 this was 294 mln. ton). From 1983 onwards recovery set in, and in 1989 292 mln. tons were handled. This process of recovery went hand in hand with changes in the structure of trade (for instance the growing importance of the Far East trade) and the form of the cargo (containerization of the general cargo).

Table 7.1   *International arrival and removal of goods in resp. from the Netherlands, 1980=100, mln. tons*

	1980	1982	1984	1986	1988	1989
Arrival	100=348.3	89	94	100	104	105
Removal	100=263.9	91	99	102	107	112

Source: CBS, Monthly Statistics on Traffic and Transport

Schiphol deals with only a small part of the flows measured in tons (in 1988 only some 800,000 tons were handled, of which 228,000 tons were related to the intra-European trucking of airfreight). In terms of value the share of airfreight is much higher, and the growth figures are impressive.

Freight transport in the Randstad is not limited to international flows. Yet the total interior transport of goods in the Netherlands is markedly smaller than the international flow. Out of the total interior flow of goods in the Netherlands, approximately 20 percent has its origin or destination in the Randstad. The flows within the Randstad account for another 35 percent.

Not only is the amount of tons handled considerable, but the contribution of the transport sector as a whole (including passenger transport) to the regional product of the Randstad is significant as well. The sector accounts directly for 8 percent of the total output, more than 9 percent of value added and nearly 10 percent of the labor volume of the region. Indirectly, however, the economic significance of the transport sector for the Randstad is even bigger. Transport can be labeled a basic sector, as it is strongly intertwined with activities like trade, banking, insurance etc. Several studies show that the indirect effect of the international transport function for the Dutch, i.e. Randstad, economy is considerable (for instance McKinsey & Company 1986; Lambooy 1984; NEI 1983).

Referring to the scheme in Figure 7.1, one can say that, from an economic point of view, it is not the growth in the flows of goods itself that is interesting. Rather, it is the factors behind these processes, and the changes they bring about in the economic structure of the Randstad that warrant study. These changes, in turn, influence the demand for infrastructure and transport, and consequently affect urban spatial development. To assess this influence, at least the following factors should be taken into account.

The 1980s were a period of economic restructuring, in which technological changes and development of world trade played a key role. After the world wide economic crisis of the late 1970s and early 1980s, international trade flows changed fundamentally, both in direction and composition. This is not the place to deal with these changes in depth. Figures from the GATT (1989, p. 8, 40-41) show that world trade grew at a faster pace than world production, reflecting a growing internationalization of the world economy. Also, the structure of world trade changed. While world trade grew by an average of four percent per annum, the share of 'manufactures' grew from 56 percent in 1980 to 73 percent in 1988. The trade between the Asian countries and the Western world, in categories like 'Office and telecom equipment', contributed significantly to this development.

For the Randstad, with its ambition to fulfil the role of 'gateway' to the Single European Market, the changes mentioned above have far-reaching consequences. This is largely because, in the growing international competition, transport and logistics are increasingly viewed as 'the last cost frontier yet open to large-scale savings'. In this context, the transport function is changing, and nodes like harbors and airports are faced with new requirements. Both Rotterdam harbor and Schiphol airport are engaged in a battle with the other European harbors and airports to position themselves as the 'mainports' of the continent. Their position in this confrontation depends to a large extent on how well they can comply with the requirements that are being posed in that segment of transport comprising high-valued goods and logistic services.

It should be remarked, however, that the above-mentioned developments concern only part of the transport sector. It is notably the market for transport of high-valued goods, for instance machine parts, foodstuffs, (express) documents, chemicals etc., that is confronted with the demand for logistic services. Transport of bulk flows like coal, grains etc. are subject to other constraints, which will not be dealt with here (for instance the stagnating population growth in Europe, or energy policy).

Thus the question is whether the Randstad is able to transform itself from its traditional role - a transport node predominantly focused on moving large flows of goods into the European hinterland - into a center that offers opportunities to the emerging segments of the transport industry. In this section we will use the conceptual scheme of Figure 7.1 to show that the interaction - between these economic developments, on the one hand, and the areas of transport, infrastructure, and urban spatial development, on the other - has several implications for the Randstad.

In short, three issues are of decisive importance to this interaction. First, from the point of view of transport, the position of the various modes is subject to change. The growing accent on road and air transport generates bottlenecks in the infrastructure of the Randstad, while exacerbating the environmental problems. Second, relating to the urban spatial development, the geographical setting of the transport function within the Netherlands shows a shift away from the Randstad. And, finally, as the organization of the European distribution networks is increasingly controlled by a select group of firms, the function the Randstad will fulfil in these networks depends on the strategy of leading firms in this segment. In this context, new demands are posed on infrastructure.

The changes in the transport of goods within the Randstad have less far-reaching consequences for transport, infrastructure, and urban spatial development. They will not be dealt with thoroughly here.

Transport and changes in the position of the various modes
As mentioned above, the growth in international transport in the second half of the 1980s went hand in hand with changes in the composition of the flows. Stam (1991a, Tables 2.1 - 2.4) shows that this is also reflected in the volume of goods entering and leaving the Netherlands, especially through the port of Rotterdam and Schiphol airport. The share of high-valued goods like food products, chemicals, and the category 'other manufactures' rose. In the interior transport, the growth between 1984 and 1989 was more evenly spread among the various categories of goods.

In regard to the position of the various transport modes, two major shifts can be attributed mainly to road transport: the growth in the late 1980s in the Netherlands' international arrival and removal of goods measured in tons moved; and the growth in interior transport (see also Visser 1990). Airfreight is also growing, but measured in tons this does not compare with road transport. In fact the 'trucking' of airfreight by road has become more popular. For the Netherlands, the international arrival and removal of freight by road grew between 1980 and 1988 by nearly 50 percent. The domestic freight transport by road grew in the same period by some 10 percent.

An even better indication of the shifts in relative importance of the various transport modes can be derived by comparing the value added that is generated in various subsectors of transport with the value of the output. Data on value added have a common denominator with an economic meaning, while tons and tonkilometers may be rather incomparable between, for instance, road and sea transport. As is shown in Stam (1990), in the 1980s telecommunications, road transport, and, to a lesser extent, air transport and transport auxiliary firms (forwarders, agents etc.) clearly made up a bigger share of value added.

These are also the segments of transport where the ratio of value added versus value of the output is relatively high. Sea transport, inland navigation, and rail transport appear to be losing ground.

Several factors have contributed to these developments. Here we will deal only briefly with the factors responsible for raising the share of road transport.

In the first place the high-valued goods are easier to transport by road, because most of the time their volume is relatively small. And the road system combines flexibility with speed of delivery. The demand by shippers for logistic services has favored road transport firms in particular (Stam 1990). In the first place, the share of transport by non-transport firms is declining. Shippers increasingly tend to board out their logistic function. Second, in the value added generated by the large road transport firms, the share derived from non-transport, i.e. 'logistic' activities, is growing fast.

The above-mentioned shifts are not unique to the Randstad or the Netherlands. When interpreting them, however, we must keep an inherent threat in mind. That is that the traditional comparative advantages of the Randstad and the Netherlands as 'European gateway' are to a large extent based on the forms of transport that seem to be losing ground.

In the international transport to and from the Netherlands, two phenomena are striking: the relatively large share of inland navigation, especially in the removal of goods (nearly 40% versus 13% in the supply); and the small share of the railways (less than 2% in supply and about 3% in removal). In other European countries, the share of rail transport is much higher, for instance nearly 37 percent in France and more than 25 percent in former West Germany (1985 resp. 1984; NEA 1990). Also pipelines play a significant role in the removal of goods; various lines for oil and its products connect between Rotterdam Europoort with its European hinterland. It is very likely Rotterdam will maintain its dominant position as a major European 'hub' for sea transport, but that will not necessarily benefit the Dutch shipping sector. Positive economic effects of this 'hub function' become more concentrated in activities like inland transport, forwarding, and distribution.

In view of these 'threats', it should be remarked that the Netherlands holds a very strong position in European transborder road traffic. With a share of 22 percent (1989, share of total tonnage moved), the Netherlands is the European market leader in this respect. However, road transport is very flexible, and less tied to the traditional modes of international transport than sea ports, for instance. As the next section will show, the growth of road transport firms is less concentrated in the Randstad.

Urban spatial development

In a geographical sense, the Randstad is engaged in a competition as a transport node at various levels. At the global level, intercontinental flows of goods seem to concentrate on a restricted number of 'mainports'. As mentioned before, the position of Schiphol airport and the port of Rotterdam in the urban hierarchy is to a large extent defined at the level of mainport. If one of them loses its mainport function, this will have a serious impact on the overall transport and distribution position of the Randstad. We will return to this point below.

The intra-European distribution is the logical follow-up of the intercontinental flows of goods. Two trends dominate this market segment: The tendency among shippers to contract out logistic functions, and the centralization of European distribution. As shown above, road transport benefits most of this development. The location of these relatively new activities - including not only the transport firms themselves, but also for instance warehouses - seem to be less tied to the traditional transport nodes. Inland locations are preferred, situated more towards the center of the European market. As a consequence, the Randstad might lose its dominant position in transport within the Netherlands. In Chapter 5, De Smidt shows that this process is an element in the spread of the urban functions over a larger region.

The third geographical context to consider is found within the urban system of the Randstad. It deals with the position of the agglomerations and the changes within them (central city versus surroundings). In this contribution we will make only cursory remarks on this aspect.

Stam (1990) shows that road transport is the subsector of transport with the least degree of concentration in the Randstad. While for most other subsectors 50 to 60 percent of the total number of firms in the Netherlands are located within the Randstad, for road transport this is true of only some 40 percent. As Figure 7.2 indicates investment by road transport firms in the Randstad is low compared with the rest of the country.

Several reasons can be given for the relatively weak position of the Randstad in road transport. The most important one is probably the distance to the center of the European market, after the adjustment precipitated by 'Europe 1992'. As in logistics, the overnight or 48-hour service is becoming more important. Warehouses and distribution centers are located in regions more towards the center of this Single European Market, for instance in the provinces of Noord Brabant and Gelderland. Other reasons are the congestion in the Randstad, the lack of room for expansion there (combined with relatively high land prices), and a lack of qualified labor.

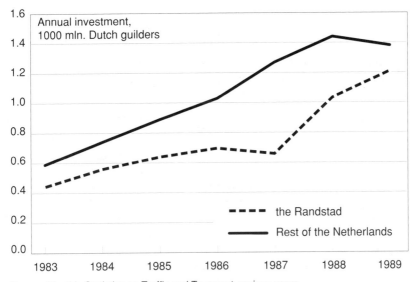

Figure 7.2   Investment by road transport firms in the Randstad versus the rest of the Netherlands, 1980-1989

Infrastructure, networks, and value added

Traditionally, the competition between various ('main')ports on the European continent was focused on issues directly related to the harbor or airport (costs, transit times etc.). The growing importance of logistic services, as well as the prospect of the Single European Market after '1992', have given an impulse to the development of intra-European distribution networks. Transport firms are confronted with a growing demand for 'door to door' transport.

These developments have resulted in a growth of international investment in transport. In the second half of the 1980s, investment by foreign firms in the Dutch transport sector has more than doubled. The foreign investments by Dutch transport firms also rose significantly (Stam 1990). It is expected that only a few firms will be able to set up a logistic network on a European scale, some of them building 'hub and spoke' systems, others using less centralized systems. The effects for the Randstad will show up along two lines. In the near future, the firms that control the European distribution networks will have a strong influence on the choice of modes, links, and nodes used in European transport. Intermodal operators, with their own networks, will control the flows of goods. For the Randstad, and especially the port of Rotterdam and Schiphol airport, their position in these networks will be decisive. Both mainports hold a strong position, but these new developments may undermine it. Rotterdam holds a rather strong position in the deep-sea (container) trade, but it is less specialized in activities to enhance the value added of the cargo. In the high-value range of goods this is becoming a disadvantage. In air-freight, Schiphol is number four among European airports. It owes this position to the strength of the home-carrier KLM in the international freight market. The effect of the 'alliance game' in the airline industry can, in this respect, have serious consequences. In the emerging market of 'integrators', the position of Schiphol is rather weak.

A second relevant feature of the networks will be the infrastructure, and especially the inland connections. An important aspect of the Dutch transport system is the relatively insignificant role of the railways in freight transport. Less then two percent of the international transport is carried by rail; for domestic transport this figure amounts to only one percent (1988). In Europe, there is a growing tendency to promote rail transport at the expense of road transport. The Dutch internal connections by rail have to be upgraded to link up with this trend.

This policy to limit (the growth of) freight transport by road was induced by concern about the environment and congestion. Besides the railways, domestic shipping might also benefit from such a policy. In both cases however, a network of combi-terminals along the overland routes is needed to accommodate these flows, since most destinations do not have direct access to rail or barge. This will reinforce the network character of inland transport and European distribution. To connect the centers of the Randstad to this network, large investments in infrastructure are needed.

Freight transport perspectives

International freight transport is an important economic basis for the Randstad as an urban center. The restructuring of the world economy in the 1980s imposed new requirements on transport. The growth in the flow of high-valued goods, as well as the increasing importance of logistics for this part of world trade, have a significant influence on transport, infrastructure, and urban spatial development of the Randstad. This gives rise to new opportunities, as well as threats.

In transport more emphasis is placed on functions that generate value added, like warehousing and distribution. This confronts the transport nodes in the Randstad, like Schiphol airport and Rotterdam harbor with a growing demand for space for these activities. It requires a restructuring of sites, which is well on its way.

Road transport firms are benefiting most from the growing demand for transport. The Netherlands has developed a rather strong position in European cross-border road traffic. However unrestrained growth of road transport has serious drawbacks in the form of congestion and pollution of the environment. In the Netherlands, rail transport of freight is relatively underdeveloped, and this is becoming a comparative disadvantage for the Randstad. This is especially threatening since the infrastructure networks towards the European hinterland have become a factor of growing importance in the competition between 'mainports'. A traditional comparative advantage of the Netherlands, the well developed inland waterways, have, until quite recently, been insufficiently used for transport of relatively high-valued goods in containers. There are, however, signs that this is changing rapidly.

In the field of urban spatial development, it is clear that road transport and distribution are less tied to traditional transport nodes like ports and airports. Inland locations, towards the center of the European market, are preferred. For the Randstad, it is very important to develop the links with these new centers. Internationally, the question is whether the Randstad holds a strong position in the networks of firms organizing the European distribution. There is some indication that Schiphol and Rotterdam harbor are less well represented in the networks of the new segments of the transport industry.

From a theoretical frame of reference, it seems that the world wide economic growth from 1984 onwards shows characteristics of the upswing of the fifth Kondratieff cycle. The restructuring of world production and world trade, to a large extent induced by technological development, demands comparable adaptations in worldwide transportation systems (see also Stam 1991b). These adaptations lag behind the pace of change in the demand for transport. As a consequence, bottlenecks in transport and infrastructure occur.

As a reaction to these bottlenecks, qualitative changes are made in the transport system. Technological innovations, organizational adaptions in transport, and geographical changes - for instance the use of inland nodes - constitute part of this process. The transportation system of the fifth Kondratieff cycle does not necessarily use the same geographical routes and nodes as the existing system.

To remain an important node in the worldwide transportation system, the Randstad will have to adapt to the qualitative changes demanded in transport and infrastructure. However, the exact nature of these changes still has to be sorted out. It seems that the 'logistic service supplies', organizing European and worldwide distribution systems, take the lead in this process.

7.3   Passenger transport in the Randstad

In the preceding section we have seen that the international dimension in freight transport in essential to the Randstad. This dimension is also clearly present in passenger transport. Schiphol airport has an important position as a node in both continental and intercontinental passenger flights. In addition, large investments are projected to extend or improve the international railway connections between the Randstad and the European railway network. For example, a high speed rail connection is planned, connecting the Randstad with Brussels, Paris, and the Channel tunnel by the end of the century. Similarly, a substantial reduction in travel time is planned by improving the connection with the German railway system. Nevertheless, it is fair to say that the local and regional dimension is very prominent in passenger transport. It is on this aspect that we will focus in this section.

We start with a short sketch of the evolution of the transport system in the Randstad during the last decades, taking into account the interrelationships with the major elements of the conceptual scheme (Figure 7.1): economic development, urban development and government policies.

Transport and infrastructure have played an important role in urban development in the Netherlands. Between 1960 and 1980 the length of the highway system and the number of passenger cars grew at an annual rate of about 10 percent. The development of the railway system stagnated during that period. After 1980 a rather different pattern emerged: the number of cars and length of the highway system grew at a much more moderate annual rate of about 2 percent, and the railway system started to grow in length. As a result, the average annual number of kilometers traveled per person increased from about 4,000 in 1960 to about 11,000 in 1990.

The economic boom during the 1960s and the early 1970s caused a massive growth of the road transport network and of the number of passenger cars. Consequently commuting patterns were no longer dominated by public transport but by the car system. This led to a process of rapid suburbanization among the major cities in the Randstad (see e.g. Klaassen et al. 1981). Government policies developed during the 1970s sought to check the process of urban sprawl by creating growth centers. These growth centers are usually located 10 to 30 kilometers from the major cities. They are preferably located *outside* of the Randstad if space is available. Examples include Alkmaar, Purmerend, Hoorn, and Almere for Amsterdam; Nieuwegein and Houten for Utrecht; and Spijkenisse for Rotterdam. A notable exception is Zoetermeer for The Hague, since the coastal setting of the Hague does not allow for an outward location of a growth center. The development of the inner part of the Randstad (the so-called Green Heart) was discouraged by strict physical planning restrictions. As a result, the road density in the Green Heart remained rather low. For example, plans to create a direct highway connection between Amsterdam and Rotterdam were cancelled.

The spatial deconcentration of population of the Randstad was followed by a deconcentration of employment (Zondag & Stijnenbosch 1989). The Randstad's share of employment in the industrial sector decreased substantially. The service sector was less and less oriented towards the centers of the large cities. Instead, employment in the service sector grew rapidly at the fringe of the larger cities and at suburban locations. The major urban agglomerations in the Randstad developed into polycentric metropolitan areas over the last two decades (Droogh et al. 1991). Various new subcenters emerged, with a rather specialized sectoral composition. From the viewpoint of transport it is important to note that the spatial direction of the deconcentration of population and employment was sometimes inconsistent. For example, the growth centers of Amsterdam were created on the northern side, whereas employment was most dynamic on the southern side. This spatial divergence induced growing commuting distances and bottlenecks in the road system, especially since adequate public transport facilities to the growth centers were not always provided. It must be added that the development of the structure of urban agglomerations in a polycentric direction offers opportunities to reduce commuting distances (cf. Gordon et al. 1988). However, the Dutch experience indicates that even when the employment/population ratio is relatively balanced per subcenter, average commuting distances may still be considerable. This is because of a mismatch between the quality of housing demanded by the workers and the actual quality available (cf. Droogh et al. 1991). Another aspect of transportation entailed by polycentric development concerns the use of public transport. In general, it is easier to provide adequate public transport to monocentric urban areas than to polycentric ones.

In view of the Dutch government's policy objective to reduce the share of the automobile in the modal split, the trend towards polycentric urban areas is clearly unfavorable (cf. Verroen 1991).

In the beginning of the 1980s, the economic recession, in combination with a reorientation of residential construction, halted the population decline of the large Randstad cities and led to a decrease in population growth in suburbs and growth centers. However, it is by no means certain that this pattern will last long (cf. Chapter 3). The combination of further economic growth and lack of space for residential construction in large cities will probably stimulate a new wave of suburbanization. As a result the spatial distribution of population will become increasingly dispersed, making it difficult to provide public transport services.

Modal choice
Urban spatial form is one of the determinants of demand for transport, as indicated in the conceptual framework (Figure 7.1). In the present section we will investigate its role in modal choice in the Randstad. Modal choice is an important aspect of transport, since the externalities caused by transport (environmental degradation, congestion) differ widely among travel modes. The Randstad provinces are characterized by a relatively high population density of approximately 900 persons per square km; the density in the rest of the Netherlands is much lower (below 300 persons per square km). From the viewpoint of transport, high densities may affect both the length of trips and modes of travel. Concerning the length of trips, high densities imply that for most types of destinations there are nearby alternatives in space, which may lead to relatively short traveling distances. For travel modes, high densities mean that there are favorable opportunities to provide public transport services. Further, high densities offer good opportunities for short distance modes, such as cycling or walking. However, as shown in Table 7.2, the differences between the Randstad and the rest of the Netherlands are rather small. The fact that the degree of urbanization is relatively unimportant as a determinant of travel behavior is also noted by De Ben et al. (1990).

Total distances traveled in the Randstad are only slightly lower compared with the Netherlands as a whole. The share of public transport in the Randstad is higher than in the rest of the Netherlands, but the difference is rather small. The share of walking in the Randstad is slightly above average, and the share of cycling is slightly below average. The latter suggests that the supply of public transport services has a negative effect on the use of the bicycle.

From an international perspective, the share of the bicycle in modal choice in the Netherlands is very high. More than one out of four trips is made by bicycle. The import-

Table 7.2   *Modal choice in the Randstad and the Netherlands (persons 12 years and older), 1989*

	average number of trips per person per day traveled		average distance per person per day (km)	
	Randstad	Netherlands	Randstad	Netherlands
Car (driver)	1.14	1.21	16.6	17.0
Car (passenger)	0.45	0.49	7.8	8.6
Public transport	0.25	0.17	4.8	3.8
Moped	0.04	0.05	0.3	0.3
Bicycle	0.94	1.01	3.1	3.2
Walking	0.68	0.60	1.0	0.9
Other	0.03	0.04	0.8	0.8
Total	3.52	3.56	34.3	34.7

Source: CBS (1990)

ance of the bicycle is even somewhat underrated in this table, since the role of the bicycle in trips with combined modes (such as bicycle and public transport) is neglected in the left part of the table. In an international comparative study Pucher (1990) noted that the share of public transport in the Netherlands is low compared with other industrialized countries. Only in the USA is the share lower. This outcome can be explained partly by the widespread use of the bicycle in the Netherlands. Yet it should be noted that in a country like Sweden, a relatively high use of the bicycle does not lead to a comparably low use of public transport.

At a lower spatial level much larger variations in modal choice can be observed. For example, in Amsterdam, quarters with a high quality public transport system (metro) have a public transport share which is 50 percent above the city average (Municipality of Amsterdam 1987). Similarly, car ownership and car use vary largely among city quarters. Some quarters in the center of Amsterdam have car ownership rates which are only 50 percent of rates observed in suburban municipalities (CBS 1989; Municipality of Amsterdam 1987).

Travel purposes
Economic structure is one of the key factors influencing transport flows, according to the conceptual scheme in Figure 7.1. In this section we will investigate the extent to which this holds true for passenger transport. As indicated in Table 7.3, about 22 percent of all trips in the Randstad relate to work (commuting and business-related trips). These trips account for about 33 percent of all passenger kilometers. Thus, in passenger transport, non-work purposes, such as social visits, shopping, and recreation, are dominant. Yet work-related traveling purposes play a major role in the political debates about the appropriateness of Dutch transport infrastructure. The reason is

Table 7.3   Traveling purposes in the Randstad and the Netherlands, 1989

	number of trips per person per day		average distance travelled per person per day		average distance per trip (km)	
Travelling purpose	Randstad	Netherlands	Randstad	Netherlands	Randstad	Netherlands
Commuting	.63	.62	8.50	8.30	13.5	13.4
Business	.16	.15	3.05	2.81	18.7	18.7
Social visits	.56	.61	7.68	7.63	13.7	12.5
Shopping	.93	.90	3.81	4.07	4.1	4.5
Education	.18	.19	1.74	1.90	9.7	10.0
Recreation	.37	.37	3.59	3.83	9.7	10.4
Other	.69	.72	5.94	6.15	8.6	8.5
Total	3.52	3.56	34.31	34.68	9.7	9.7

Source: CBS (1990)

Table 7.4   Road distances between urban centers in the Randstad

	Rotterdam	The Hague	Amsterdam	Utrecht
Rotterdam	-	27	78	58
The Hague	27	-	61	62
Amsterdam	78	61	-	39
Utrecht	58	62	39	-

that commuting is the major traveling purpose during rush hours. Improvements and extensions of the transport infrastructure network in congested areas will primarily benefit work-related trips.

Table 7.3 shows that economic and spatial conditions specific to the Randstad area hardly influence the mobility pattern of Randstad residents compared with other Dutch residents, if measured at this level of spatial aggregation. The Netherlands is so homogeneous from an economic point of view (in terms of labor market participation or income levels) that interregional differences in mobility patterns are slight.

The average distance per trip is about 10 km in the Randstad. For work-related motives it is somewhat higher: about 13 km for commuting and 19 km for business-related passenger trips. These distances are relatively short, compared with the road distances between the major urban centers in the Randstad, as shown in Table 7.4. In the next section we will see what this implies for functional interdependencies in the Randstad.

Spatial interaction patterns in the Randstad
Fifty percent of all trips by Randstad residents are shorter than 3.5 km. The share
of long-distance trips (more than 50 km) is only about four percent. This implies that
the share of passenger trips between urban agglomerations must be very small compared
with the share of trips within agglomerations. Based on a spatial division of the Randstad
in 10 larger and smaller urban agglomerations, it is found that 89 percent of all passenger
trips take place within these agglomerations (see Table 7.5). Of the remaining trips,
only two percent take place between the four large agglomerations indicated above.
From the viewpoint of passenger transport, these results underline the polycentric
nature of the Randstad (see also Cortie & Ostendorf 1986).

The weakest degree of spatial interdependence in the Randstad is observed for
passenger transport with 'other' purposes, which include social visits, recreation, shopping,
etc. For commuting, a higher degree of interdependence is found: 15 percent of all
commuters in the Randstad cross boundaries between urban agglomerations on their
trips from home to work. This rather low figure means that the Randstad does not
consist of one spatially well-integrated labor market, but instead, of a number of spatially
separated sub markets. This applies to the labor market in general. For specific jobs
requiring high qualifications, transport commuting distances are much longer than
average, however (CBS 1990).

For business-related passenger trips, a higher degree of spatial interdependence can
be observed in the Randstad. About 20 percent of such trips are between urban
agglomerations. For freight transport, this figure is even considerably higher (31%).
These results indicate the wide variation in the degree of functional integration within
the Randstad. It is very low for leisure-related activities, such as shopping, recreation,
and social visits. Functional integration is also low for major segments of the labor
market. The figures for business-related passenger flows, and especially for freight
flows indicate that functional integration is considerable for the production system
in the Randstad.

Table 7.5   *Daily trips between major urban areas in the Randstad, workdays, 1986*

	Amsterdam	Utrecht	The Hague	Rotterdam
Amsterdam	1444	24	18	11
Utrecht	26	626	12	7
The Hague	18	12	1135	48
Rotterdam	12	8	51	1340

Source: DVK (1990), CBS, INRO (1988)

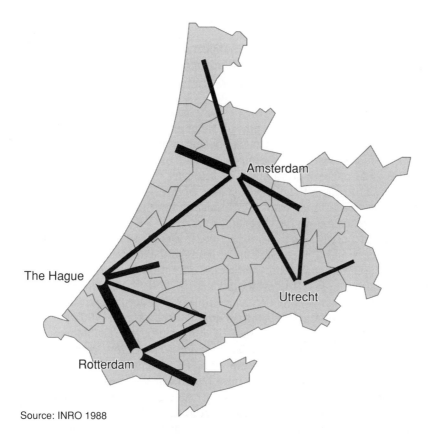

Source: INRO 1988

Figure 7.3   Most important passenger flows within the Randstad

At a more detailed level, it can be shown that from the viewpoint of passenger trips (all traveling purposes taken together), the Randstad consists of two wings: a Northern wing, consisting of Amsterdam, Utrecht and some smaller cities in the northern part of the Randstad and a southern wing, with Rotterdam and The Hague as the major urban centers (see Figure 7.3). As can be inferred from Table 7.5, the level of interaction between the two wings, measured by the interactions between the major urban agglomerations, is very low indeed. This implies that the extensive road-and railway system connecting the major cities of the Randstad is primarily used for short-distance passenger trips. The share of persons using these networks for long-distance trips (including international trips) is small.

7.4   Transport, infrastructure and the future of the Randstad

We can distinguish three spatial levels that pertain to the discussion of the future role
of transport and infrastructure in the Randstad:
- within agglomerations in the Randstad
- between agglomerations in the Randstad
- between the Randstad and the rest of the world

Transport of goods and passengers play a role at all three spatial levels. But it is clear
that short distances are most important for passenger transport. This is nicely illustrated
by Figure 7.4, which shows the traffic intensity on the main road connecting the Randstad
with Central and Southern Germany. The intensity is very high near Utrecht, where
the road serves as a link in the highway system of the agglomeration. The traffic gradually decreases with distance from the Randstad; near the border it is only about 10
percent of that near the city of Utrecht.

We now turn to a discussion of transport and infrastructure at various spatial levels.
As indicated in Section 7.3, adequate infrastructure at the metropolitan level is important
for the functioning of urban labor markets. Congestion on roads is mainly found in
Dutch metropolitan areas. It is estimated that in 1990 more than 90 percent of all
time lost on Dutch highways due to backen-up traffic occured within 20 kilometers
of the four major cities of the Randstad (Dienst Verkeerskunde 1990). Public transport
is generally assigned the important task of mitigating these problems in the future.
The quality of public transport in the larger cities is rather low, compared with cities
like Paris and London, although it is improving (Bruinsma & Rietveld 1991). Subway
systems or advanced light rail systems have been built only rather recently. The total
length of these systems is still limited, however, so that much of the urban population
still depends on slow modes of public transport. A further improvement of rapid public
transport is essential in order to reduce the growth of car use in these areas. Around
1990, the larger cities of the Randstad formulated ambitious investment plans to make
these improvements. But it is unlikely that these plans can be realized, given the
budgetary constraints of the central government.

The second spatial level concerns the linkages between the urban agglomerations
in the Randstad. As demonstrated in Section 7.3, the economic importance of these
linkages is not determined primarily by labor market considerations but by the functional
interdependence in the Randstad production system. This is demonstrated by the figures
on business-related traffic and freight, in particular. At this spatial level, road traffic
is the only viable transport mode for these types of spatial interaction. In the highway
system, business-related traffic and freight transport are mixed with passenger traffic,
which tends to make use of the highways for relatively short trips. Especially during
rush hours, a conflict of interest emerges between the various road users. A system
of (electronic) tolls has the potential to produce a more efficient use of highway capacity
in such a case.

The third spatial level is interregional/international. Traditionally, (Western) Germany,
Belgium, and Luxembourg have been the most important hinterland of Dutch transport.

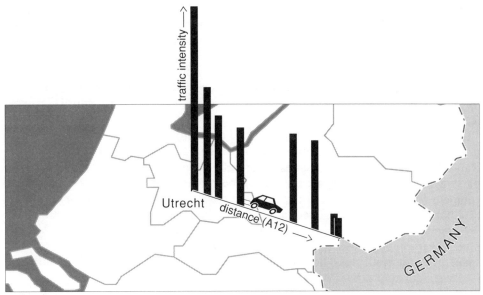

Source: DVK 1990

Figure 7.4   Traffic intensity as a function of distance from the Randstad

In 1989, 64 percent of total removal of goods from the Netherlands had its destination in these countries.

The changing economic structures of Europe, increasing emphasis on distribution networks fitted to the Single European Market, and 'door to door' transport requirements, stress the importance of developing infrastructural links with newly emerging regions in Europe. It is, however, rather uncertain what exactly can be expected in this field.

The expected economic development of (former) Eastern Europe might very well benefit the Northern German ports more than Rotterdam. Also, Berlin might become a serious competitor for Schiphol in the battle for a European 'hub' function. On the other hand, it is clear that the restructuring of the East European economies will take many years. Several recent studies suggest that the economic development of Europe shows a tendency towards more dynamic growth in the Alpine regions, like Southern Germany, Switzerland, Northern Italy, and the eastern part of France. Yet it is doubtful whether this is still true (see for instance NEI 1989). So these geographical shifts are by no means clear perspectives. It seems unlikely that they will change the trade patterns in Europe in the near future.

NEA (1990) shows that the infrastructure links of the Randstad are still predominantly oriented towards traditional industrial centers in Europe. This entails a risk for the future, since the newly developing centers are less accessible by barge, the traditional comparative advantage of the Dutch infrastructure network. The growing emphasis on the rail network in Europe might be a serious handicap for the Netherlands, where freight transport by rail is clearly underdeveloped. It is thus no surprise to see that a great deal of political effort is directed toward improving the railway connections with the German hinterland. An example is the proposal to construct the Betuwe line for freight transport by rail as a connection between Rotterdam and Central Germany (see also Chapter 8).

For the road system, the above-mentioned elements of demand for transport lead to conflicting claims on the limited capacity. The conflicts are most severe in the Randstad area near the large cities, where all spatial levels come together for both passenger and freight transport. It is here, for example, that short-distance commuters compete for the available road space with truckers on their way to international destinations. As will be explained in Chapter 8, the Dutch government intends to give preferential treatment to freight transport and business-related passenger trips. Various policy instruments have been proposed to reduce the claim of commuters on road space. It is not at all clear, however, whether the proposed policies will be effective (see also Nijkamp et al. 1991).

7.5   Addressing the deficiencies

In transport, the central issue is to maintain the position of the Randstad as an international distribution center while securing the quality of life. How can this conflict of interest be resolved? Three elements are of vital importance in addressing this issue.

In the first place, to get the trucks off the road, it is essential to stimulate intermodal transport; long-haul distances should be covered by train or barge, while the truck is to fulfil fine-meshed distribution functions. To this end, plans have been developed to create inland intermodal transport centers, where the transfer between train/barge and truck can take place. Here the Netherlands is hampered by its small geographical scale. Distances to destinations in the Netherlands alone are too short to justify the use of rail and barge, followed by transfer to truck. The transfer costs limit the use of intermodal transport to distances longer than 300 to 500 km. Especially in rail transport, this means that these plans rely heavily on international cooperation, which is not well developed among the European railroads.

A second element in this respect is the issue of restructuring. This entails developing sites for housing and economic activities in such a way that the rate of growth of mobility decreases.

The last element we will consider is the creation of adequate infrastructure for telematics. The further introduction of telematics is expected to lead to an increase in efficiency of transport, which may help to reduce its negative environmental impacts. In this field we can differentiate between hardware and software. The hardware does not seem to pose serious problems. In regard to software, it is the communication between the various parties in transport that is the focal point at the moment. By the 1980s, most parties had developed their own in-house communication system. To make optimum use of the possibilities of EDI, the systems of the various parties have to be linked. So-called 'community-systems' have been developed to this end (like Cargonaut at Schiphol and INTIS in Rotterdam).

It is difficult to say whether the Netherlands, and the Randstad in particular, holds a strong position in the telematics infrastructure. Problems abound, but that seems to be the case in other countries and regions as well. However, in the long run, an adequate information infrastructure will be a decisive element in transport.

References

Bruinsma, F. & P. Rietveld (1991), Infrastructuur en stedelijke ontwikkelingen in Europa. Werkstukken Stedelijke Netwerken 27. Amsterdam: Stedelijke Netwerken.

Ben, L.J.C. de, L.H. Immers & H.C. van Evert (1990), Bevolkingsgroepen met een homogeen en in de tijd stabiel verplaatsingsgedrag. In: J.M. Jager (ed), Colloquium Vervoersplanologisch Speurwerk, pp. 63-82. Delft: CVS.

Cheshire, P. (1990) Explaining the recent performance of the European Community major urban regions. Urban Studies 27, pp. 331-333.

Cortie, C. & W. Ostendorf (1986), Suburbanisatie en gentrification: sociaal-ruimtelijke dynamiek in de Randstad na 1970. Geografisch Tijdschrift 20, pp. 64-83.

CBS (Centraal Bureau voor de Statistiek) (z.j.), De mobiliteit van de Nederlandse bevolking, 's Gravenhage: CBS.

Dienst Verkeerskunde (1990), Verkeersgegevens 1990, Rotterdam: Ministerie van Verkeer en Waterstaat.

Droogh, D.A.A., A. Buys & C. Cortie (1991), Op overbrugbare afstand?, wonen en werken in een polycentrisch stadsgewest. Amsterdam: Universiteit van Amsterdam.

Dienst Verkeerskunde (1990), Het Landelijk Model Systeem (LMS), Rotterdam: Ministerie van Verkeer en Waterstaat.

GATT (General Agreement on Tariffs and Trade) (1989), Developments in World Trade. In: GATT International Trade 88- 89, pp. 5-22. Geneva: GATT.

Gordon, P., A. Kumar & H.W. Richardson (1988), Beyond the Journey to Work. Los Angeles: University of Southern California.

INRO (1988), Interaktiepatronen in de Randstad, Delft.

Klaassen, L.H., J.A. Boudrez, & J. Volmuller (1981), Transport and Reurbanisation. Aldershot: Gower.

Koopman, G.J. (1990), Nederland vervoersland. Economisch Statistische Berichten 3788, pp. 1231-1236.

Lambooy, J.G. (1984), De regionaal economische betekenis van Schiphol. Deel 2: de uitstralingseffecten, pp. 1-31, Haarlem: Provinciaal Planologische Dienst, Noord-

Holland.

McKinsey & Company (1986), Gateway Holland, vormgeven aan een initiatie. Samenvatting van een studie voor de Commissie Nederland Distributieland. Amsterdam: McKinsey.

Municipality of Amsterdam (1987), Amsterdam in Cijfers, jaarboek. Amsterdam: Gemeente Amsterdam.

Musterd, S. (1991), Dynamiek in randstedelijke woonmilieus; urbanisatie en suburbanisatie. In: S. Musterd & P. Hooimeijer (eds), De Randstad, balans van winst en verlies, deel 2, Stedelijke Netwerken, pp. 93-108. Amsterdam/Utrecht: Stedelijke Netwerken.

NEA (1990), Infrastructuur en concurrentiekracht, achtergrondstudies. Rijswijk: NEA.

NEI (Nederlands Economisch Instituut), EBWW (Economisch Bureau voor het Weg- en Watervervoer) (1983), Nederland als stapelplaats. Rotterdam: NEI.

NEI (Nederlands Economisch Instituut) (1989), Verschuiving van economische zwaartepunten in Noordwest-Europa: Fictie of realiteit? Rotterdam: NEI.

Nijkamp, P., P. Rietveld & J. Simons (1991), Multimodel Options for Commodity and Person Transport: Conflicts and Compromises in the Dutch Randstad, paper presented at OECD Conference on Transport Policy. Paris.

Ottens, H.F.L. (1989), Verstedelijking en stadsontwikkeling. Assen: Van Gorcum.

Pucher, J. (1990), A competetive analysis of policies and travel behavior in the Soviet Union, Eastern and Western Europe and North America. Transportation Quarterly 44, pp. 446-465.

Stam, W.J. (1990), De transportsector in beweging, Werkstukken Stedelijke Netwerken 23. Delft: Stedelijke Netwerken.

Stam, W.J. (1991a), Enkele aspecten van de Randstad als logistiek knooppunt, OTB Werkdocument 91-07. Delft: Delftse Universitaire Pers.

Stam, W.J. (1991b), Technische ontwikkelingen en mobiliteit. Infrastructuur, transport en logistiek 4. Delft: Delftse Universitaire Pers.

Verroen, E. (1991), Lokatiebeleid woningbouw en werkgelegenheid. Paper presented at Conference Urban Development, Infrastructure and Transport in the Randstad, Amsterdam: Stedelijke Netwerken.

Visser, J.G. (1990), Goederentransport en de Randstad. In: H. Priemus & H. van der Heyden (eds), Randstad: toplokatie of probleemakkumulatiegebied. pp. 31-48. Technisch-Bestuurskundige Verkenningen 10. Delft: Delftse Universitaire Pers.

Zondag, H. & M.H. Stijnenbosch (1989), Struktuur van de werkgelegenheid en de bedrijvigheid in de vier Randstadgewesten. Werkstukken Stedelijke Netwerken 13. Utrecht: Stedelijke Netwerken.

Prof.dr. P. Rietveld
Faculty of Economics
Free University of Amsterdam
P.O. Box 7161
1007 MC Amsterdam
The Netherlands

Drs. W. Stam
Ministry of Transport Public Works and Water Management
Directorate-General of Transport
P.O. Box 20901
2500 EX The Hague
The Netherlands

8. RANDSTAD POLICY ON INFRASTRUCTURE AND TRANSPORTATION: HIGH AMBITIONS, POOR RESULTS

H. Priemus & P. Nijkamp

8.1 Introduction and objective

The Netherlands has the highest density of automobiles (cars/km2) on earth. Within the country, the density is highest in the Randstad. Compared with greater Tokyo, greater London and Paris, the situation can hardly be called dramatic. Nevertheless, a coherent policy on infrastructure and transport is still highly important for the Randstad.

The Dutch government reformulated its policy on infrastructure and transportation recently in the Second Transport Structure Plan (SVV2). Part A appeared in 1988: the policy outline (Minister van Verkeer en Waterstaat en Minister van VROM 1988). After a change in the cabinet, Part D was published in 1990: the government's decision (Minister van Verkeer en Waterstaat en Minister van VROM 1990).

The strategy presented in SVV2, Part A, was based on the intention to deal most adequately with the tension between individual freedom, accessibility and liveability. Part D takes a sustainable society as the point of reference for the policy it proposes. A sustainable society implies developments that satisfy the needs of the current generation without jeopardizing the possibility to also satisfy the needs of future generations.

The Dutch government seeks to limit the negative externalities of traffic and transportation by placing restrictions on air pollution, energy consumption, noise pollution, the number of traffic accidents, the devastation of nature, the decline of liveability in the cities, and the usurpation of space.

On the authority of the Central Planning Office, SVV2 Part D also assumes that the level of affluence will continue to increase over the next 20 years. "We owe our affluence largely to our location along the major transportation axes of Europe. To keep and buttress the country's transport and distribution function based on that location, in addition to the role of locational factor for international enterprises, constitutes an important goal of government policy" (p. 9). The mainports of Schiphol and Rotterdam are identified as engines of the Dutch economy, which must have access to good connections by road, waterways, rail, and telecommunications.

Intelligent and creative solutions have to be found in the area of traffic and transport, solutions that make economic growth possible within the context of a sustainable society.

F. M. Dieleman and S. Musterd (eds.), The Randstad: A Research and Policy Laboratory, 165–191.
© 1992 *Kluwer Academic Publishers. Printed in the Netherlands.*

SVV2, Part D, concludes as follows (p. 9): "That requires controlling mobility." This control over mobility applies first and foremost to automobile traffic. But SVV2, Part D, also intends to curb the growth of commuting distances, by public transport as well.

The authors observe that the current low price of mobility does not reflect the real costs incurred for infrastructure, the environment, and public health. "The low price is more of an incentive to mobility than an obstacle" (p. 9).

The 'strategy' of SVV2, Part D (p. 10) can be analytically divided into five steps:
1. Tackle the problem at its source. Vehicles must be as clean, economical, safe, and quiet as possible.
2. Reduce and restrict mobility. Incidentally, this implies that only the growth in number of kilometers must be reduced in passenger and freight transport. The government intends to develop a balanced location policy for housing, employment and recreation. In addition, the price of mobility as such must be raised.
3. Improve alternatives to the automobile. The bicycle and collective transport should be emphasized.
4. Provide selective accessibility by road. The accessibility of the mainports has highest priority.
5. Strengthen the basis. This includes communications, administrative cooperation, financing, maintenance and research.

A number of policy aims are quantified in SVV2, Part D. We do not elaborate on these here. Rather, we now turn to the question of which policy instruments are implemented in order to operationalize the strategy that has been formulated. In this vein, we focus on Steps 2 and 3 of the strategy:
- to reduce mobility
- to change the modal split, from car to collective transportation.

In this Chapter, we pose a four-pronged objective:
- What infrastructure and transportation policy is being followed in the Randstad? This question is treated in Sections 8.2 through 8.4.
- What policy instruments are used to implement this policy? This issue is elaborated on in Section 8.5.
- How effective is this policy in light of the intention to change the modal split from automobile to collective transportation? This issue is discussed in Section 8.6.
- How effective is this policy in terms of the aim to control mobility? This is the focus of Section 8.7.

These considerations lead to the formulation of several conclusions and recommendations (Section 8.8). This Chapter emphasizes passenger transportation. Freight transport is treated extensively in Chapter 7, elsewhere in this volume. This limitation implies that the accessibility aim of the government policy receives less attention than the mobility issue and, accordingly, the goal of liveability.

The policy on infrastructure and transportation, related to the Randstad, consists of a number of components. In this Chapter, we limit our discussion to the most important of these. First we give attention (in Section 8.2) to the location policy that is being followed. Where will new residential and employment locations be sited in the near future (the Fourth Memorandum on Physical Planning Extra sets the planning horizon at the year 2015). Secondly, we treat the most important plans to improve the rail infrastructure (Section 8.3). The plan of the Dutch Railways, entitled 'Rail 21', and the projected incorporation of the Netherlands into the European network of high-speed trains. This link is particularly vital to the Randstad. Further, we highlight some strategic policy intentions regarding the road infrastructure (Section 8.4). This includes the plan to install five toll tunnels in the Randstad in order to relieve the bottlenecks in road traffic. It also includes the government's intention to discourage home-work commuting by car in the Randstad by installing numerous socalled toll stations. It is no exaggeration to state that the components mentioned here create the image of the current policy on infrastructure and transportation that the Dutch government is now applying to the Randstad. Yet another image-building component does not enter our analysis: the plans to develop Schiphol. This topic would go beyond the scope of the present discussion, and indeed it deserves a Chapter of its own. For an overview of the most important physical plans for the Randstad, we refer the interested reader to Bentvelsen (1990).

8.2   Location policy in the Randstad

The Fourth Memorandum on Physical Planning, of which the policy intention (Part A) appeared in March 1988, sketches the Randstad as an area facing opportunities and dangers. In Part D of the Fourth Memorandum (Minister van VROM en Minister President 1988b), the Randstad is placed in the field of tension between economic growth potential and liveability:

"At a European and a global scale, there are signs of increasing competition between cities. The Randstad has the opportunities to join the competition. The best points of departure for an internationally competitive metropolitan locational environment are the agglomerations of Amsterdam, Rotterdam and The Hague. The Randstad is not only an area of opportunity. Nowhere else in the Netherlands do so many people live and work, or is there so much unemployment, nor are so many people on the move. Nowhere else is there so much pressure on the liveability of the cities, the opportunities to move around, and the quality of the rural areas."

The Fourth Memorandum sketches a development perspective that is focused on the following issues:
- improvement of the internationally competitive metropolitan locational environment in the Randstad to serve the international business services sector, with a strong emphasis on Amsterdam, Rotterdam and The Hague, as well as on the cohesion between these cities;
- utilization of the development opportunities of the Green Heart in connection with the developing green structure of the Randstad, particularly in regard to agriculture,

nature, tourism and open-air recreation, in part to enhance the international location environment in the Randstad;
- guarantees for accessibility of the four big cities, both mainports of Schiphol and Rotterdam Harbor, and the other large concentrations of industry;
- continuation of a labor-market and housing policy for the weak socioeconomic groups in the big cities.

New construction sites in the Randstad will lie either within or contiguous to the cities; the Green Heart is to be protected. The growth-center policy still in effect will be tapered off. In the so-called letter of intent (Minister van VROM 1990a) and in the Fourth Memorandum Extra, known as VINEX (Minister van VROM 1990b, 1991a, 1991b), the political product of a new government coalition, the policy of the Fourth Memorandum is refined. Specifically, the care for the environment, the so-called social innovation, and the renewal of the administrative climate form points for attention. Locations for expansion are linked more closely to public transportation. At new locations for concentrations of employment, maximum norms are imposed for the number of parking spaces. As of 1995, maximum parking norms will be enforced at firms and services at B locations and (more strictly) at A locations (Minister van Verkeer en Waterstaat en Minister van VROM 1990). The policy concerning residential and employment locations seeks to reduce home-work distances, on the one hand, and on the other, to stimulate the use of public transport to bridge the home-work distances. Every major construction site is located at a high-quality public transport link.

In practice, the policy-makers had to rack their brains to operationalize the location policy. When can we say that a connection is of high quality? Is a tram line sufficient? How do multinationals, developers and investors react to a restriction on parking space? Are A locations, as defined by the government, indeed attractive places for private-sector establishments? Or does the business community prefer B and C locations?

Furthermore, there is a notable difference in policy direction as formulated in the White Paper on Housing in the 1990s (Staatssecretaris van VROM 1988, 1989) and in the Second Transport Structure Plan, Part D (Minister van Verkeer en Waterstaat en Minister van VROM 1990). In the Heerma Memorandum, subtitled 'from building to housing', the emphasis is on the task of managing the existing housing stock. The residential construction programs will have to be cut back structurally in the nineties. New construction will play a lesser role. But in VINEX, the accent lies on a "thorough location policy for housing, employment and recreation," partly in order to reduce mobility. Yet it is insufficiently recognized that the existing pattern of the built environment in the Netherlands, and certainly that in the Randstad, is a fact that can hardly be changed. Because of this emphasis in housing policy on unsubsidized residential construction, the central government is losing its grip on location policy. 'Intensification on the ring' was the motto of VINEX, illustrating that planners take the present pattern of settlements as the point of departure for the Randstad, and that they attempt to reinforce this pattern by selective new construction. The suggestion in VINEX and SVV2 that a 'balanced location policy' would open entirely new opportunities is not realistic in combination with the current housing policy. This conclusion notwithstanding, it is worthwhile to give the relation between infrastructure and location policy some serious thought.

8.3   The Randstad and plans to improve the rail infrastructure

Rail 21
The Fourth Memorandum Extra and the Second Structure Plan for Traffic and Transport (Minister van Verkeer en Waterstaat 1988, 1990) announced a considerable expansion of the rail infrastructure. This expansion is elaborated in the studies 'Rail 21' and 'Railcargo' published by the Dutch Railways. 'Railcargo' (NS 1990) sketches a perspective for freight transport by rail. Especially the Betuwe line is an ambitious project and is strategically important to the Dutch Railways and to Rotterdam Europoort.

'Rail 21' (NS 1988) is aimed at a new model for train timetables, which will be introduced around the year 2015. That timetable has a hierarchic structure with a far-reaching separation of functions, attuned to the differentiated demand of the clientele. In addition to the existing intercity and local trains, a Eurocity/Intercity (EC/IC) network will be set up, consisting of a limited number of routes that link the five national centers in the Randstad (Amsterdam, The Hague, Rotterdam, Utrecht and Schiphol) with the 15 regional centers outside the Randstad (Figure 8.1).

These routes extend outside the country to form part of the new Eurocity network. The maximum speed in the Netherlands is between 160 and 200 km per hour. The trains depart at one-hour intervals and the service connects to other EC/IC trains. The traveling time is reduced by about one-third. According to 'Rail 21' (NS 1988), the EC/IC network fulfills three functions:
- a very rapid link between the five national centers in the Randstad;
- a very rapid link of the Randstad centers with the regions of Groningen, Twente, Southeast Gelderland, the large cities of North Brabant, and South Limburg;
- a very rapid link between the Randstad centers and the major national centers in the neighboring countries within a radius of about 500 km, such as Hamburg, Hannover, the Ruhr area, Cologne, Brussels, Paris, and London.

In the Randstad, the Dutch Railways distinguishes a triangle formed by Amsterdam-Schiphol, The Hague-Rotterdam, and Utrecht at the corners. Physical planners usually call this the Randstad ring (Figure 8.2).

Two trains per hour connect Amsterdam/Schiphol with The Hague/Rotterdam. The same holds for the route Schiphol/Amsterdam-Utrecht, respectively The Hague/Rotterdam-Utrecht. Each of the urban centers of the Randstad is allocated four EC/IC train connections, which link them with virtually all major domestic centers and those in neighboring countries by very rapid hourly service.

'Rail 21' emphasizes rapid train connections for relatively great distances. Another task of collective transportation is to make the network denser in order to shorten the door-to-door travel time. This affects the way the train stations are linked to

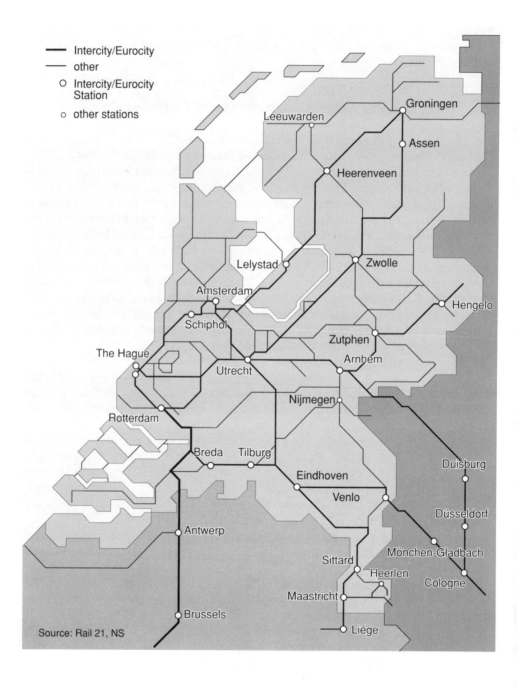

Figure 8.1   The planned Eurocity/Intercity network

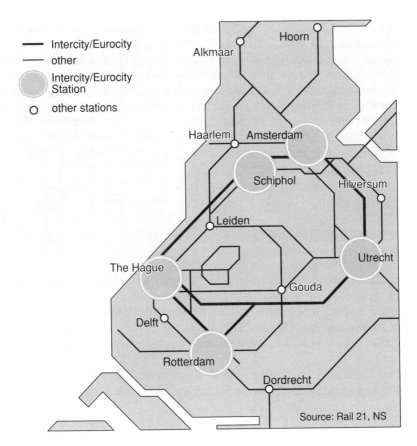

Figure 8.2   *The Randstad rail-triangle*

residential and employment locations by bus and tram lines. The solution is sought in establishing 'agglonets'. The SVV2 confidently allocates this task to the transport regions that are supposed to take care of the regional coordination of transport. At present, there is still little known about the strategies that are followed at the regional level. The memorandum 'Bestuur op niveau' (Administration at the right level) (1991) produced by the Ministry of Domestic Affairs provides a policy framework for identifying the numerous coordination problems that occur at the regional level but are not convincingly resolved.

High-speed rail link
An important component of the infrastructure policy for the Randstad is the connection of the Randstad to the European network of high-speed rail links (CEMT 1989;

Community of European Railways 1989). In 1981, France started a new high-speed line between Paris and Lyon. This route (TGV (train à grande vitesse) Sud-Est) was a commercial success. In West Germany, the Intercity Express (ICE) was developed as a high-speed line. Unlike the TGV, the ICE is also intended to transport freight.

The Netherlands, and the Randstad in particular, is especially interested in the TGV Nord, the route connecting Paris, Brussels, Amsterdam, Cologne, and London. In 1977, the Working Group Routing Study for the High-Speed line Amsterdam-Rotterdam-Belgian Border published a report (Minister van Verkeer en Waterstaat 1977). The conclusion was then already drawn that it was feasible to build a HSL (high-speed link), even though some radical measures were considered imperative to limit the negative effects on the environment.

In 1984, the Roundtable of European Industrialists published a report called 'Missing Links' advocating a comprehensive program of overland connections, by road and rail, between European countries (Roundtable of European Industrialists 1984). Three projects were assigned top priority: The Channel Tunnel, the connection between Scandinavia and Northern Germany, and the European network of high-speed trains. Since 1984, the Netherlands has been involved in international committees on the high-speed line. In 1987, the Minister of Transport and Public Works produced a provisional memorandum proposing the implementation of an activity for which an environmental impact assessment had to be prepared (Minister van Verkeer en Waterstaat en Minister van VROM 1987). It was then almost certain that a high-speed line would have to be developed. The discussion has focused ever since on determining the route and the stops. The coordination with the plans for Schiphol and the links to the Dutch Railway networks are also strategic issues.

The SVV2, Part D, established that the Netherlands will have a high-quality connection to the European high-speed network. To the east (ICE), it will follow the existing route (Amsterdam-Utrecht-Arnhem), which will be adapted to accommodate speeds up to 200 km per hour. The southern connection requires a new route, which has to accommodate speeds up to 300 km per hour. Stops are planned for Rotterdam, Schiphol, and Amsterdam (the municipality of The Hague feels bypassed).

The Hoge-Snelheidslijnnota (HSL Memorandum) was published in March 1991 (Minister van Verkeer en Waterstaat 1991a). In principle, the route for the line from Rotterdam to the Belgian border was drawn to the west of Roosendaal. The Minister intends to develop the Brabant portion of the HSL first, and the Randstad route will follow at a later date. Furthermore, the preference is expressed for a new connection between Rotterdam and Schiphol, with alternative routes to the east and west of Zoetermeer (see Figure 8.3). It has recently been acknowledged that the use of existing routes in the Randstad forms a viable alternative. In the course of 1992, a parliamentary decision on the route can be expected. In 1995 the actual construction of the HSL can be started. The high-speed line in the Randstad can be put into operation just before the turn of the century (1998/1999).

The official policy documents devote remarkably little attention to the aims of a high-speed railroad line. Obviously, the primary task is passenger transportation, and

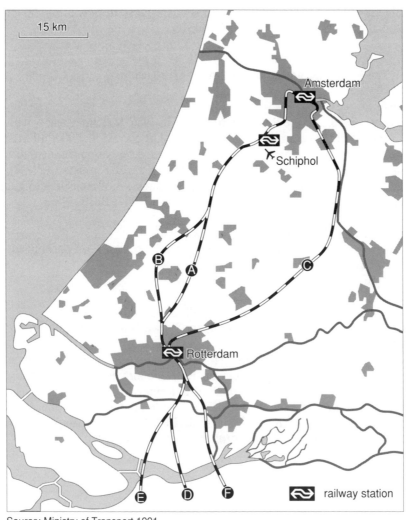

Source: Ministry of Transport 1991

Figure 8.3   High-speed link alternatives in the Randstad

freight is only of limited concern. The emphasis of the discussion was originally placed on the (small volume of) substitution of air travel by train trips. The possibility of substituting a large amount of automobile traffic by rail transport was recognized only later. The discussions then emphasized the environmental benefits of the HSL. But the fact that some want to route such an environmentally sound HSL right across the

Green Heart is not appreciated by the environmental lobby. It seems that the HSL may not be as 'environmentally friendly' as some suggest, in view of the benefits that Schiphol Airport stands to gain from the HSL.

8.4   The Randstad and plans for road infrastructure

Toll tunnels
Traffic jams have plagued the Randstad for years. In 1986, McKinsey and Co. estimated the social cost of traffic congestion in the Randstad at about Dfl. 700 million annually (McKinsey en Co. 1986). In 1987, the affected provinces, large municipalities, and departments formed a Project Group Mobility Scenario Randstad (PMR), which published a report in that same year proposing a package of measures to guarantee the accessibility of the Randstad (McKinsey en Co. 1987; PMR 1988):
- increase in the price of fuel
- toll charge on certain new tunnels
- expansion of paid-parking zones to areas with high pressure on parking space and good public transport
- optimization of public transport
- optimization of the highway network
- extra investment in road infrastructure (Dfl. 300 million annually)
- expansion of public transport in, around, and between the big agglomerations (Dfl. 100 million extra annually)
The report advances the idea of imposing tolls on certain new tunnels, since then known as toll tunnels. A supplementary report by the PMR elaborates further on the imposition of tolls and the private financing of the traffic tunnels.

In December 1987 the cabinet decided to implement the 'Bereikbaarheidsplan Randstad' [Accessibility Plan for the Randstad] (PBR 1988). This comprised numerous infrastructure projects, including five toll tunnels (Figure 8.4):
- De Noord Tunnel
- Wijk Tunnel
- Second Benelux Tunnel
- Second Coen Tunnel
- Blankenburg Tunnel
As it turned out, not everybody was happy with the intention to build these toll tunnels. The business community and the freight transport sector raised objections to the costs. The environmental movement is wary of the pull effects of increased capacity of the road infrastructure, and they advocate a greater emphasis on the expansion of the rail infrastructure.

SVV2, Part D (Minister van Verkeer en Waterstaat 1990, 1991b) provided this emphasis, but did not abolish the idea of toll tunnels. That document states:
"Taking into account the results of the mobility-steering policy (135 index points in 2010 and interim points of reference) and the formulated quality requirements regarding

Source: Visser and Bentvelsen (forthcoming)

Figure 8.4   Planned toll tunnels in the Randstad

congestion of 2% and 5%, for the time being this Part D retains the intention to improve the connections, including the necessary infrastructure such as tunnels. Further research will have to determine whether all of these are indeed necessary."

The tunnel under the River De Noord is currently under construction. The Wijk Tunnel can be started when the financing is available. The planning procedures concerning the Second Coen Tunnel are now in an advanced stage. The procedures for the Benelux Tunnel are still in an early stage. For the Blankenburg Tunnel, a procedure to determine the route still has to be carried out.

Toll stations
Of the bottlenecks belonging to the 'top-20 traffic line-ups' of 1990, 16 are situated in the Randstad. The traffic congestion in the Netherlands is thus largely concentrated in the Randstad. Not only is the capacity of the road network inadequate at certain times (morning and evening rush hours), but the air traffic above Schiphol and the rail infrastructure are running above capacity.

Kreutzberger & Vleugel (1992) reveal that the capacity of the material infrastructure is not only an issue of hardware but also (and sometimes primarily) determined by organization, management and policy, in a way similar to the application of information systems.

Through overuse of the material infrastructure, two vital issues clash in the Randstad: the accessibility of parts of the Randstad is undermined and the quality of the environment is damaged. The Second Transport Structure Plan is aimed at securing both the accessibility and the liveability. In the Fourth Memorandum Extra, as pointed out above, a similar area of tension is defined. On the one hand, the quality of the

Table 8.1   Top-20 traffic line-ups in 1990

		line-ups	km
1.	Brienenoord Bridge (Rotterdam)	326	1444
2.	Coen Tunnel (Zaandam)	263	1045
3.	Coen Tunnel (Amsterdam)	232	1007
4.	Velsen Tunnel (Haarlem)	217	940
5.	Velsen Tunnel (Velsen)	215	860
6.	Lek Bridge Vianen ('s-Hertogenbosch)	228	811
7.	Everd./Ouderijn (Utrecht)	114	568
8.	Lek Bridge Vianen ('s-Hertogenbosch) (other direction)	147	656
9.	A2 Zaltbommel (Maastricht)	135	543
10.	Brienenoord Bridge (Dordrecht)	125	526
11.	A10 RAI/A2 (Utrecht)	141	580
12.	A2 Bullewijk (Utrecht)	127	566
13.	Velperbroek (Arnhem)	93	452
14.	A15, De Noord (Gorinchem)	81	340
15.	A1 at Diemen (Amsterdam)	57	287
16.	A2 Holendrecht (Amsterdam)	60	288
17.	Benelux Tunnel (Hoogvliet)	95	335
18.	Gaasperdammerweg	69	295
19.	A2 Holendrecht (Amsterdam)	42	208
20.	Utrechtsebaan (The Hague)	66	321

Source: Dienst Verkeerskunde, Rijkswaterstaat

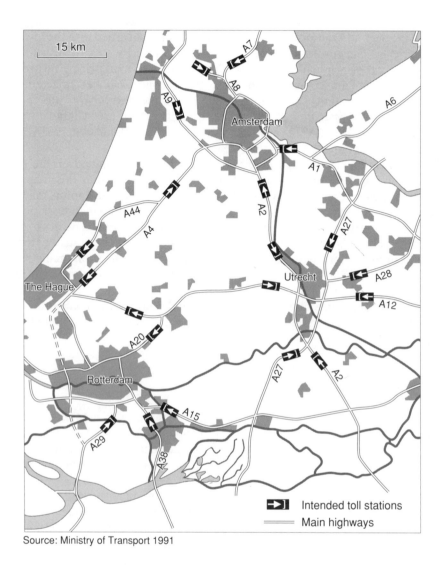

Source: Ministry of Transport 1991

Figure 8.5   Intended toll stations in the Randstad

daily living environment has to be protected, while on the other hand the Randstad
has to be able to compete internationally. As an environment for firms to establish
premises, the Randstad is only attractive if the accessibility by road, air, water, and
rail is guaranteed.

According to the Accessibility Plan for the Randstad, the congestion could be abated by relieving bottlenecks, while the idea of a system of road pricing gained ground. Part A of the Second Transport Structure Plan is largely concerned with the instrument of road pricing. The government was too hasty in choosing a specific instrument for the fundamental principle of user charge. Yet the idea of road pricing turned out to be abandoned in Part D, partially because the Second Chamber rejected it. The instrument of toll stations came in its place. Again, the government was too quick in adopting another specific instrument for the principle of user charge.

The revised Part D of SVV2 (Minister van Verkeer en Waterstaat 1991b) has the following to say about the toll station idea:

"The toll locations in the highway network should be determined on the basis of the enclosed map (see Figure 8.5). It should be pointed out that this map is only indicative and that adaptations in regard to the location of the fee points may ensue. The restrictive character of the number of toll locations on the map does not apply to possible toll locations that may be installed in the subsidiary road network to prevent traffic from taking other routes to circumvent the toll road [...]. The State is determined to exert its utmost effort to prevent, as much as possible, traffic from taking recourse to secondary roads in order to avoid paying the toll, and will do so by way of infrastructural measures and traffic regulations."

Regional coordination groups will be involved in this policy. In the meantime, it has become highly uncertain if there is actually a majority in the Second Chamber in favor of instituting toll stations.

8.5   Implemented policy instruments

A new location policy, a high-speed line, an extended railroad infrastructure, a handful of tunnels and a series of toll stations do not just appear by themselves. Concrete policy instruments are needed to give the policy on infrastructure and transportation in the Randstad a concrete form. In the following we offer a brief overview of these instruments.

First, there are traditional instruments of physical planning: the socalled destination plan at municipal level, the structural plan at municipal or intermunicipal level, the regional plan at regional level (to be initiated by the province), and the allocation authority of the Minister of Housing, Physical Planning and the Environment - which, incidentally, is only invoked in unusual situations. These instruments have a primarily coordinating function and are mostly very time-consuming in practice.

Secondly, there is the aspect of the financing of the infrastructure works. The revised Part D (p. 7) gives an overview of the financial resources that are involved in the implementation of the SVV2 (see Table 8.2). Huge amounts of money are required, which is incompatible with the central government's intention to reduce its substantial budgetary deficit. It was arranged to put an Infrastructure Fund into operation as of January 1992, to pay for infrastructure expenditure. The aim of the Infrastructure Fund is to create more flexibility in time and allocation per traffic sector. In addition, extensive

Table 8.2 Financial resources involved in the implementation of SVV2 (in 1991 prices)

	Total required for SVV, billions of guilders	Total available until 2010, billions of guilders	1991-1995, annual average, millions of guilders	1996-2000, annual average, millions of guilders	2001-2010, annual average, millions of guilders	> 2010 required, billions of guilders
Collective transportation						
- Dutch Railways (1)	17.5	14.1	540	760	760	3.4
- city/region	6.9	6.3	300	310	330	0.6
- management	74.8	74.8	3450	3545	3980	-
- high-speed link (2)	2.8	2.7	50	270	115	0.1
Highways						
- maintenance (3)	17.3	17.3	695	780	995	-
- utilization	2.1	2.1	105	105	105	-
- construction	17.7	13.5	690	620	690	4.2
- tunnels (4)	2.1	-	-	-	-	-
Waterways						
- construction	4.2	3.5	215	190	150	0.7
- maintenance	6.7	6.7	345	315	340	-
Railroads, freight						
- Betuwe line (5)	2.4	2.3	30	235	100	0.1
- other infrastructure	1.5	1.3	65	65	65	0.2
- management (6)	1.3	1.3	35	65	80	-
Traffic safety	3.0	2.6	140	130	130	0.4
City traffic	2.2	1.4	105	60	55	0.8
Promotion/Research (7)	6.4	6.1	300	300	315	0.3
Total	168.9	156.0	7065	7750	8210	10.8

(1) These amounts include the payments of interest and principal on the prefinancing by the Dutch Railways (as of 1994, 60 million per year; total is 1,020 million).

(2) This includes government funding (à fonds perdu) and the payments of interest and principal (1,457 million) on the 50% of the financing from other sources.

(3) In addition, funds amounting to 2.4 billion are reserved for the current restructuring operation.

(4) The tunnels are financed privately.

(5) This includes government funding and the payments of interest and principal (1,304 million) on the 50% private financing.

(6) The budget for management of rail (freight) does not include the structural contribution of the Dutch Railways in the order of 7 million per year.

(7) The definition of stimulation has been changed from that given in SVV Part D. Now stimulation includes business transport and several items that were previously subsumed under management of public transportation.

use will be made of the financing capacity of institutional investors. To that end public-private partnerships will be set up.

Like in other West European countries (CEMT 1990), the public investment in traffic infrastructure has declined in the Netherlands since the mid-1970s. Recently there has been a shift away from investment in roads to investment in rail infrastructure. Between Part A and Part D of the SVV2, the priority of investment in collective transportation has increased sharply. The investment in collective means of transport rose from about Dfl. 12 billion in Part A to more than Dfl. 20 billion in Part D. The budget for the construction and extension of roads was lowered considerably in the same period.

A third instrument is the 'Meerjarenplan Infrastructuur en Transport' (Multiyear Plan Infrastructure and Transportation), which is annually adjusted and is used to monitor progress. The arguments expressed in VINEX and SVV2 led to a text of a so-called key planning decision (PKB). The PKB text of the SVV2 concerns the period up to 2010. The Long-term Plan for Infrastructure and Transport (MIT) 1990-94 reveals that in the Randstad more is invested in infrastructure for rail transport than in roads. Investment in roads is still greater than in rail infrastructure in the rest of the Netherlands (Kreutzberger 1990).

A fourth category of instruments relates to the price attached to the use of transportation. On the one hand, there are high subsidies on collective transportation, which stimulate the use of these collective means of transport. On the other hand, the variable costs of auto mobility are raised by road tax, fuel tax, and tolls. Parking fees also contribute to this increase. Furthermore, the rush-hour permit sticker and road pricing were under discussion, but both have been rejected by parliament for the time being.

Finally, the fifth category is organizational instruments. These include realizing the concept of transport regions, integrated public transport systems, the corridor approach, and fostering an adequate implementation management.

8.6   Changing the modal split and the effectiveness of policy instruments

The policy on infrastructure and transportation seeks to bring about a considerable change in choice of mode of transport.

The fact that change of the modal split is a policy aim is a relatively recent phenomenon. Over the past decades, billions of guilders have been invested in highways and interchanges to serve the automobile, while the railroad infrastructure lost ground. Numerous unprofitable railroad lines were abandoned, many stations were closed. This was hardly compensated by the slight investment in new rail infrastructure (the railroad through the Flevo Polder, the Zoetermeer line, the Schiphol Airport connection, the light rail system in Utrecht).

The rail network has insufficiently followed the development of the spatial environment of the Netherlands in the course of time. The network thus does not correspond well to the current transport relations.

The Accessibility Plan for the Randstad (see McKinsey en Co. 1987; Projectgroep Mobiliteitsprogramma Randstad 1987; Projectgroep Bereikbaarheidsplan Randstad 1988) was still based on the customary modal split. And in fact, the plan for the five new toll tunnels presaged more of the same. In the Mobiliteitsscenario Randstad, abatement of traffic line-ups is a priority. The Project Group Mobility Program Randstad has a preferred set of measures, and this includes a reduction of auto mobility by increasing the share of public transport in home-work travel and by placing greater emphasis on the compact city as a planning principle.

Part A of the Second Transport Structure Plan (Ministerie van Verkeer en Waterstaat 1988) shows signs of a transition in the way of thinking, though it still follows incompatible assumptions. This memorandum pays a great deal of lip service to environmental concerns, but does not question the freedom of choice of the automobile user, and the planned investments in road infrastructure still exceed those in railroad infrastructure. The shift is manifest, in political terms, in Part D of the Second Transport Structure Plan (Minister van Verkeer en Waterstaat en Minister van VROM 1990), reinforced by the NMP+ (Ministerie van VROM et al. 1990) and the Fourth Memorandum Extra (Ministerie van VROM 1990b).

'Rail 21' (NS 1988) and 'Railcargo' (NS 1990) form the main lines of the investment policy for rail infrastructure. This might be considered the design for the pull factors of the policy, directed towards changing the modal split. Yet it will be many years before the rail infrastructure is expanded. In the meantime, the government is also attempting to mobilize push factors. This is demonstrated by the increase in fuel tax effective as of 1 July 1991, by the tentative plans for road pricing, and the still projected toll stations. This package of measures is popularly known as 'auto baiting'. As long as the alternative of a competitive public transport system is not forthcoming, the effectiveness of the push measures have to be seriously doubted.

In regard to the change in the modal split between air and train travel, the high-speed rail link is of some importance.

Decision-making in regard to the development of Schiphol has given far more credit to accessibility criteria than to liveability criteria. The attractive perspective of Schiphol as one of the few mainports in Western Europe has led to spectacular investment programs for the airport. Arguments for a high-speed line, which would link Schiphol with Brussels and the French TGV, are based on the assumption that this entails an environmentally sound substitute for relatively short air connections. A stop on the HSL route, in combination with the mainport or megaport function of Schiphol (Blaas et al. 1991) does not only mean that passengers board there (e.g., for Paris) to bridge the distance by train rather than by plane; it also means that passengers disembark there to transfer to their flight to New York, for instance, leaving from Schiphol and not from Brussels or Cologne. It is expected that the incorporation of Schiphol into the high-speed line will strengthen the position of this airport as a mainport. It remains to be seen whether the rapid rail connection serving Schiphol will eventually lead to fewer or to more kilometers flown.

The impact of the location policy for the change in the modal split will be limited because the main pattern of the built-up area in the Randstad is largely fixed. The location policy should be considered as primarily symbolic (Droogh & Cortie 1991). Even inadvertent effects are conceivable. If a stringent location policy were actually implemented in the Randstad, firms and residents would be more likely to move to more peripheral areas outside the Randstad, which would then encourage automobile use rather than discourage it.

Furthermore, it seems that little concrete attention is given to refining the web of links in the public transport system at the regional level, which might reduce the door-to-door travel time. It is disappointing that relatively little attention is given to subway systems within the metropolitan agglomeration and at the level of the Randstad. And finally, it should be noted that passenger transport is central to most discussions, whereas freight transport has a low profile. There are hardly any initiatives to develop the traffic on the inland waterways as a serious substitute for trucking.

8.7   Restrictions on mobility and the effectiveness of the policy instruments

Previously, traffic and transportation policy were designed to foster mobility. Mobility was considered as a sign of affluence, a symbol of a civilized and dynamic way of life, a merit good. The more kilometers one traveled each day, the better. The annual kilometer record was taken as a mobility indicator. In 1990 the Dutch population ran up a total of 169 billion kilometers; ten years before, the figure was 143 billion km. Thus, in ten years the mobility increased by 18%. In 1990 mobility rose by nearly 2%. Yet that percentage is not spectacular compared to the growth rate of GNP. Gradually, people are also starting to question the point of and the need for this growth in mobility.

Table 8.3   Distance travelled per person per day, in kilometers, 1989

Motive	
Commute to/from work	8.3
Business trip	3.5
Social trip	7.6
Shopping	4.1
Schooling	1.9
Recreation/sport	3.8
Tourism/walking	2.3
Other	3.8
Total	35.4

Source: CBS 1990, in: Kruythoff 1991

Table 8.4   *Index figures for auto mobility 1986-2010*

1986	1990	1995	2000	2010
100	115	124	130	135

Source: Ministerie van Verkeer en Waterstaat en Minister van VROM 1990

Table 8.5   *Home-work distance for dual-income and single-income households in the Randstad, percentages*

| | | dual income | | single income |
	head	partner	longest commute	
0-9 km	43.6	66.0	36.1	42.5
10-19 km	19.6	16.4	21.4	19.3
20-29 km	11.7	7.1	13.1	11.6
30-39 km	5.8	3.3	6.7	5.7
40 or more km	7.5	3.4	8.6	7.4
Varying	11.8	3.8	14.1	13.6

Source: WBO 1985/1986, data processed by Directorate General of Housing

In the period 1985-1989 the total distance traveled per person per day increased from 32.6 to 35.4 km. The growth is primarily connected with the increasing commuting distance (from 6.9 to 8.3 km). Most of the mobility is not business-related but for leisure. The commuter traffic accounts for only a quarter of the kilometers traveled, but it causes the lion's share of line-ups.

Part D of SVV2 explicitly discusses a policy aimed at reduction of mobility. But upon closer reading, this policy only refers to the reduction in growth of mobility. Table 8.4 presents the index figures for auto mobility (weekday averages) that are utilized in SVV2 Part D.

Kruythoff (1991) investigated the commuting distance for households with a single income and for the head of a dual-income household (Table 8.5). These commutes are considerable. The distances have probably increased in the course of time. Dual-income households top single-income households in this respect. The commuter with the longest trip in dual-income families covers greater distances than the breadwinner in single-income households. And then the distances covered by the partner with the shorter commute have to be added to the total for the dual-income household. Since the share of dual-income households will rise in the coming years, this factor alone gives us grounds to anticipate a further increase in home-work commuting distance.

Furthermore, Kruythoff investigated the degree to which the home-work distance

Table 8.6   *Working households in the Randstad according to type of residential environment and home-work distance for the partner with the longest commute, in percentages*

	Metropolitan areas	Urbanized areas	Moderately urbanized areas	Weakly urbanized areas	Growth centers	Randstad
0-10 km	52.6	52.2	47.1	36.4	24.4	42.5
10-19 km	22.6	15.5	17.8	19.1	24.0	19.2
20-29 km	8.0	12.0	10.5	12.1	18.3	11.6
30-39 km	2.9	2.6	4.9	7.4	7.1	5.7
40 or more km	3.5	6.3	6.5	8.8	13.4	7.4
Varying	10.4	11.5	13.2	16.1	12.7	13.6

Source: WBO 1985/1986, data processed by Directorate General of Housing

is related to the type of residential environment where the households live.

The shortest travel distances are found, as expected, in the metropolitan and urbanized areas. The longest travel distances are not only covered in the most weakly urbanized areas, but they are also, and primarily, found in the growth centers. We can then observe that the government policy enforced in the 1970s and 1980s was unable to steer the development of mobility. In fact, the policy only fostered mobility, in as far as commuting is concerned. Part of the traffic line-ups are due to the implemented policy, although Table 8.6 does not give a definitive answer to the question of which commuting mode was used: car, train, bus, or bicycle.

To what extent are policy instruments now being implemented by the central government to control mobility? First of all, this could involve raising the price of both individual and collective transportation.

In setting public transport fares, the aim is to cover more of the costs. The price differential between using public transport and the private car has been improved, as much as possible, in the favor of public facilities (SVV2, revised Part D, p. 5).

The hike in fuel tax could be considered a mobility-reducing instrument. But the justification for this tax is primarily its potential contribution to the change in the modal split. Public transport receives substantial subsidies; rather than restricting mobility, this promotes it. The 'free' public transportation year passes for students constitutes an extremely clear example of an instrument that fosters mobility.

Currently, there is no policy to reduce kilometers on public transportation, either for rail or air travel. Efforts are being made to cut back auto mobility, however, essentially seeking to change the modal split, though perhaps to help control overall mobility as well. The policies under consideration are for the most part financial instruments, such as rush-hour permit stickers, road pricing, toll tunnels and/or toll stations.

Rush-hour permits are intended to cut down the traffic peak by imposing a tax on driving in the rush hour. There is no difference in price for a driver who is in rush-hour traffic only incidentally and the regular rush-hour driver. Someone who might get into rush-hour traffic a few times a year will thus probably obtain a permit sticker. But obviously, enforcement of control for permit stickers during rush-hour is no easy task. The combination of the low efficiency and the difficult (expensive) enforcement made the rush-hour permit an unattractive instrument. Thus, there should be no regrets about the fact that this option no longer appears on the political agenda.

Road pricing is in principle a sophisticated instrument. The fee can be differentiated according to time and place. And a net of checkpoints can be set up in such a way that the drivers cannot escape notice by taking an alternative route. Part A of SVV2 originally advocated road pricing as the primary central instrument to regulate the use of the automobile. The idea was to reach three goals in one stroke:
- facilitate private financing for infrastructure projects
- take the top off the traffic peak
- limit auto mobility

Nevertheless, the instrument was rejected by the Second Chamber of Parliament. There are indeed some major drawbacks to road pricing as a general instrument:

a. If road pricing would only be imposed in the Randstad, it would create a negative location factor for that part of the country and would increase the trend to disperse industry and housing. Incidentally, the social costs of the Randstad are also the highest in the country, which could conceivably justify higher variable costs for automobile use.

b. The Dutch parliament has had to acknowledge that it is not yet possible to produce a passport invincible to fraud. And road pricing has hardly been put into practice anywhere. The policy-makers are wary of start-up problems, as well as of an unknown repertory of tricks people will invent to escape paying. These might include vandalizing the checkpoints, adapting the car to circumvent the system, etc. An important consideration in rejecting road pricing as the key solution is the protection of privacy. A comprehensive system of road pricing makes it possible in principle for the authorities to check the routes of every motorized citizen. This could assist the police in finding delinquents, but in general this is a worrisome venture. Finally, there is little known for certain about the cost of implementing the system. The income for the recipient (which could be the government, but might also be a private firm) has to be weighed against the yet unknown but probably high expense of installing the system (appliance in every car, installation of checkpoints), the repair of malfunctions, and the security, maintenance, enforcement, and administration of the system. The system is most likely highly vulnerable and, if the social support would prove inadequate, could turn out to be very expensive. Finally, investors do not like the fact that road pricing is so highly dependent on government intervention. Thus, they cannot determine beforehand how much profit they stand to gain from investments in infrastructure. It seems difficult, if not impossible, to foresee all the situations that could occur, and therefore no firm contract can be made between the government and a private investor. It is obvious that road pricing will not be privatized but will be implemented by the government, which itself determines the risks to a large degree. But such pressure on the central government budget (and here too, outlays have to precede income) is not welcome at a time when the government is trying to reduce the budget deficit.

Toll tunnels are proposed in order to allow private financing of new infrastructure projects. This involves a highly selective fee, which will have little or no effect on the volume of automobile traffic. A well-known problem is that of drivers taking alternative routes, whereby the traffic line-ups are just moved and the income for the financing institution does not meet expectations. For strategically located tunnels, this problem of alternative routes can sometimes be reasonably controlled. The amount of the toll can take the alternative route into account. If the toll is so high that it is worth taking a detour, the instrument is not effective. Incidental tunnel tolls form an acceptable instrument, but it is an insignificant instrument for restricting the use of cars. A more effective way to reach that goal would be to not build the tunnel. The remaining alternative is that of toll stations, which is (still?) current policy. The Key Planning Decision of VINEX stipulates reserving space around the Randstad for a toll system. As of 1995, this system will have to cover a large part of the traffic and transport expenditure.

Toll stations entail the same advantages and drawbacks as road pricing.
a. First of all, toll stations in the Randstad would also constitute an instrument to foster dispersal. It becomes attractive for firms and residents to locate outside of the Randstad.
b. The planning procedures that have to be carried out in order to install toll stations are of long duration and are readily underestimated.
c. Toll stations contribute to a further fragmentation of the landscape and can generate traffic line-ups. This is contrary to the goals of the environmental policy.
d. The cost of implementation of toll collection by installing toll stations is probably substantial.
e. Since fixed fees are intended, regardless of the time of day, toll stations do not help limit the peak in rush-hour traffic.
f. Toll stations are also conducive to the development of alternative routes, even though the Ministry of Transport and Public Works is watching.

If the government would discard the toll station as a policy instrument, a replacement would have to be found as a source of income. In this regard, a further increase in fuel tax could be considered; this would have to be instituted at a European level, in order to prevent unfavorable effects in border areas.

A fundamental reconsideration of the user charge for traffic infrastructure is very important. It is unwise for the government to keep jumping to conclusions. In the (often justified) criticism of specific proposals advanced by the government, the critics should be wary of throwing out the baby with the bath water.

8.8   Conclusions and recommendations

For the Randstad, a coherent policy on infrastructure and transport is considered to be imperative.
The following components of such a policy are important:
- policy concerning residential and employment locations in the Randstad
- the plan 'Rail 21' of the Dutch Railways
- the connection of the Randstad with the European network of high-speed train routes
- the construction of five toll tunnels in the Randstad
- the construction of a large number of toll stations in and around the Randstad

The components of policy mentioned here were supported by policy instruments in the area of physical planning, financing (Infrastructure Fund and public-private partnerships with investors), the Long-term Plan for Infrastructure and Transport, organizational instruments, public transport subsidies, and numerous fees (road tax, fuel tax, tolls, parking fees). A segmented approach to individual mainports and cities must be avoided. What is needed is a comprehensive policy, aimed at creating sophisticated infrastructure rather than the conventional infrastructure that dominates the scene at present.

Mobility restriction
The effort to restrict mobility seems to be essential a token policy. The mobility is still growing and there is no consistent implementation of policy to curb it. It is clear that freight transport is assigned an important economic function. For economic reasons, a high priority is given to excellent accessibility of mainport Schiphol and Rotterdam Harbor. The restriction of mobility in the area of freight transport is difficult, if not impossible. The goal of restricting mobility will thus have to be pursued in relation to passenger transportation. Subsidies for public transport and free public transport year passes also stimulate mobility. Moreover, no restrictions are placed on car ownership.
    What remains is the goal to change the modal split. On this point, it is salient that no consistent policy has been formulated to substitute air kilometers by train kilometers. The high-speed train does compete with short-distance flights, but at the same time it constitutes an ideal feeder for Schiphol, which only reinforces the function of Schiphol as an intercontinental airport. Nor do we observe much effort to replace truck transport by inland waterway shipping.
    The intended change in preferred mode of transport proves to be focused primarily (or perhaps exclusively) on the substitution of automobile traffic by collective transport. In this decision-making arena, we can distinguish a number of push and pull factors.

Pull factors
First, an attractive alternative for the car has to be provided. This requires new rail infrastructure and more locomotives and rolling stock; it also entails increasing the

quality of public transport and improving the service orientation. More attention should be given to the high-density local routes of regional public transport (tram, bus), to shorten door-to-door travel time. At present the focus is too one-sided, emphasizing the fast TGV and EC/IC trains. More creative thought will have to be put into designing underground transport: subway routes within the metropolitan agglomerations and at the level of the Randstad as a whole.

If the intention is to build an extensive public transport network that will remain manageable in the future, then the subsidies on public transportation will have to be tapered off. Subsidy reduction is also advisable from the point of view of mobility control. This step can be taken on the condition (which was also noted in the revised Part D of SVV2) that the price of public transport will rise more slowly than the cost of using a car.

Push factors

The use of the automobile can be reduced through a combination of measures: increasing fuel tax, imposing a high road tax, charging parking fees, and not expanding the road infrastructure. Car ownership can be restricted by instituting parking fees in residential areas and by raising the thresholds for environmental regulations. These measures would lead to higher car prices and higher taxes on car ownership, particularly on cars that do not meet environmental requirements (Priemus 1991). The principle that the polluter pays should also apply to drivers. The theoretical legitimation for imposing such charges is found in the statistical correlation between automobile ownership and automobile use, as well as in the likelihood of extremely high negative externalities of the use of cars (OECD 1989). The social costs of road transport in developed countries fall in the range of 2.5-3.0% of GDP, or even higher (Himanen et al. 1989).

The negative externalities of auto use apply not only to emissions, noise, and landscape degradation, but also to traffic safety, or rather the lack of it. In the Netherlands, traffic accidents take an annual toll of about 1,500 lives, and about 50,000 people are injured (Minister van Verkeer en Waterstaat en Minister van VROM 1990).

The construction of toll tunnels does not fit in with the effort to restrict mobility, nor with the goal of changing the modal split. Toll tunnels can help thin-out traffic jams and reduce waiting time. These social benefits may be only temporary, because of the attraction exerted by new infrastructural capacity. If the travel time by car is reduced by the construction of tunnels, this provides a disincentive to change over to public transport. Every guilder spent by the government or an investor on the construction of a toll tunnel cannot be spent on improving public transportation. Also this point entails a conflict with the previously formulated policy goals.

The installation of toll stations fragments the landscape and creates traffic line-ups. This is in conflict with the aims of environmental policy. Toll stations can inadvertently lead to a dispersal of firms and population to locations outside the Randstad. In short, toll stations do not correspond well with the intended policy goals either.

The most effective strategy is probably a combination of extending the rail infrastructure for collective transport, supplemented by metropolitan subway systems for high-density collective transportation, a gradual reduction of subsidies on public transport, a virtual moratorium on new road infrastructure for cars, an increase in the cost of car ownership (high environmental norms, leading to price increases for cars, and parking fees in the direct vicinity of the home), and a tax on use of the automobile, with a European scope, specifically in the form of higher taxes on fuel. A great deal depends on the success of this policy mix - for instance, the future of the Randstad.

Acknowledgement:
The authors wish to thank Ir. E. Kreutzberger and Ir. J.C.S.N. Visser for their comments on a previous draft of this Chapter.

References

Bentvelsen, T. (1990), Naar een inrichtingsplan voor de Randstad? Een inventarisatie van actuele voorstellen. Delft: OTB.
Blaas, E.W., P. Nijkamp & J.M. Vleugel (1991), Randstad megaport, een studie rond het thema: economisch overwegen. Amsterdam: Vrije Universiteit.
Cemt (1986), International Traffic and Infrastructural Needs. Paris: OECD.
Cemt (1989), Rail Network Co-operation in the Age of Information Technology and High Speed. Paris: OECD.
Community of European Railways (1989), Proposals for a European High-speed Network.
Droogh, D.J.A. & C. Cortie (1991), Meer verkeer hoort erbij; wonen en werken in een polycentrisch stadsgewest. Stedebouw en Volkshuisvesting 72, pp. 16-21.
Himanen, V., K. Makela, K. Alppivuori, P. Aaltonen & J. Loukelainen (1989), The Monetary Valuation of Road Traffic's Environmental Hazards. Research Report 943. Espoo: Technical Research Centre of Finland.
McKinsey & Company (1986), Afrekenen met files. 's Gravenhage: McKinsey & Company.
McKinsey & Company (1987), Vrij baan in de Randstad. Samenvattende eindrapportage in opdracht van de Projectgroep.
Mobiliteitsscenario Randstad van het Ministerie van Verkeer en Waterstaat. 's-Gravenhage: McKinsey & Company.
Kreutzberger, E. (1990), Vernieuwing van de infrastructuur in de Randstad. In: W.J. Stam (ed), De internationale concurrentiepositie van de Randstad. Technisch-Bestuurskundige Verkenningen. pp. 99-122. Delft: Delftse Universitaire Pers.
Kreutzberger, E. & J.M. Vleugel (1992), Capaciteit en benutting van infrastructuur. Capaciteitsbegrippen en infrastructuurgebruik in de binnenvaart en het lucht-, rail-

en wegvervoer. Delft: Delftse Universitaire Pers.

Kruythoff, H.M. (1991), Tweeverdieners vergeleken. Woonmilieudifferentiatie van tweeverdieners, eenverdieners en geenverdieners in de Randstad. Werkstukken Stedelijke Netwerken Werkstukken 30. Utrecht: Stedelijke Netwerken.

Ministerie van Verkeer en Waterstaat (1977), Amrobel, globale verkenning van tracé's voor een Hoge Snelheidslijn Amsterdam - Rotterdam - Belgische grens. 's Gravenhage: SDU-Uitgeverij.

Ministerie van Verkeer en Waterstaat & Ministerie van Volkshuisvesting, Ruimtelijke Ordening en Milieubeheer (1987), Startnotitie voor de Milieu-effectrapportage betreffende het Nederlandse deel van de Hoge Snelheidsspoorlijn Parijs-Brussel-Keulen/Amsterdam. 's Gravenhage: SDU-Uitgeverij.

Ministerie van Verkeer en Waterstaat (1988), Tweede Structuurschema Verkeer en Vervoer. Deel a: Beleidsvoornemens. 's Gravenhage: SDU-Uitgeverij.

Ministerie van Verkeer en Waterstaat & Ministerie van Volkshuisvesting, Ruimtelijke Ordening en Milieubeheer (1990), Tweede Structuurschema Verkeer en Vervoer. Deel d: Regeringsbeslissing. 's Gravenhage: SDU-Uitgeverij.

Ministerie van Verkeer en Waterstaat (1991a), Nederlands deel hogesnelheids-spoorverbinding Amsterdam-Brussel-Parijs, ontwerp PKB/tracénota/milieu-effectrapportage. 's Gravenhage: SDU-Uitgeverij.

Ministerie van Verkeer en Waterstaat & Ministerie van Volkshuisvesting, Ruimtelijke Ordening en Milieubeheer (1991b), Tweede Structuurschema Verkeer en Vervoer. Aangepast deel d. 's Gravenhage: SDU-Uitgeverij.

Ministerie van Volkshuisvesting, Ruimtelijke Ordening en Milieubeheer (1988a), Vierde Nota over de Ruimtelijke Ordening, deel a: Beleidsvoornemens. 's Gravenhage: SDU-Uitgeverij.

Ministerie van Volkshuisvesting, Ruimtelijke Ordening en Milieubeheer (1988b), Vierde nota over de Ruimtelijke Ordening. Deel d: Regeringsbeslissing. 's Gravenhage: SDU-Uitgeverij.

Ministerie van Volkshuisvesting, Ruimtelijke Ordening en Milieubeheer (1990a), Vierde Nota over de Ruimtelijke Ordening, Brief van de Minister van VROM. Stellingname. 's Gravenhage: SDU-Uitgeverij.

Ministerie van Volkshuisvesting, Ruimtelijke Ordening en Milieubeheer (1990b), Vierde Nota over de Ruimtelijke Ordening Extra, deel I. 's Gravenhage: SDU-Uitgeverij.

Minister van Volkshuisvesting, Ruimtelijke Ordening en Milieubeheer (1991a), Vierde Nota over de Ruimtelijke Ordening Extra deel II. 's Gravenhage: SDU-Uitgeverij.

Ministerie van Volkshuisvesting, Ruimtelijke Ordening en Milieubeheer (1991b), Vierde Nota over de Ruimtelijke Ordening Extra deel III. 's Gravenhage: SDU-Uitgeverij.

Ministerie van Volkshuisvesting, Ruimtelijke Ordening en Milieubeheer, Ministerie van Economische Zaken, Ministerie van Landbouw, Natuurbeheer en Visserij & Ministerie van Verkeer en Waterstaat (1989), Nationaal Milieubeleidsplan Kiezen of Verliezen. 's Gravenhage: SDU-Uitgeverij.

Ministerie van Volkshuisvesting, Ruimtelijke Ordening en Milieubeheer, Ministerie van Economische Zaken, Ministerie van Landbouw, Natuurbeheer en Visserij &

Ministerie van Verkeer en Waterstaat (1990), Nationaal Milieubeleidsplan-plus. 's-Gravenhage: SDU-Uitgeverij.
Nederlandse Spoorwegen (1988), Rail 21, Sporen naar een nieuwe eeuw. Utrecht: NS.
Nederlandse Spoorwegen (1990), Rail 21, Cargo. Toekomstplan voor het goederenbedrijf, Utrecht: NS.
OECD (1989), The Social Costs of Land Transport. Environment Directorate. Paris: OECD.
Priemus, H. (1991), Niet alleen autogebruik belasten maar ook autobezit. Staatscourant 5 juni.
Projektgroep Bereikbaarheidsplan Randstad (1988), Werkprogramma infrastructuur-investeringen Bereikbaarheidsplan Randstad. 's Gravenhage.
Projektgroep Mobiliteitsscenario Randstad (1988), Mobiliteitsscenario Randstad. 's-Gravenhage.
Roundtable of European Industrialists (1984), Missing Links, Upgrading Europe's Transborder Ground Transport Infrastructure. Brussel.
Staatssecretaris van Volkshuisvesting, Ruimtelijke Ordening en Milieubeheer (1988), Ontwerp-Nota Volkshuisvesting in de jaren negentig; van bouwen naar wonen. 's-Gravenhage: SDU-Uitgeverij.
Staatssecretaris van Volkshuisvesting, Ruimtelijke Ordening en Milieubeheer (1989), Nota Volkshuisvesting in de jaren negentig; van bouwen naar wonen. 's Gravenhage: SDU-Uitgeverij.
Visser, J.G.S.N. & T.G.M. Bentvelsen (1992), Toltunnels in de Randstad (forthcoming). Delft: Delftse Universitaire Pers.

Prof.dr.ir. H. Priemus
Research Institute for Policy Sciences and Technology
Delft University of Technology
P.O. Box 5030
2600 GA Delft
The Netherlands

Prof.dr. P. Nijkamp
Faculty of Economics
Free University of Amsterdam
P.O. Box 7161
1007 MC Amsterdam
The Netherlands

9. THE PROVISION AND USE OF PUBLIC SERVICES AND FACILITIES IN THE RANDSTAD

G. Molenaar & J. Floor

9.1 Introduction

In the Dutch welfare state, many services and facilities are provided in the public realm. These include health care and social services, education, culture, sports, and recreation. The provision of such services and their facilities is either the direct responsibility of government agencies or else it is influenced by subsidies or regulation. Also the use of these amenities is subject to government intervention. There are several grounds for such involvement. First, many public services differ from purely collective goods, of which the provision is uniform everywhere and no one is denied access or can refuse to use them. On the contrary, the quantity and the quality of other services and facilities commonly differ among regions. These differences have an administrative component; local authorities are often responsible for the provision of these services. In addition, there are some typically geographical influences. Many public services and facilities are localized. This implies an impact of distance decay and externalities, which can diminish the collective character of public services (Pinch 1985). The motivation for public intervention is sometimes the desire to correct such situations.

Secondly, the need for public intervention is based on market imperfections. Obviously, many facilities and services can be provided by the private sector. But undesired situations can emerge from the point of view of the distribution standards set by the public sector, both categorically and geographically. The aims of equity, equality, and efficiency then form the grounds for intervention (Lineberry 1977; Curtis 1989).

Thirdly, the intervention in market processes is argued on the grounds of 'merit' (Hartog 1980). The authorities assign a higher utility to the supply and use of certain services and facilities than individuals do. Objectives such as fostering the cultural heritage, public health, and general human development require the implementation of policies with respect to museums, the performing arts, libraries, and sports. The authorities can target subsidies to influence the market, whereby they can assure that such facilities become sufficiently available, accessible, and used.

During the 1980s, privatization increasingly became the policy model for the supply and use of public facilities and services. The need for budget cuts, along with the desire to reduce government involvement in general, are the main motives for this change (SCP 1988). At the same time, there has been a definite shift from 'equity' to 'efficiency'

F. M. Dieleman and S. Musterd (eds.), The Randstad: A Research and Policy Laboratory, 193–218.

goals. Critics speak of the demolition of the welfare state. The more neutral terms used for this shift are 'reconsideration' and 'privatization'. In addition, the government tries to maintain some distance in its commitment. Thus, on top of the direct provision of services by the public sector, the private sector is increasingly allowed to provide services and create facilities. Yet, the public and the private sector involvement in public service provision remain strongly intertwined. At the moment, more attention is given to the output of services than the input of resources.

Another relevant development is the tendency toward governmental decentralization. In many policy fields, the central government has transferred its responsibilities to local authorities. This topic is elaborated in Chapter 10.

In addition to changes in government policy, many social developments exert an influence on the supply and use of public services and facilities. In this respect, the 1980s were a turbulent period. This was expressed in several ways: for instance, in the initial decline and subsequent gradual recovery of the number of jobs; the graying and de-greening of the population (more elderly and fewer children, both in absolute numbers and in relative terms); the explosive increase in the number of singles; as well as the steady increase in the amount of leisure time and the concomitant problem of how to spend it. These processes affect the demand for and the supply of public services and facilities. There are many areas of quantitative and qualitative imbalances (Schouw & Den Draak 1986; Alessie et al. 1987). These reflect from the diversified character of social processes that influence each other, both positively and negatively.

This chapter elaborates on the shifts in the supply of and the demand for some public services and facilities in the Randstad. It deals, for instance, with the spatial pattern of supply and demand within the Randstad and the changes therein that have occurred during the 1980s. The central question is how these shifts can be explained. Are they brought about by changes in the population composition? Do various population groups alter their use of services? What are the roles of autonomous changes and of those that are (partially) instigated by policy with respect to the nature, the volume, and the distribution of services?

It is evident that only a limited number of services and facilities can be studied. Our selection includes a few amenities in the areas of health care, culture, and recreation. This chapter is structured as follows. First, a few theoretical notions providing the context for the study are discussed. Subsequently, the supply and use of services and facilities in the Randstad is dealt with. The focus is on spatial differentiation within the Randstad, and the changes thereof. The chapter concludes by linking the empirical analysis to the theoretical notions discussed at the beginning.

9.2   Theoretical perspectives

Spatial developments in the supply and the use of services and facilities can be defined as macro phenomena, i.e. developments at an aggregated level. Yet they result from the numerous actions of and interactions between individuals. The explanation therefore needs to start at the micro level, the level of individual actors. "Because data are so often gathered at the level of individuals or other units below the level of the system whose behavior is to be explained, it is natural to begin the explanation of system behavior by starting at the level at which observations are made, then 'composing' or 'synthesizing' the systematic behavior from the actions of these units" (Coleman 1990, p. 3). This leads to the problem of how individual behavior and collective phenomena are related. The issues are the aggregated effects of individual behavior, as well as the impact of collective phenomena on individual behavior. In other words, it concerns the relationships between higher (macro) and lower (micro) levels of analysis, which implies both the transition from macro to micro and from micro to macro levels (Ritzer 1990).

The transition from the one level to the other is not simple or direct. The macro to micro transition refers to the ways in which the social context or the geographical setting influences the individual. This implies a wide range of socio-cultural, economic, and political influences. The other transition, i.e. the move from micro to macro, has two dimensions, namely the interdependence of the activities of an individual and the way in which their aggregation results in macro-level phenomena. Individual behavior emerges from a process of interaction with others. "The interaction among individuals is seen to result in emergent phenomena at the systems level, that is phenomena that were neither intended nor predicted by the individuals" (Coleman 1990, p. 5).

The notions of micro-macro relationships do not preclude widely disparate starting points for theory formulation about the social reality and human activities. How is the relationship between individual and society interpreted? Is the initiator the individual who shapes the social reality through his or her activities? Or do social and spatial structures condition individual behavior?

For a long time, there were clear lines of division among theorists, who took either the actor or the structure as their point of departure. But in recent decades, attempts have been made to bridge the gap (Ritzer 1990). Two approaches that are preeminent in the current discourse are summarized here. These are Giddens' (1984) structuration theory and the notion of structural individualism (Hechter 1983; Coleman 1990).

The central notion in Giddens' approach is that society and the individual are linked in dynamic interaction. Giddens calls this 'structuration'. Society is shaped by individual activities, but at the same time these activities take place within social structures. Human activity is competent and purposeful, but it is also contextual because structural characteristics influence these activities. This dual relationship is referred to as the duality of structures. Structures offer opportunities but also impose restrictions. Freedom of action is therefore subject to constraints; in addition, it is influenced by the (positive and negative) externalities resulting from earlier actions. The 'social practices' that result from the actions of individuals are not incidental or purely voluntaristic; they evince a certain degree of regularity and order (Moos & Dear 1986; Clark 1990). Thus, social reality cannot be isolated from the contexts of time and space within which human action is situated and social developments occur.

The approach of structural individualism has at its core the individual's freedom of choice. That freedom is constrained by social structures, but these do not fully determine human behavior. "In such an approach the structure first determines, to a greater or lesser extent, the constraints under which individuals act. While these constraints define the limits of the individual's possible action, they are insufficient to determine his or her behavior. In no way does this imply that individual attributes should be given greater weight than structural constraints; it merely asserts that social phenomena cannot be understood without taking the intentions and consequences of individual action into account" (Hechter 1983, p. 8).

This should make it clear that the theory concerning the actions of people is of central importance. An important element in this approach is the rational choice theory. This depicts people beings who act rationally and try to achieve certain goals (e.g. physical well-being, social recognition) by means of the resources they command, and under the influence of various constraints (Wippler 1990). The resources include, besides income and financial assets, also knowledge and skills, time and social contacts, etc.

How relevant are these theoretical notions to the supply and use of public services and facilities in the Randstad? The benefit of these approaches is that they highlight the relationships between social practices (structuration theory), individual actions (structural individualism), and social and spatial contexts. This is relevant when studying spatial patterns of the use of services and facilities, because such use is influenced by the nature, volume, and distribution of these and other aspects of the residential environment as macro-level characteristics. At the same time, it must be emphasized that the use of services and facilities at an aggregate level reflects the collective result of the processes of individual choice at the micro level; it reflects numerous individual decisions to use the services or not. Individuals make their choices within a social context, which is conditioned by institutions in the widest sense of the word. This is depicted schematically in Figure 9.1.

In principle, shifts in the pattern of the use of services and facilities at the aggregate level can result from changes in the composition of the population, or of changed behavior of people with respect to these. The presence of population groups who do or do not use them, or who use them frequently or infrequently, is subject to change as a result of such demographic developments as de-greening or graying, as well as the development of the number of households, especially those of single persons. In addition, there are period effects and cohort effects. Because people representing different generations have different experiences, depending on the period of history in which they have lived, differences in patterns of behavior result. Changes in the living conditions and social circumstances of people have consequences for their use of services. In other words, the decision regarding whether or not they will use services and facilities will be different, also because their resources and the constraints on their actions are very dynamic.

While the use of services and facilities cannot take place without their supply, the existence of demand for these is a necessary condition for their proper functioning. Some services face a loss of support because of changing use patterns. Others lack the capacity to meet growing demand, which can result in waiting lists, etc. At the

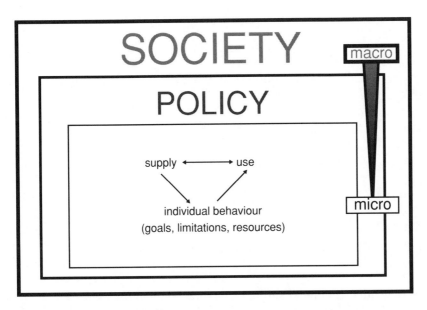

Figure 9.1　　*Conceptual model*

same time, the nature, volume, and distribution of services and facilities are subject to economic, technological, and policy developments.

On the one hand, the threshold for the economic functioning of services and facilities has increased because of such processes as their expanding scale of operation, diversification, and specialization. Pinch (1989) has pointed out that the notions of economic restructuring in manufacturing sectors are also valid for the analysis of public services. But on the other hand, public service provision is subject to social pressures, as political interests, pressure groups, and special interest groups attempt to influence its development. Contrary to the private sector, the deliberations concerning public services are not only sensitive to the notion of efficiency, but to some extent they also respond to equity considerations and (territorial) equality. The availability and accessibility of public services, seen from the supply side, are partially determined by these criteria (compare Chapter 10). This influences the use that people can and wish to make of the public services and facilities.

Within the Randstad, considerable differences exist in the use of services and facilities. The presence of user groups and their relative sizes is an important factor, in addition to the availability of the services. Within the Randstad there are clear differences in the composition of the population, as well as with respect to the nature, volume, and distribution of services. These differences can be noted among categories of munici-

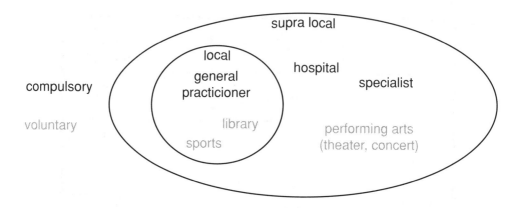

Figure 9.2   Classification of selected services and facilities

palities (big cities, commuter settlements, rural communities, etc.), as well as among the regional subdivisions of the area. In addition, there is a considerable degree of dynamism. Clear shifts in the supply and use of services have occurred during the 1980s.

   In the following sections of this chapter, several public services and facilities are analyzed in more detail. The focus of analysis is on the relationship between the macro and micro levels. The performing arts, libraries and sport facilities, and medical facilities are reviewed, in that order. The selection of these amenities was based on two considerations. On the one hand, these services and facilities represent the range from voluntary to compulsory, as far as usage is concerned. On the other hand, they range from local to regional in character. In Figure 9.2, the selected services and facilities are presented as a diagram.

9.3   The performing arts

The performing arts can be defined as regional services. Their supply is largely concentrated in cities. Amsterdam assumes the undisputed leadership position. This city has the most theaters and concert halls, the largest number of performances, and in addition it is the seat of many theater companies, orchestras, and similar organizations (Van Kempen 1982; CBS 1990). Table 9.1 presents some data on the number and relative shares of theater performances and concerts in the Randstad, in as far as these are subsidized by the national government. This shows unequivocally that Amsterdam has further strengthened its position. The increase by more than ten percent of its share of both forms of the performing arts reinforces Amsterdam's primacy. The overall

Table 9.1   *The number of theater performances and concerts in the Randstad subsidized by the national government in 1980/81 and 1987/88, absolute numbers and percentage shares of the total number of performances in the Randstad*

	theatre		concert	
	1980/81	1987/88	1980/81	1987/88
Big cities	74.7	84.7	68.5	79.5
Amsterdam	35.6	47.2	29.6	40.8
Rotterdam	12.2	11.1	11.6	11.2
The Hague	20.2	22.2	17.9	20.3
Utrecht	6.6	4.2	9.4	7.4
Randstad (100%)	3126	1984	971	767

Source: CBS

decline in number of performances has predominantly occurred outside the big cities. This may be inferred from the fact that the other big cities in the Randstad have managed to consolidate their position.

Studies in other countries of participation in cultural events confirm the predominantly urban character of theater and concert attendance (Hantrais & Kamphorst 1987). A French study (Samuel 1987) shows that the percentage of the population that goes to the theater or to concerts is eight times larger in Paris (1982) than in rural areas. Obviously, differences in the availability of various cultural facilities are an important factor. It is no surprise that Paris ranks first in the country as far as the provision of theaters and concert halls is concerned. The same applies to a city like London. "The contrast in provision between London and the regions is noteworthy, and studies by geographers show that there are 'cultural belts' and 'cultural deserts', even within regions" (Hantrais 1987, p. 122). Yet, this does not imply that performances and the provision of cultural facilities is a sufficient condition for attendance: "Although it is easy to gauge that the lack of facilities will prevent attendance, the converse is not necessarily true" (Hantrais 1987, p. 12).

In which ways do the inhabitants of the Randstad differ with respect to their attendance at performing arts events? Participation in culture is part of the activity patterns of a select segment of the population. The selectivity applies not only to the share of the population that participates but especially to its composition. In 1987, approximately 30 percent of the population would occasionally attend a theater performance or a concert. That group is dominated by people with a higher education or a relatively high income. This corresponds to the situation in other countries. "In the advanced capitalist societies, the arts were found to be the privileged domain of a predominantly male, well-educated, relatively wealthy high status public" (Hantrais 1987, p. 227).

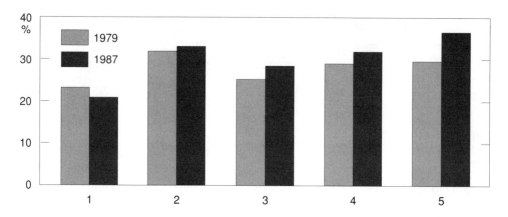

1 = (urbanized) rural municipalities
2 = commuter areas
3 = small cities (< 50,000 pop.)
4 = medium-sized cities (> 50,000 pop. excluding 5)
5 = the four big cities (Amsterdam, The Hague, Rotterdam, Utrecht)

Source: AVO 1979 and 1987

Figure 9.3   Attendance at theater performances and concerts in the municipalities of the Randstad by degree of urbanization, 1979 and 1987 (percentages)

Increasingly, this cultural elite tends to live in the large cities. In other words, the potential attendees live relatively close to the cultural facilities (Maas et al. 1990). The variations in participation among types of municipalities within the Randstad are to a major extent the result of differences in local performances and in the composition of the population. In the cities, there are far more single persons and two-person households, students and well-educated people; outside the cities, families with children are the characteristic population group.

Attendance at theater performances and concerts in the Randstad also shows a tendency toward spatial divergence, parallel to the trend in the supply. In general, the 1980s have witnessed a modest increase in the share of people who sometimes attend a theater performance or concert. But the frequency of visits has decreased, resulting in a drop in attendance in spite of the broadening of the audience. Figure 9.3 shows that the increase in attendance does not take place everywhere in the Randstad to the same extent. The inhabitants of rural municipalities and small cities have become increasingly underrepresented in the audiences, while the medium-sized and large cities remain clearly at the head. In other words, as far as these manifestations of participation in culture are concerned, they have increasingly become an urban affair. As far as attendance is concerned, these cultural activities have assumed an increasingly

Table 9.2   *Attendance at theater performances and/or concerts in the Randstad by education and income, 1979 and 1987 (percentages)*

| | low income | | high income | |
	1979	1987	1979	1987
Primary school	13.3	12.3	33.4	26.6
Secondary school/ Lower vocational school	23.9	23.9	30.1	37.3
College-preparatory/ Vocational high school	43.6	46.8	42.9	49.4
University/ Technical college	53.5	53.4	58.0	60.3

Source: AVO 1979 en 1987

local function (Knol 1988). But from the perspective of the supply, this is most certainly not the case: the importance of cultural facilities reaches far beyond the city on account of its innovative character.

During the 1980s, the differences between the groups that do and do not attend events of the performing arts have continued to increase. There are no fundamental changes in the pattern of attendance, but nevertheless there is a shift towards a more select audience. Table 9.2 demonstrates the increased attendance among people with a high income and a high educational level. Knulst (1989) suggests that the increased selectivity may have resulted from the increase of alternative ways to spend leisure time in general, which affects the performing arts in particular; they are particularly sensitive to the competition from various forms of home entertainment. Consequently, the balance of cost and benefit has changed. Nowadays, attendance at performances outside the home must be weighed against the many options for home entertainment. The results are very much dependent on one's household situation, acquired cultural abilities, and social status. In other words, the changes at the macro level affect the choices of people at the micro level. Conversely, the collective result of these individual decisions is a change in the size and composition of the audience of the performing arts.

Obviously, geographers tend to emphasize the influence of the place of residence on the pattern of attendance at events staged by the performing arts. Controlling for such personal characteristics as age, education, income, and type of household, the category of place of residence adds to the explanation of the observed variations in attendance. The resulting pattern fits the expectations. The inhabitants of rural areas attend less often than could be expected on the basis of their personal characteristics, while living in a large city proves to be a stimulant to attend theater performances or concerts. These differences have increased during the 1980s.

The causes of this pattern are identified as the availability and accessibility of these particular facilities. Verhoeff (1991) has shown that distance influences the attendance rate, even when controlling for differences in population composition. This also shows up when the attendance pattern is expressed in time units; the average traveling time is 20 minutes, while the median is approximately a quarter of an hour. Yet, the nature of the performances also plays a major role. This is not so much related to the location where they take place as to the type of performance. Performances with a high-quality rating, as well as amateur performances in which acquaintances play a role, attract audiences from a greater distance. This is a clear example of a macro-micro relationship: the trouble that people are willing to take to overcome constraints is partly related to the characteristics of what is being offered.

For decades, considerations of social and geographic distribution have affected policy on the performing arts (Honigh 1985; Ganzeboom 1989; Bevers 1990; Maas et al. 1990). The effects of a policy of social dissemination, i.e. the promotion of attendance at cultural events among all strata of the population, may only be expected to yield results in the long term. Geographical redistribution has a short-term impact. Offering performances in a more dispersed pattern broadens the potential audience. Previously, the reaching-out principle of 'performances-to-the-audience' was dominant. At the moment, also the reverse strategy is emphasized: 'audience-to-the-performance'. It is assumed that increased mobility (automobile ownership), as well as various transportation arrangements promoted by the theaters themselves, have decreased the constraints of distance. The policy now aims at changing the micro-level constraints that kept people from attending a performance. But budget cuts have also played a role in this change in policy. The tighter financial constraints have led to a decrease in the number of performances away from the seat of residence of the theater companies and orchestras. At the same time it is being argued that the fragmentation inherent in tours threatens quality. Cities are widely seen as the cradles of culture, with circumstances favorable to performing arts productions. But the fact that these performances have increasingly become an urban phenomenon implies that people who live outside the large cities of the Randstad have to make a greater effort to attend an event.

9.4   Public libraries and sports accommodations

In contrast to the performing arts, public libraries and sports accommodations are facilities that serve a local clientele. Most municipalities have made such facilities available. Obviously, there are variations in their capacity. In comparison with the variations in the performing arts, however, these are modest. Therefore, that aspect is less pronounced in this discussion.

Major changes with respect to the public libraries and sports accommodations occurred during the 1970s and 1980s. The national figures show that the availability of these facilities increased substantially; there were also changes with respect to their composition. Especially places with a large residential construction program and consequent population growth needed to expand their services. But in addition, there are clear indications of a general improvement of the level of services. This was, however, more typical of the 1970s than of the 1980s.

The expansion of the library services pertains especially to the enlargement of their book collections (NBLC 1990). In comparison to 1977, the collections of books had almost doubled by 1988, while the availability of audio-visual items quadrupled. But also the number of libraries increased, from nearly 800 nationwide in 1973 to over 1200 in 1988. More than one-third of these are located in the Randstad. Almost every municipality now has a library at its disposal.

The most notable change with respect to sports accommodations is that during the 1970-1985 period, the number of open-air playing fields and courts almost doubled (CBS 1986). This increase was much more rapid than the population growth, which means a doubling in relative terms. But major differences emerge when the particular types of sports are considered individually. The number of tennis courts tripled between 1970 and 1985. There are now more tennis courts than soccer fields. The expansion of the number of soccer fields has been much slower since the early 1980s. The fields and courts for other sports, such as softball, cricket, rugby, etc., have increased even much more rapidly in a very short time. This is also true of indoor facilities.

In spite of the expansion of facilities, there has been a need for restructuring since the early 1980s. Libraries as well as sports accommodations are confronted with budget cuts. Frequently, these are disguised as a decentralization of responsibilities to lower-level authorities (SCP 1988). The restructuring aims at increasing the efficiency of these services. With respect to the libraries, this mostly implied that a further expansion of the services was curtailed, while in the larger municipalities also branch libraries were closed. Nevertheless, the emergence of the 'information society' forces the libraries to broaden their services drastically. Apart from their traditional supply of books, libraries need to meet the need for other vehicles of information (electronic and audio-visual means, etc.) that can be used on the spot. It is obvious that not every library can meet this demand. This has forced libraries to cooperate within a hierarchically structured network of facilities.

With regard to sports accommodations, discrepancies between supply and demand have emerged. Many facilities have been negatively affected by the changes in the public's interest. The sports that can be performed freely on an individual basis outside an organization have enjoyed a growing popularity. In addition, people now tend to participate in more than one sport. These changes have had a negative impact on the traditional field sports, which are mostly played as teams. An international comparative study by Kamphorst & Roberts (1989) shows that these shifts, which they define as pluralism, diversification, and differentiation, are occurring in many countries. Furthermore, such demographic trends as de-greening and graying have important implications for sports participation.

Because of these developments, soccer has steadily been losing players for years. An investigation in the large cities has shown that the decrease in the number of soccer teams during the 1980s was approximately 25 percent stronger than could have been expected to result from the demographic changes alone (Molenaar & Floor 1990). Consequently, the soccer fields remain un(der)utilized. The size of the surplus depends on the norms that are applied. On the basis of the norms used by the cities themselves,

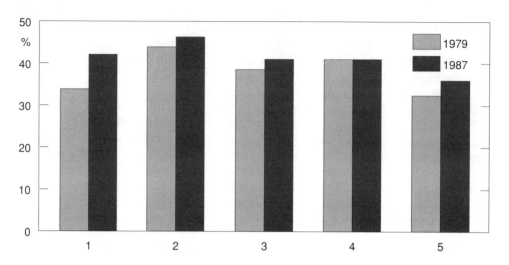

1 = (urbanized) rural municipalities
2 = commuter areas
3 = small cities (< 50,000 pop.)
4 = medium-sized cities (> 50,000 pop. excluding 5)
5 = the four big cities (Amsterdam, The Hague, Rotterdam, Utrecht)

Source: AVO 1979 and 1987

Figure 9.4   *Membership of public libraries in the municipalities of the Randstad by degree of urbanization, 1979 and 1987 (percentages)*

the actual supply of playing fields is about one-and-a-half times the number needed. In the meantime, numerous measures have been taken to decrease the oversupply. This proves to be a rather tedious process, however, since the interests of the parties involved (municipal authorities, sports associations, residents' associations, etc.) are often conflicting. One of the issues is whether or not the playing fields are to be re-used for sports or for other activities. Another concerns consolidation or other cooperative arrangements between sports clubs (Van der Knaap et al. 1990; WVC 1990). Therefore, the discrepancies between supply and demand in the large cities have hardly diminished. The decrease in the number of teams has been much more rapid than the decrease in the number of playing fields (Molenaar 1991).

The fact that most municipalities have libraries and sports accommodations does not imply that there are no variations in the use of these facilities. Figures 9.4 and 9.5 show that within the Randstad considerable variations remain among types of municipalities in the share of the population that utilizes these facilities. For both types of facilities, the use in the large cities is less than in the other municipalities; conversely,

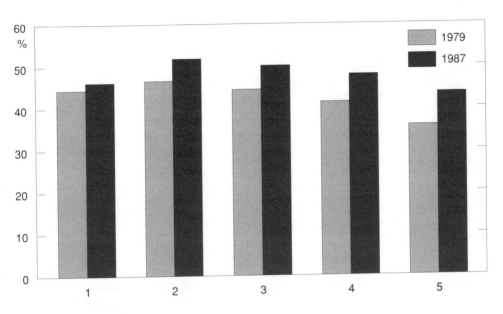

1 = (urbanized) rural municipalities
2 = commuter areas
3 = small cities (< 50,000 pop.)
4 = medium-sized cities (> 50,000 pop. excluding 5)
5 = the four big cities (Amsterdam, The Hague, Rotterdam, Utrecht)

Source: AVO 1979 and 1987

Figure 9.5   *Sports participation (tied to accommodations) in the municipalities of the Randstad by degree of urbanization, 1979 and 1987 (percentages)*

in commuter settlements and small cities, many more people participate in sports and join the public library. Such differences are mostly the result of differences in the population composition, especially with respect to the age distribution. The large cities contain relatively many elderly people, while the commuter settlements are (still) the realm of families.

The growth of the number of sports practitioners and library members during the 1980s has not been equally strong in all types of municipalities. The percentage of library members increased most in the rural municipalities; this is partially the result of opening up libraries in these places. The increase in the area of sports shows a much more balanced pattern. The increases partially paper over the qualitative shifts in the use of both types of facilities.

Over time, shifts have occurred in the user profiles of the libraries and the sports accommodations. On the one hand, these result from the changed share of a particular group in the total population. De-greening and graying lead to changes in the age composition of the population. Although these are general processes, the rate of change is not equal in all parts of the Randstad. The number of youthful users of libraries and sports accommodations is decreasing. There is evidence of a graying user population. For instance in Amsterdam, the ratio of little league to adult soccer teams changed from 48:52 in 1980 to 34:66 in 1989. With respect to the share of youthful members of the Amsterdam public library, a decrease of six percent to 39 percent took place between 1980 and 1987.

On the other hand, the behavior patterns of certain groups change. An increasing proportion of the youth join the public library. By 1987, the percentage of members 6 to 18 years of age had increased by more than six percent to 79 percent in comparison to 1979. The participation rate among the elderly has also increased (Table 9.3). More and more, elderly people prove to have a past record of library use (Knulst 1987; SCP 1990). In comparison to earlier cohorts, they have attained a higher educational level and a higher income.

Such shifts are also typical for sports participation (Table 9.4). Among the youth, almost 70 percent is involved in some sport. Although a clear age effect remains, the increased participation in sports among the middle-aged and the elderly is notable. These are not so much new recruits from among the adult population, but rather people who keep practicing the sport they were involved in as youths (SCP 1988; Roosen & Kropman 1989). In addition, Table 9.4 demonstrates that the differences in educational levels have decreased between 1979 and 1987. The participation rate of people with a higher education is apparently also attained by less-educated people, albeit with a time lag of a few years.

The significance of income for the use of libraries or sports accommodations is also changing. During the 1980s, the income thresholds preventing people from joining the library were removed. But given the current discussion of raising membership fees and introducing borrowing fees, it remains to be seen whether the thresholds will remain low. With respect to sports participation, the significance of income has increased. The higher costs of practicing a sport (membership fees, equipment, and other additional expenses) have deterred especially people with a low income (Schelvis 1985; Manders & Kropman 1987). The introduction of the principle that the user must bear the cost, which underlies these increases, has a negative effect on participation among these social groups. Once more, this is a clear example of a change at the macro level that puts constraints on participation in sports at the micro level. The application of this principle in the realm of sports policy formulated by the authorities in the 1980s is seen by Kamphorst & Roberts (1989) as the result of a "change in perception and definition, from sport as a collective right, to sport as an individual option" (p. 395). Their study suggests that also in this respect, the Dutch situation is not fundamentally different from that in the surrounding countries.

Table 9.3   *Membership of the public library in the Randstad in 1979 and 1987, by age and educational level (percentages)*

	18-44 years		45-54 years		55 years and older	
	1979	1987	1979	1987	1979	1987
Primary school	19.7	24.4	11.8	14.8	15.1	16.4
Secondary school/ Lower vocational school	29.3	29.8	23.0	28.0	20.1	30.3
College-preparatory/ Vocational high school	42.9	42.9	38.8	31.9	29.9	37.0
University/ Technical college	42.7	46.6	29.8	45.9	28.1	37.6

Source: AVO 1979 en 1987

Table 9.4   *Sports participation (tied to accommodations) in the Randstad in 1979 and 1987, by age and educational level (percentages)*

	18-44 years		45-54 years		55 years and older	
	1979	1987	1979	1987	1979	1987
Primary school	32.6	42.2	14.1	26.8	6.5	14.4
Secondary school/ Lower vocational school	48.7	51.6	19.9	33.3	10.2	24.6
College-preparatory/ Vocational high school	57.4	57.2	25.0	39.4	16.2	27.8
University/ Technical college	53.2	58.6	35.1	43.4	18.3	26.7

Source: AVO 1979 en 1987

9.5   Health care

Health care is quite different from the other services and facilities discussed here. People attend shows of the preforming arts, participate in sports, and use libraries largely because they choose to do so. The use of these facilities is voluntary and expresses preferences. In contrast, people are usually compelled to use health care services, namely because of health problems. In order to be cured, they need to call upon doctors. People are therefore in a dependent position, acquiescing to the decisions of experts (De Swaan 1988). Therefore, the functioning of the health care system itself exerts a clear influence on the consumption of medical provisions (Sluijs et al. 1985; Sanders et al. 1988). In other words, factors at the macro level determine to a large extent the medical consumption at the micro level. (For the services and facilities discussed above, this is only one of several influences.) After a consultation with a

Table 9.5   *Consultations with general practitioners and specialists (during the preceding three months) and hospital visits (during the preceding year) in the Randstad, by age in 1987 (percentages)*

	general practitioner	specialist	hospital
6-17	23.9	14.1	3.9
18-44	38.1	16.1	9.2
45-54	36.6	22.5	10.3
55-65	45.5	29.6	13.2
65+	54.5	33.5	14.0
Total	38.0	19.8	9.3

Source: AVO 1979 en 1987

general practitioner, he or she may take the initiative to schedule subsequent visits. The general practitioner can refer a patient to a specialist or to a hospital, at the request of the patient or of his or her own volition. In a hospital, the actions of specialists or the policy of the management influence such decisions as the degree to which the facility fill up the bids, the length of the nursing period, and the balance between clinical and out-patient care. In short, the patients are far from autonomous in their relationship to medical facilities. De Swaan (1985) even speaks in terms of a 'medical regime'.

The investigation focused on the differences in medical consumption in the Randstad among people and among municipalities and sub-regions (Molenaar 1992). It is obvious that the first determinant of visits to a general practitioner, a specialist, or a hospital is the incidence of health problems, which correlate closely with age. This is a micro relationship of a compulsory character. This relationship between age and consumption of medical services is expressed in various popular adages, such as 'with age come problems' (Table 9.5). Only the frequent contacts of infants and toddlers with the medical sector interrupts a basically positive statistical relationship. Compared to age, the importance of other personal characteristics is modest. Nevertheless, there are many variations in the patterns of use of medical services that cannot simply be explained by reference to age.

One of the regularities is that people in a lower socioeconomic position use the medical services more frequently than people with a higher status (Sluijs et al. 1985). This is partly due to socioeconomic differentials in the health of a population. The explanation for these differences is rather complicated. On the one hand, people with medical problems have less opportunity for upward social mobility than healthy people. On the other hand, people from lower social status environments have more medical problems. The relationship results from the interaction of these two causes (SCP 1988). The question remains to what extent the difference is related to the quality of housing and of respective social conditions. At one time, this connection was clearly established.

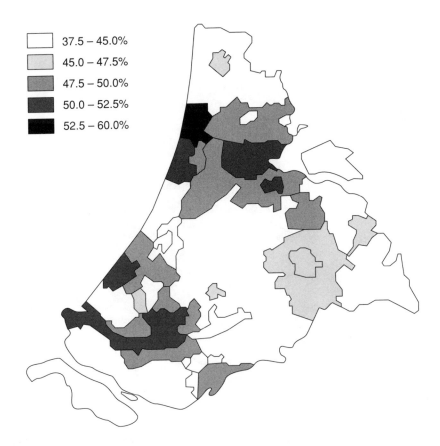

Figure 9.6   Visits to general practitioners, specialists, and hospitals in the Randstad in 1987 (percentages)

But compared to a few decades ago, poor material conditions no longer have a great impact on the health differential.

The differences in the consumption of medical services have been the subject of many investigations (Giggs 1979; Sanders et al. 1988). Epidemiological and, above all, demographic factors have been shown to explain much of the variation, though they do not offer a full explanation. At the macro level, many interacting factors related to the supply of medical services contribute to the existence of regional variations. Among these are the density of the pattern of general practitioners and specialists, the referral policy of general practitioners, and the methods of treatment by specialists,

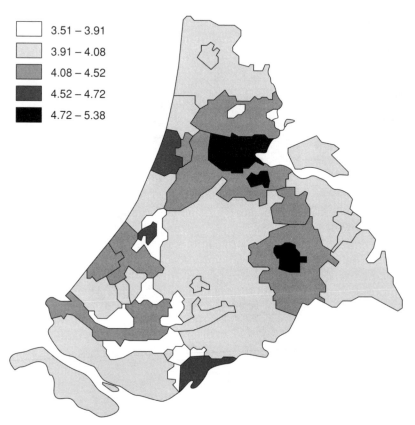

☐	3.51 – 3.91
☐	3.91 – 4.08
☐	4.08 – 4.52
☐	4.52 – 4.72
■	4.72 – 5.38

Figure 9.7   *The number of general practitioners per 10,000 inhabitants in the Randstad in 1987*

characteristics of the management of hospitals, and geographical factors such as the location of facilities and their accessibility (Groenewegen et al. 1987; KNMG 1989).

Figure 9.6 depicts the visits to general practitioners, specialists, and hospitals in the Randstad in relative terms. It is obvious from this figure that substantial differences exist between cities and rural municipalities. In the cities, especially in the larger ones, the proportion of patients in the population is substantially higher. Obviously, differences in age structure play a role. But the variations among municipalities and sub-regions within the Randstad in medical consumption also show a distinct positive relationship with the presence of general practitioners, specialists, and hospital services (Figure 9.7 and 9.8).

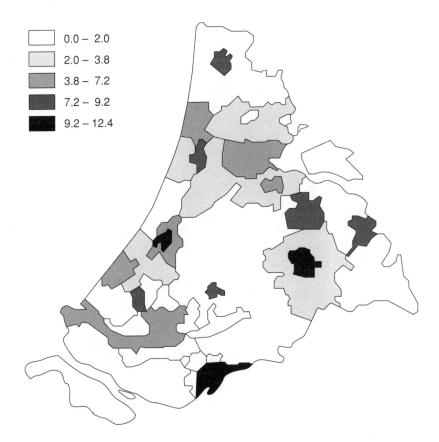

Figure 9.8   *The number of beds in general hospitals and in university-affiliated hospitals*
per 1000 inhabitants in the Randstad in 1987

By means of regression analysis, the differences between parts of the Randstad with
respect to the use of medical services have been studied more closely (Molenaar 1992).
This analysis shows the obvious influence of age, but it also demonstrates the independent effect of supply factors. Over 25 percent of the variation in the rate of visits to
the general practitioner are explained by the differences in the relative supply of general
practitioners. No less than 41 percent of the variation in the visits to specialists are
explained by the relative supply of family doctors. When there are more general
practitioners per 10,000 inhabitants, the visits to both the general practitioner and
the specialist increase.

The use of hospitals, the clinical consumption, has been measured in a number of
ways, namely the percentage of the population that has had clinical treatment, the
number of admissions, and the number of nursing days. These are different entities,

each of which elucidates a different aspect of the use of hospitals. The percentage of people who have received hospital treatment correlates strongly with the visits to specialists (almost 48 percent explained variation). The variation in the number of admissions to the hospital correlates with the capacity of hospital beds and the relative number of general practitioners, which account for almost forty and six percent, respectively, of the total variation. These results are in line with Roemer's law: "A built bed is a filled bed") (Van Doorslaer & Van Vliet 1989).

As suggested above, differences in the population composition among areas form an additional factor. Age composition in particular is significant. For instance, the percentage of the elderly (65 years and older) explains almost 58 percent of the variation in the number of nursing days. In short, at the aggregated level, the effect of the nature, volume, and distribution of medical facilities on their use is evident. However, these macro relationships are the combined result of the behavior of patients and medical professionals, which are micro-level variables. Nevertheless, their activities are partially a reaction to the differences in the presence and the capacity of the various services. General practitioners are influenced in their referrals by the availability of specialists and clinical facilities. Specialists and hospital managers, in turn, influence the number of admissions and the number of nursing days.

Since the early 1970s, the attempt to bring the costs of health care under control has been a central issue in Dutch policy. Various means have been identified to reach this end. The first way is by limiting the capacity of clinical health care. The reduction of the number of hospital beds is an important strategy. The dual aim is to reduce overcapacity as well as to make more efficient use of existing capacity. The second way is by shifting from clinical care to out-patient treatment, from 'cure' to 'care', from treatment to prevention. The policy aims to prevent admissions to the hospital in less urgent cases and, if admission is necessary, to discharge patients earlier and to continue their care at home. Finally, the changes in the structure and financing of health care are subject to heated debate. The aim is to develop a less expensive and more efficient health care system, whereby the responsibility of achieving this goal is in the hands of the health care workers and the insurance companies. This strategy involves the introduction of market elements in the health care system (cf. Chapter 10). But until now, the multitude of policy proposals contrast sharply with actual progress in restructuring of the health care system.

The patterns of supply of medical facilities prove to be highly resistant to change (Daniels 1985; Pinch 1985). The restructuring process is tedious and slow. The hospitals are a clear case in point. Dutch authorities have resolved to reduce the number of hospital beds to 3.4 per 1000 inhabitants by the year 1995. During the 1980-1988 period, the number of beds were reduced from 5.2 to 4.6 per thousand (SCP 1990). This reduction in capacity is often carried out by consolidation of facilities and closure of small hospitals. Consequently, the location pattern of hospitals is becoming increasingly concentrated (Stijnenbosch 1983; Buit & Nozeman 1988). Nevertheless, the use of hospitals has hardly declined; instead, the average time spent in a hospital has been reduced. At present, the average nursing period runs 12 days; in 1951, this was three weeks (Biesheuvel & Stijnenbosch 1987). The reduction of the number of beds affects only part of the production capacity of hospitals. This is clearly expressed in the strong rise in the number of out-patients (KNMG 1989). The decreasing length of nursing, the introduction of various forms of out-patient care, and the ageing of the population all contribute to an increase in the need for health care. During the time patients are hospitalized, they require more intensive care. This has clearly increased the work load of the staff (SCP 1990).

Although the changes described here are clearly not unique to the Netherlands, a comparison of the situation with the state of health care in other countries is far from straightforward. The differences in the health care systems of the respective countries are simply too great. These differences go beyond the structure, ways of financing, and health insurance models. For instance, a patient can directly consult a specialist in Germany, while in the Netherlands a referral by a general practitioner is the rule. With respect to the number of hospital beds and the number of doctors per 1000 inhabitants, the Netherlands occupies a relatively low position in comparison with other European countries. This may be the result of the advantaged position of the Netherlands with respect to numerous health indicators. In addition, the Netherlands does have a reasonably well-functioning system of home care in comparison with the surrounding countries (SCP 1990).

9.6   Conclusions

This chapter reviewed the developments of supply and demand of a number of services and facilities in the Randstad. This was not a complete description; only a few significant trends were indicated. Yet it was shown that in spite of all the differences, these services display some similarities. The common trends are related to changes in the context within which these services operate. Efficiency criteria regarding the provision of public services now play a much more dominant role than before. Input and output are taken much more into consideration to achieve an optimal supply of services within the constraints of available budgets.

In practice, this leads to processes of concentration and increasing scales of operation. Each of the services under discussion has been affected by these trends to some degree. At the root of this lies not only the desire to reduce budgets but also the desire to broaden the range of services provided or to achieve a higher degree of specialization. The trend towards greater efficiency is also notable on the part of the users. The costs of services have been made more visible by introducing new user fees or by the reduction of subsidies. This has led to the individualization of the use of services and facilities. Consequently, the conditions that determine whether or not people use the services have shifted to the individual resources and constraints. Obviously, this applies especially to the services and facilities that are essentially used on a voluntary basis.

Population group		Share of group using facilities	
high educational level	+	performing arts	+
low educational level	-		-
youth 6-17 years old	-	sports	+
adults 45-54 years old	0		+
adults 18-44 years old	-	libraries	+
households of four or more	-		0

Figure 9.9   *Situations illustrating the changes in use of services by specified population groups in relation to their changing representation in the population as a whole*

The theoretical notions introduced at the beginning of this chapter offer the interpretation framework for the reviewed developments in the supply and use of the public services and facilities. Both approaches contain many relevant elements. The reappraisal of the role of the individual who is seen as acting purposefully within the context of the societal structures, which are also the result of that action, has enriched that theoretical perspective. An important element is the notion that relationships exist between micro and macro levels.

The review of the various services and facilities has clearly drawn out the interactions between the two levels. The changes in the pattern of supply and demand take place in this interaction. Policy changes with regard to the supply can be seen as one of the factors that influence the use of services and facilities. These policies are part of a broader societal framework, wherein the values, norms, and institutions are also shifting. The impact of this is exerted through the individual, who experiences changing constraints (options and limitations), and reaches his or her decisions within their framework. Obviously, the primary factor is thereby the balancing of the costs and benefits of the individual's use of services and facilities. The externalities of these numerous individual decisions manifest themselves at the macro level as qualitative and quantitative discrepancies between the supply of and the demand for public services.

The identified population groups exhibit a changing pattern of use of the services and facilities under discussion. At the same time, the proportions of these groups in the population as a whole are changing. Several examples of this were reviewed. Figure 9.9 presents a comprehensive picture of a number of changes that occurred in the Randstad during the 1980s.

The performing arts attract an increasingly select audience; this change is partly induced by the emergence of various forms of home entertainment and other alternative ways to spend leisure time. The public library also encounters a shift in the composition of its user population. As a consequence of the de-greening and graying of the population and changing participation patterns, the libraries have to meet different demands. The combined effects of changes in the number and composition of the population and shifts in interests also manifest themselves in the realm of sports. This can lead to an erosion of the base of one type of accommodation, while at the same time other sports facilities have to resort to the introduction of waiting lists. Health care is especially affected by demographic change, which shows up in an increased use of health care services and facilities as a consequence of the aging of the population. This is the collective result of an unavoidable relationship at the micro level, namely that between age and health problems. The actions of the health care professionals determine to a large extent the volume and nature of the use of the facilities, a macro level phenomenon.

These examples demonstrate the importance of the mutual relationships of micro and macro levels. The notion of the interactions between the two levels greatly enhances our understanding of the changes in the supply of and demand for public services and facilities. For both suppliers of these services and their clients, constraints develop as a consequence of new and evolving circumstances. Within this complex context, patterns of use and supply of public services and facilities emerge and develop.

References

Alessie, R.J.M., P.B. Boorsma & F.A.J. van de Bosch. (1987), Demografische veranderingen en economische ontwikkelingen. Leiden/Antwerpen: Stenfert Kroese.

Bevers, A.M. (1990), Cultuurspreiding en publieksbereik. Van volksverheffing tot marktstrategie. In: I.van den Berg & S. de Sitter (eds), Kunst en overheid: Beleid en praktijk, pp. 61-82. Amsterdam: Boekmanstichting/Universiteit van Amsterdam.

Biesheuvel, A. & M.H. Stijnenbosch (1987), Concentratie en deconcentratie van intramurale gezondheidsvoorzieningen. In: P.P.Groenewegen, J.P. Mackenbach & M.H. Stijnenbosch (eds) (1987), Geografie van gezondheid en gezondheidszorg, pp. 87-95. Nederlandse Geografische Studies 24. Amsterdam/Utrecht: KNAG/Geografisch Instituut, Rijksuniversiteit Utrecht.

Buit, J. & E.F. Nozeman (1988), Ruimtelijke gevolgen van ziekenhuisconcentraties. Verkenningen 42 (a&b). Amsterdam: Planologisch Demografisch Instituut, Universiteit van Amsterdam.

CBS (Centraal Bureau voor de Statistiek) (1986), Accommodatie-onderzoeken, Inventarisatie Sportaccommodaties 1985. 's Gravenhage: SDU-Uigeverij.

CBS (Centraal Bureau voor de Statistiek) (1990), Podiumkunsten 1988. Voor burg/Heerlen: CBS.

Clark, J. (1990), Anthony Giddens, sociology and modern social theory. In: J.Clark, C. Modgil & S. Modgil (eds), Anthony Giddens. Consensus and Controversy, pp. 21-27. London/New York: Falmer Press.

Coleman, J.S. (1990), Foundations of Social Theory. Cambridge, Mass./London: Belknap Press.

Curtis, S. (1989), The Geography of Public Welfare provision. London/New York: Routledge.

Daniels, P.W. (1985), Service Industries, A Geographical Appraisal. London/New York: Methuen.

Doorslaer, E.K.A. van & R.C.J.A. van Vliet (1989), "A Built Bed is a Filled Bed?" An empirical re-examination. Social Science & Medicine 28, pp. 155-164.

Ganzeboom, H. (1989), Cultuurdeelname in Nederland. Een empirisch-theoretisch onderzoek naar determinanten van deelname aan culturele activiteiten. Assen/Maastricht: Van Gorcum.

Giddens, A. (1984), The Constitution of Society, Outline of the Theory of Structuration. Cambridge: Polity Press.

Giggs, J.A. (1979), Human health problems in urban areas. In: D.T.Herbert, & D.M. Smith (eds), Social Problems and the City. Geographical Perspectives, pp.84-116. Oxford: Oxford University Press.

Groenewegen, P.P., J.P. Mackenbach & M.H. Stijnenbosch (eds) (1987), Geografie van gezondheid en gezondheidszorg. Nederlandse Geografische Studies 24. Amsterdam/Utrecht: KNAG/Geografisch Instituut, Rijksuniversiteit Utrecht.

Hantrais, L. (1987), The arts in Great Britain. In: L.Hantrais & T.J. Kamphorst (eds) (1987), Trends in the Arts. A Multinational Perspective, pp. 113-143. Amersfoort: Giordano Bruno.

Hantrais, L. & T.J. Kamphorst (eds) (1987), Trends in the Arts. A Multinational Perspective. Amersfoort: Giordano Bruno.

Hartog, F. (1980), Toegepaste welvaartstheorie. Leiden: Stenfert Kroese.

Hechter, M. (ed) (1983), The Microfoundations of Macrosociology. Philadelphia: Temple University Press.

Honigh, M. (1985), Doeltreffend beleid. Een empirische vergelijking van beleidssectoren. Assen: Van Gorcum.

Kamphorst, T.J. & K. Roberts (eds) (1989), Trends in Sports. A Multinational Perspective. Culemborg: Giordano Bruno.

Kempen, E.T. van (1982), Amsterdam als centrum van cultuurproduktie. Geografisch Tijdschrift 16, pp. 80-393.

Knaap, M.A.M. van der, J. den Draak, J. Th. Gantvoort & D. Frielink (1990), Aanpassing van het aanbod van wijkvoorzieningen aan bevolkingsveranderingen. Deel 2: verslag van drie case-studies. OSPA-rapport 26. Delft: Delft University Press.

KNMG (Koninklijke Nederlandse Maatschappij ter bevordering van de Geneeskunst) (1989), Verschillen tussen gezondheidsregio's in gebruik van ziekenhuisvoorzieningen, 1985. Rapport van de Commissie Hoefnagels. Utrecht: Koninklijke Nederlandse Maatschappij ter Bevordering van de Geneeskunst.

Knol, F.A. (1988), Veranderingen in het ruimtelijk patroon van het gebruik van culturele voorzieningen. Rooilijn 1988, pp. 9-15.

Knulst, W.P. (1987), Bibliotheken in een veranderende samenleving. Bibliotheek en Samenleving 15, pp. 263-270.

Knulst, W.P. (1989), Van vaudeville tot video. Sociale en Culturele Studies 12. Rijswijk: Sociaal en Cultureel Planbureau.

Lineberry, R.L. (1977), Equality and Urban Policy. The Distribution of Municipal Public Services. Sage Library of Social Research 39. London: Sage.

Maas, I., R. Verhoeff & H. Ganzeboom (1990), Podiumkunsten en publiek. Een empirisch-theoretisch onderzoek naar omvang en samenstelling van het publiek van de podiumkunsten. Utrecht: Vakgroep Empirisch-Theoretische Sociologie, Rijksuniversiteit Utrecht.

Manders, Th & J. Kropman (1987), Sport: ontwikkelingen en kosten. Samenvatting. Nijmegen: Instituut Toegepaste Sociologie, Katholieke Universiteit Nijmegen.

Molenaar, G. & J. Floor (1990), Sociaal-culturele voorzieningen in een grootstedelijk perspectief. Werkstukken Stedelijke Netwerken 19. Utrecht: Stedelijke Netwerken.

Molenaar, G. (1991), Velden te over, maar waar blijven de spelers? Implicaties van trends in de sportbeoefening voor de vraag naar voetbalvelden in de grote steden. Planologische Discussiebijdragen, deel 1, pp. 361-370. Delft: Stichting Planologische Discussiedagen.

Molenaar, G. (1992), Randstad in gebruik. Een sociaal-geografische analyse van het gebruik van enkele publieke voorzieningen in de Randstad. (forthcoming).

Moos, A.I. & M.J. Dear (1986), Structuration theory in urban analysis: 1. Theoretical exegesis. Environment and Planning A 18, pp. 231-252.

NBLC (1990), Jaarboek Openbare Bibliotheken 1989. 's Gravenhage: NBLC.

Pinch, S. (1985), Cities and Services. The Geography of Collective Consumption. London: Routledge & Kegan Paul.

Pinch, S. (1989), The restructuring thesis and the study of public services. Environment and Planning A 21, pp. 905-926.

Ritzer, G. (1990), Micro-macro linkage in sociological theory: applying a metatheoretical tool. In: G.Ritzer (ed), Frontiers of Social Theory. The New Syntheses, pp. 437-370. New York: Columbia University Press.

Roosen, J. & J. Kropman (1989), Ouderen en sport: naar een permanente sportbeoefening. Nijmegen: Instituut Toegepaste Sociologie, Katholieke Universiteit Nijmegen.

Samuel, N. (1987), The arts in France. In: L. Hantrais & T.J. Kamphorst, (eds) (1987), Trends in the Arts. A Multinational Perspective, pp. 87-112. Amersfoort: Giordano Bruno.

Sanders, D., A. Coulter & K. McPherson (1988), Variations in Hospital Admission Rates: A Review of the Literature. KF Project Paper 79. London: Department of Health & Social Security.

Schelvis, N. (1985), Zuinig met sport. Rijswijk: Ministerie van Welzijn, Volksgzondheid en Cultuur.

Schouw, R.J. & J. den Draak (1986), Bevolking en voorzieningen in beweging. Rapport 53. Delft: Delft University Press.

SCP (Sociaal en Cultureel Planbureau) (1988), Sociaal en Cultureel Rapport 1988. Alphen aan den Rijn: Samson.

SCP (Sociaal en Cultureel Planbureau) (1990), Sociaal en Cultureel Rapport 1990. 's Gravenhage: VUGA.

Sluijs, E.M., J.P. Dopheide & J. van der Zee (eds) (1985), Overzichtsstudie onderzoek eerstelijn. Stand van het wetenschappelijk onderzoek in en over de eerstelijnsgezondheidszorg en haar raakvlakken. Utrecht: Nederlands Instituut Voor Eerste Lijnsonderzoek.

Stijnenbosch, M.H. (1983), Non-profit sektor en intramurale gezondheidszorg. Een sociaal-geografische analyse. Utrechtse Geografische Studies 28. Utrecht: Geografisch Instituut Rijksuniversiteit Utrecht.

Swaan, A. de (1985), Het medisch regiem. Amsterdam: Meulenhoff.

Swaan, A. de (1988), In Care of the State. Health Care, Education and Welfare in Europe and the USA in the Modern Era. Cambridge: Polity Press.

Verhoeff, R. (1991), Plaats en publiek. Geografische aspecten van podiumbezoek. In: R.Verhoeff & H.B.G.Ganzeboom (eds), Cultuur en publiek, Multidisciplinaire opstellen over de publieke belangstelling voor kunst en cultuur in Nederland, pp. 55-68. SISWO-publikatie 353. Amsterdam: Stichting Interuniversitair Instituut voor Sociaal-Wetenschappelijk Onderzoek.

Wippler, R. (1990), Cultural resources and participation in high culture. In: M.Hechter, K.D. Opp & R. Wippler (eds) (1990), Social Institutions: Their Emergence, Maintenance and Effects. Berlin/New York: Walter de Gruyter.

WVC (Ministerie van Welzijn, Volksgezondheid en Cultuur) (1990), Herstructurering sportaccommodaties. Momentopname met perspectieven. Samenvatting Onderzoek naar de wijze waarop het herstructureringsproces van buitensportvoorzieningen in gemeenten verloopt. Rijswijk: Ministerie van Welzijn, Volksgezondheid en Cultuur.

Drs. G. Molenaar
City Council of Ede
P.O. Box 9022
6710 HK Ede
The Netherlands

Dr. H. Floor
Faculty of Geographical Sciences
University of Utrecht
P.O. Box 80.115
3508 TC Utrecht
The Netherlands

10. PROVISION OF SERVICES AND THE WELFARE STATE

A.P.N. Nauta & H. van der Wusten

10.1 Introduction

Public service is an ambiguous concept. Normally it refers to facilities to which people have a right, but services may back up obligations (the taxman). There are also traditional combinations, as in compulsory education. The state has long been a major provider of services, although these have not always been solicited as anxiously as many of them are now. Judicial structures to regulate property rights, guaranteed money as a generally accepted means of payment and standard of value, and armed forces to provide security were the initial services provided by the early territorial 'absolutist' states in Europe. These were imposed on the citizenry, but they provided a service, however valued, that materialized in a set of facilities: courts, central banks, barracks (initially on a temporary basis only) (Giddens 1987).

The evolution of the nation-state and its acceptance as a universally applicable political arrangement was accompanied by an astonishing increase in the range and scope of state actions. This occurred particularly in the twentieth century. After 1945 they took the form of welfare states. The 1980s have been characterized by efforts to at least curb further increases in public welfare provision, which is regulated and in many cases financed by the central state, and by efforts to prune what came to be seen as excesses of the current system.

The main emphasis in the increase of state activity has been in the field of welfare in the widest sense of the word. These actions are based on the idea that after guaranteeing civil and political rights, the state should also guarantee minimum levels of welfare for the whole populace (Marshall 1973). The implementation of this idea sparked major debates on the definition of what should be called minimal, not to mention how the actual guarantee should be realized once that level had been defined. These debates became intertwined and were recently even overshadowed by a focus on issues of (negative and positive) freedom, equality of opportunity, and the ideal of equality itself.

This chapter discusses a number of policy issues related to the provision of welfare services by the state. Considerations of effectiveness, efficiency, equity, and accountability apply. They affect the design of the structure of service provision. Structures are also conditioned by the nature of the service. In the case of medical services, direct personal

F. M. Dieleman and S. Musterd (eds.), The Randstad: A Research and Policy Laboratory, 219–236.
© 1992 *Kluwer Academic Publishers. Printed in the Netherlands.*

contact is almost impossible to avoid, whereas social security payments leave greater leeway in that respect. Payments can be made through the mail and the banking system or through a multitude of offices with employees engaging in some form of direct contact. Considerations of efficiency may in this case favor impersonal, centralized provision, whereas considerations of effectiveness may lead to more personalized provision at a number of locations. Recently a major overhaul of the system of student loans was implemented in the Netherlands. Initially this was to be administered from a single central point (located in a very peripheral location in the country), but it soon became clear that some face-to-face contact was necessary. At certain times of the year, telephone and postal services to and from the office broke down. Consequently, a number of regional support points were opened in order to redirect the information flow. Effectiveness and efficiency were greatly improved in this way.

The range of services that can be studied is very large. We limit ourselves to a small number that have been at the core of the debates concerning the welfare state: education, social welfare, and health care. In regard to education, we are particularly concerned with that part of the system aimed at age groups for whom education is compulsory. Social welfare embodies a wide array of programs aiming at the full participation of population categories in modern society (subsidies for libraries, youth clubs, and ethnic minorities fall under that heading). Health care includes not only the sector of the medical profession but also care systems from nursing to assistance with household chores available for the elderly and the handicapped. In addition to these three sectors we briefly consider a very different service, the police. In this case, notions derived from the welfare state ideal (the police as a provider of social services) are at odds with older notions concerning the role of the state (the police as an instrument to repress unlawful behavior).

We focus on the following questions:
- What considerations normally shape the pattern of facilities? What are the major factors that have recently affected these considerations? And what are the practical policy options taken into account to reshape the patterns of public service provision?
- Does the Randstad differentiate with respect to the provision of services? Is the Randstad as a whole different from the rest of the country? What are the most important internal variations within the Randstad?

10.2   Changing patterns and policy options

Generally speaking, the spatial pattern of facilities will reflect the geographical distribution of clients, though with a time lag. This is either the effect of market forces, or it results from some set of planning rules designed for that purpose. The medical specialist provides a service that is only public in the sense of being highly regulated as to quality aspects and financed through a publicly controlled system of insurance. That specialist is free to decide for himself where to establish his/her practice, on the basis of where the potential patients are likely to be. At the other end of the scale, the distribution of primary schools is strictly regulated by a cumbersome set of criteria regarding the expected number of pupils, size of the local community, denominational considerations, etcetera.

The welfare state is characterized by a large number of services. The patterns of their spatial distribution and the mechanisms that produce them are of a bewildering variety, as exemplified by the instances just mentioned. Three considerations are normally taken into account.

a) Most planned distributions start explicitly from a minimal territorial unit as a base. This unit is chosen with a view to the distances between the clients and the facility. It is also selected because of its social or cultural significance (a 'small settlement' within a larger rural municipality), its administrative or political function (a municipality), or simply for technical reasons. In the last case it is only a statistical entity. In contrast, under market conditions the pattern of facilities is strongly affected by the distance potential clients are willing to travel to make use of the service.

b) There is usually a relation to the number of users or potential users. The definition of a user or a client may vary greatly and can even be disputed. All sorts of political and ideological considerations may play a role: for instance, denominational and ethnic background of primary school children. The number of clients partly determines the size of a facility; these clients should as a rule be found within the territorial unit for which the facility has been established.

c) Considerations of minimal size in view of cost, and quality considerations limit what may be socially or politically desirable. Complex provisions like hospitals require a minimal number of different specialized departments (internal medicine, general surgery, obstetrics, neurology, etc.) and of clinical and day care facilities in order to function at all. This differentiation is considered necessary. It indicates a considerable minimal size, which for public services is of course politically determined (see GS 1988). Where small facilities are considered viable but result in extra costs, minimal size may also be prescribed. Obviously this too is a political decision.

Limits with respect to distances, numbers of people, and size are somewhat arbitrary and often negotiable in planning systems. The combined efforts of politicians, planners, and private or semi-public agencies to apply rules derived from these considerations have resulted in a dense pattern of provisions. Actually, a number of patterns, according to the type of provision that may form networks (between schools of different levels; between intra- and extra-mural facilities in health care). They all have spatial distributions, which have developed historically as a joint product of allocative principles and a process of bargaining between actors who dominate the various policy and planning arenas (witness the numerous 'exceptions' made in the field of education precluding the closure of small rural primary schools in particular). The present structure reflects the conditions of the past. In most cases the historical pattern can only be changed abruptly by incurring capital loss, an often costly interruption of routines, and the breakup of a crust of vested interests. As some of these conditions seem to have changed significantly in recent years, how will they affect that spatial distribution?

Several dynamic factors influence the spatial distribution of welfare state provisions: migration, needs, transport facilities, innovations in the structure of provisions, political attitudes, administrative capabilities, etc. Three of these factors have been paramount in recent years: the changing demographic structure, the strong political urge to control and cut public expenditure, and the change in thinking about how public services should be managed and how public administration should function.

A major development potentially affecting the demand for services at present and in the near future is the changing age structure of the Dutch population. Many services are used differently by specific age groups or are even exclusively targeted to one user group. As demand declines or grows, the size of a facility is immediately affected. Depending on a sufficient population base within the territorial unit to which the facility is targeted, its very existence may be threatened or the establishment of an extra facility may be considered.

The process of ageing involves diminishing mortality figures at younger ages and a low but fairly steady birth rate due to the preference for few children or intentional childlessness. Consequently, as the total population increases slightly, young cohorts are stabilizing after a dramatic fall in the 1970s and 1980s; cohorts of older people will increase substantially in the coming years. Due mainly to different age distributions but also to different migration patterns, these trends differ somewhat in various parts of the country, though not dramatically. In the next 25 years the four big cities, all situated in the Randstad, will hardly register any increase in the population over 65 years old. They already have a high percentage at the moment. Later these cities will again follow the national upward trend (Leering & Relou 1990; for the overall picture see Laslett 1989).

There is a tendency to 'even out' the consequences of demographic change. A natural increase in actual or potential users is not fully reflected in an equivalent growth of provisions. Similarly a decrease is not translated into a proportional shrinkage. Growth is not fully 'rewarded' because decrease is not fully 'punished', which detracts from the available financial means. The decrease in facilities for the younger age groups in the 1970s and 1980s lagged behind the demographic decline of youth. Likewise, the provisions on behalf of the elderly did not keep up with the surge in numbers that characterized the older age groups (SCP 1984).

The resistance to the reduction or elimination of a welfare facility may have to do with common motives, such as the fear of unemployment, loss of capital and expertise, reluctance to transfer and move, and resistance to change in general. There are specific motives too, as in the case of primary schools where various denominations jealously protect their interests against each other and the state. In conclusion, there has been a basic redistribution of age groups, and this has undoubtedly resulted in changes in the provision of public services. However, the redistribution of services from younger to older age cohorts has by no means proceeded at the same rate as the demographic changes.

During the 1980s the widespread political support for significant cuts in public expenditure coincided with a renewed discussion on the nature of the welfare state.

The cost of the provision of services may be cut back in various ways. This 'technical' discussion was accompanied by a reassessment of the politico-administrative structures that should regulate and administer these systems of services. This review was motivated partly by their cost, but also because of broader concerns with effectiveness, efficiency, equity, and accountability.

Up to the 1980s the Dutch welfare state showed little concern for the efficiency of its provisions. There was in fact rarely a pressing need for such concerns. A growing economy facilitated the expansion of the public sector. Policy-makers were mainly interested in satisfying the multifarious public needs that came to the fore and demanded financial aid. In planning these provisions, notions of equity (easy access, low thresholds) tended on the whole to overshadow efficiency. Then in the 1980s the political climate changed. Recession set in, and an urgent need was felt to curb the expansion of the public sector. Budget cuts were proposed. In general, the new trend gave rise to a growing interest in ways to reduce expenses in the public sector, even by reducing the level of help and service, but preferably by increasing productivity while maintaining previous output.

Reductions were planned on three different levels. In the first place, cuts were proposed and justified by arguments of a general political nature. The satisfaction of certain needs was no longer regarded as a task of government. Instead, the market should take its legitimate place, or non-professional forms of aid should again come to the fore. This kind of reasoning in favor of various kinds of 'privatization' was particularly applied to the social welfare sector, and less or not at all to health care or education. This is apparently related to differences in the general acceptance of professionalism in these sectors. Secondly, a tendency emerged to rationalize the structure of provisions: by assigning new tasks and abolishing others, by explicit delineations of tasks and improved allocation. In the field of health and social services, an extensive process of substitution from intramural to extramural and from expensive to cheaper provisions started and is still underway. Finally, measures were imposed to increase the efficiency of the single facility, notably by aiming to achieve its optimal size. This was a major point in the debate on the provision of education. Changing the size distribution has a direct impact on the spatial pattern of the service. This is because a change in size is immediately reflected in the location pattern of facilities or in the trip pattern of customers and clients. In the case of a repackaging of facilities at different levels (e.g. intra- and extramural), a very intricate rearrangement of facilities occurs. At least a further increase of more expensive higher-level facilities is curbed. And lower-level facilities become larger, more aggregated (e.g. several general practitioners pool their resources), and more differentiated (a general health clinic type of facility may develop).

We direct our discussion primarily to the issue of optimum size with a view to efficiency. Research supports the idea that optimization of size could help trim the cost of provisions and personnel without jeopardizing the amount and quality of services rendered (SCP 1989). It was found, for instance, that small public libraries tended

cost per unit of output
(index of average institution = 100)

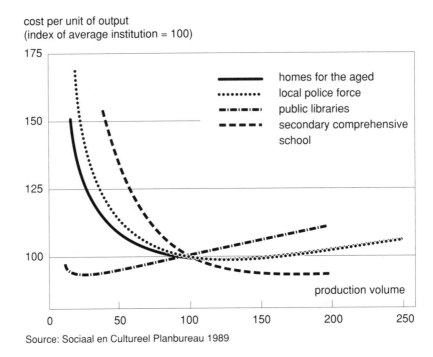

Source: Sociaal en Cultureel Planbureau 1989

Figure 10.1   Production volume and cost per unit of output

to be more productive than the larger ones. So small is sometimes indeed beautiful, even from an efficiency perspective! Yet the opposite applies to institutions for secondary education, and the optimal size of homes for the elderly was about 150 'beds'. The main results of this study are presented in Figure 10.1. The idea that it could be useful to adjust the size of a number of provisions found its way into the package of financial reductions proposed by the government in a new round of budget cuts in 1991. Studies to substantiate these claims are in progress at the time of writing. At a constant level of provision, this could give rise to a spatial rearrangement accompanied by budget cuts.

In the field of primary education, the policy of increasing the size of individual schools (thereby reducing the number of schools) has recently been more vigorously debated. The resulting policy is now being implemented against great odds. Though the average size of schools in the Netherlands is not particularly small compared with other countries (Table 10.1), the network of schools is comparatively dense. This reflects the overall high population density, which allows large schools and favorable accessibility at the same time. There were additional reasons to reduce the number of small schools. Besides

Table 10.1   *Average size and dispersal of primary schools*

	Average no. of pupils	No. of school years per school	Sq. km per school
Netherlands	175	8	5
Great Britain	174	6	10
Belgium	167	6	7
Denmark	158	6	17
France	86	5	11
West Germany	116	4	13

Source: UNESCO (1988)

being cost-saving, larger schools can be suitably equipped with a number of extra facilities, like remedial teaching, adapted education for retarded children, extra classes for immigrant children, etc. This creates a more differentiated facility. Finally there are indications that larger schools did not score worse in terms of test results but actually better (SCP 1990a).

A number of simulations were carried out, leading to four alternatives (SCP 1990a). These range from the current set of regulations, but without the many exceptions made in practice, to a minimum of 250 pupils in all cases. Not surprisingly, the more radical the model, the greater the financial gain, ranging from about two to ten percent. Accessibility, of course, was affected. Yet even in the most radical model 92 percent of the children could find a school in the settlement where they live. In urban areas distance is never a serious problem, but accessibility may be limited due to traffic barriers. The consequences for the distribution in terms of the continued presence of denominational schools of various kinds do not seem drastic.

An endless flow of minor variations on these models can be produced. This happened in negotiations during the first half of 1991. These will most likely result, at the end of the century, in the closure of about 1,000 of the 8,000 to 9,000 primary schools in the country. Small communities are generally permitted to maintain their small schools.

Despite drawbacks and compromises, the manipulation of the size of facilities to enhance their efficiency seems now fairly well ingrained at the national level. In due course this could well result in major adaptation of spatial distributions. But overall results will probably be less clear-cut, because other policies aiming at privatization and decentralization in various sectors impede the development of uniform patterns throughout the country.

As a consequence of a thorough reconsideration of the way the Dutch welfare state functions, various efforts have been made during the last two decades to decentralize programs and provisions from the national level to the provinces and municipalities. The present situation in education, health care, and social welfare is discussed here. We consider this process of decentralization to be important for our subject because of its influence on the allocation of facilities. In general, decentralization supposedly leads to a higher degree of variation. When decision-making is transferred from the one national level to more than 700 municipalities comprising the Netherlands, the degree of diversity will increase. Much, of course, depends on how much of real power is transferred.

The starting point is a relatively highly centralized state. This can best be demonstrated by the financial position of Dutch municipalities. In terms of percentage of GNP, the revenues of local authorities in the Netherlands are not particularly low: 12 percent in 1987, compared to five percent in Germany, 10 percent in the UK, and 28 percent in Denmark (Council of Europe 1990). However, in terms of the composition of the revenues, a large part of the municipal income is derived from earmarked transfers from the national government to the local authorities.

Efforts at decentralization have become more serious and more insistent over the last 15 years. They were targeted against this extreme degree of centralization. Some authors maintain that even with such financial (and other) central control, the degree of autonomy of individual municipalities should not be underestimated (Toonen 1987). The central government sought to reallocate responsibilities and jurisdictions within the system of public administration between levels of government. It was the general skepticism regarding the functioning of the heavy and cumbersome central bureaucracy, its real or alleged inefficiency, that motivated the decentralization movement. This discussion was inspired by the international climate of opinion that changed in this direction during the 1970s and by the he need to cut expenditure. The idea of increasing the reponsibilities of the province or municipality for their own sake, however, never played an important role. There was no strong 'new municipality' ideology as a corollary to the 'new federalism' in the US. Still less was this expansion of authority a right wrest by the provincial and municipal authorities from the national government. However, it should be added that traditionally the municipalities, and more recently also the provinces, have well-established collective lobbies in The Hague that look after their interests.

The government cabinet that came into office in 1989 made 'social renovation' one of the keystones of its political program. The principal aim of 'social renovation' at the local level was to combat various kinds of social deprivation: in housing, employment (or rather unemployment), ethnic discrimination, education, etc. It resulted in a number of neighborhood programs on the one hand and target-group programs on the other hand (SCP 1991b). Social renovation was to be accomplished through a further transfer of jurisdictions from the national to the municipal level. The financial transfers on behalf of some 25 programs are merged into one undivided whole, which can be used by the municipal authority according to its own political and administrative priorities. The amount thus available was Dfl. 1,552 million in 1990 and will reach 1,735 million in 1994 (from 3% to 3.5% of total municipal expenses). This is clearly one more step on the road to further decentralization. Ideas on much bolder steps toward financial decentralization are circulating.

The situation with respect to decentralization in the three policy sectors discussed here is far from uniform. Educational policy is still very much concentrated at the national level, where the department has to deal with the organized representatives of private schools (most of them denominational) and the municipalities representing the state schools. This is the result of a political compromise after a fierce battle in 1917. It was then written in the constitution that private and public schools would be financed by public funds on an equal footing. Since then a jealously guarded intricate system of rules has developed. It is managed at the national level by the ministry and a number of organizations representing the various interests.

There is hardly any role for the province. The municipality plays in fact two roles. It is first and foremost responsible for the public (state) schools (the state sector covers about a third of compulsory education nationwide) to direct and implement policy. In the second place, the municipality is also responsible for all education within its territory. The second responsibility, though, is mainly of a derivative and shared nature. As a result, the activities and the influence of local authorities in the field of education are rather restricted (WRR 1990). No political consensus to bring about changes in this respect can be discerned. Recent proposals are primarily aimed at deregulation. They try to dismantle the enormous web of rules and regulations that tie the ministry to schools and school boards. A transfer of some elements of authority to the school level is being proposed, mostly accompanied by an increase in school size.

The other public service sectors were traditionally organized according to rules that were not too different from those in education. But there were no constitutional guarantees, and they developed in different directions. In the future, the allocation of health and care facilities will be influenced by a new system, which is now in preparation and will be implemented in the 1990s. The system is designed to bring market forces into play. It purports to establish a garanteed package of health and care services for all and a supplementary insurance on a voluntary basis. The insurers (financiers) and the suppliers of services (hospitals, centers for the elderly, etc.) are put in a bargaining position towards each other. The hope is that competition can thus play a role. The first signs, though, indicate that processes of monopolization on a regional basis are taking place. The new system does not assign a significant role to provincial and local authorities.

The present system functions under strict central rules, the provinces being charged with the planning of the provisions. It is assumed that these procedures do not allow for much variation throughout the country. The new system will most likely foster regional and local variation as a consequence of regionally or locally conducted bargaining processes.

Arguably, the most important group of provisions to be decentralized from the national to the local level is connected with social welfare. The 21 provisions covered by the program range from public libraries to youth services, child care centers and immigrant welfare services. Under the 'Welfare Act', implemented in 1987, the responsibility for these provisions is assigned to the local authorities, the financing being provided by the general fund (without earmarking).

An extensive evaluation was made of the process and outcomes of this decentralization for the years 1980 - 1989 (SCP 1991a; SCP 1991b). The evaluation is of a continuous nature. So far the following main conclusions have been drawn.

In the first place the principal fear regarding decentralization, namely that municipalities will refrain from financing welfare provisions and give priority to more 'respectable' political objectives ('lampposts instead of social workers', as the saying goes), is unjustified. On the contrary, it was found that municipalities tended to compensate the cuts that the central government imposed in the field of social welfare. It is uncertain, however, whether or to what degree such supplementary financing can be continued in the future. There is some doubt as to the municipalities' financial capability to do so.

In the second place there were major differences in public expenditure per capita for welfare. For the municipalities in this study, amounts ranged from Dfl. 204 to Dfl. 45 per annum.

Thirdly, larger municipalities spent more on welfare (in terms of guilders per capita) than smaller ones. Randstad municipalities did not spend any differently than others, if size is taken into account. There was no correlation between spending and position in the political spectrum from right to left.

In the fourth place, when cuts were indeed imposed by the municipal authorities within the social welfare sector, they tended to spare the more established provisions. Thus, expenses for public libraries remained on a high level and even increased, despite declining contributions from the central government. Though lampposts did not beat social workers in the budgetary contest, books apparently did.

Finally, the municipalities, as a rule, were concerned with a careful and balanced allocation of provisions over their territories. Equity considerations, as prompted by accessibility issues, were clearly part of the municipal policy process.

In general we may conclude that the municipalities operated in a responsible manner. They endeavored to make their own mark on welfare provisions inside their territories and seem to be reasonably successful in doing so. Several moves towards reorganization, fusion, etc. were made.

Social welfare, health care, and even education are all part of the welfare state layer of public services. Older services are currently also the object of attempts at renewal. The police forms a late outgrowth of the armed personnel that provided internal and external security in the initial stages of development of the European states. Views on the police, for a long time wavering between a social service institution and an effective force against disorder and crime, have resulted in a drawn-out process of reorganizations.

In the police forces of the larger cities there has been from the 1970s onwards, a conscious effort at deconcentration, decentralization, and despecialization. The aim has been to transform one homogeneous force - with a number of technical branches at the central level - into a set of neighborhood police teams. This puts the social service point of view into practice, stressing an active and preventive approach to police work. On the other hand, serious crime has increased. This has led to a large-scale reorganization, where one police corps soon will cover a whole city region and new branches of specialists have been formed, particularly for fighting serious crime. In this reorganization the repressive task of police work has been strengthened. Yet from the point of efficiency, as measured in the study cited above, a new police organization of this size seems hardly the best solution. It indicates optimal efficiency at far lower manpower levels (SCP 1989).

In the big cities of the Randstad, where crime levels are much higher than elsewhere, these contradictory policies have been promoted with great vigor. In addition, due to manpower shortages and rising crime, private security agencies have sprung up in parts of these same cities. The police provides an interesting example of cross-pressures on institutional renewal that give rise to hybrid solutions.

We started this chapter by pointing out that the first large-scale territorial states in Europe initially forced their services upon their citizens. Citizens then learned to use at least some of these services for their own benefit. The bureaucratization of new service provisions after World War II buried client preferences under a mountain of rules and regulations. Efforts are now underway to deregulate, privatize, and decentralize. Hopefully this will restore a more balanced relation between freedom of choice and equity considerations, and at the same time result in greater efficiency and efficacy. The simultaneous realization of all these requirements is obviously elusive.

10.3   A special position for the Randstad?

The Dutch welfare state has recently been critically reassessed from various angles. In this section we focus on the impact these changes will eventually have on the Randstad. For background, we first draw a thumbnail sketch of the Randstad's features that will probably be most relevant in that respect.

Many foreign firms and international institutions located in the Netherlands are found in the Randstad (cf. Chapter 5). As a consequence a number of places in the Randstad have large numbers of highly skilled foreigners in their midst, adding to the modest vertical differentiation that exists. The Randstad has in recent decades also been the major destination of various waves of immigrants of more limited means. A large part of this immigrant population was employed in traditional industrial sectors that have been severely hit by the economic crisis around 1980. Together with the Dutch labor force formerly employed in those sectors, they are the core of the population of permanently unemployed living in the major Dutch cities. The large share of subsidized housing in the total housing market has prevented sharp segregation according to ethnic origin or class. The social security system has perhaps produced a somewhat dependent, passive, and quiescent attitude among large numbers of these people. Nonetheless, it has prevented the emergence of a sharply distinctive, despondent 'underclass'. A transformation of initially temporary immigrant populations into permanent social minorities is possible, but by no means certain. Still, the high number of permanently unemployed, to some extent overlapping with immigrant populations who are largely confined to low-skilled jobs, if there are any, generates extra vertical differentiation and horizontal segmentation of the population in Randstad cities compared to most urban places elsewhere in the country.

It should be added that, unlike the world cities the Randstad consists of a number of distinctive urban places that are fairly small and not too severely polarized, at the same time maintaining a culturally very diverse population (Soja 1991). Pronounced cultural diversity and relatively steep stratification in Dutch terms result in a modest degree of spatial segregation. This is particularly evident in comparison to many European and American metropoles. Diversity and stratification will affect the system of public services in the Randstad.

The Randstad is, of course, the most thoroughly urbanized part of the country. The dynamics of modern urbanization apply there more than elsewhere. In many newly built neighborhoods the pattern of services often fluctuates considerably through time. This happens when young cohorts move into newly built neighborhoods and tend to stay there for the rest of their lives, either because they are trapped or because they lack positive incentives to leave. This has happened in and immediately around the Randstad, where largely uncontrolled suburbanization occurred during the 1960s and early 1970s and more concentrated expansion in designated growth centers occurred in the 1970s and early 1980s (cf. Chapter 4).

In those circumstances child care centers are put into place as the new inhabitants move in. In the course of time, they have to be converted into recreation centers for teenagers, and are finally refurbished to serve their first early retired clients. This is accompanied by changes in the character of health care provision at the neighborhood level and in the equipment of public spaces (playgrounds and the like vs esthetically pleasing public parks). In the case of attractive older suburbs dating from the early decades of the century, this process may start all over again as an older generation dies and a new generation moves in. Generally changes become less sharp as the transfers are less sharply concentrated in time. In particular the growth centers described elsewhere in this volume do need to manage this problem on a major scale.

Of the three fields considered, education in the Randstad shows a number of distinctive features in terms of service provision, despite its strong central regulation. 'Basic schools' (the recent mergers of kindergartens and primary schools) are meticulously regulated from the national level. This regulation is of a corporatist nature with interest groups and the minister taking part in complicated negotiations. As compromises are made at the national level, these hardly make sense in a local or regional context.

As the relevant age cohorts dramatically dwindled, particularly during the 1970s, school size has been allowed to decrease. This was particularly important where it had already been small (in the less densely populated countryside of the North in particular) but also where selective outmigration aggravated the impact of lower birth rates (in inner city areas that lost most of their school-going population in the last few decades, and in some areas partly compensated by incoming migrant families). In densely settled areas, even those with a large influx of families with children of school age such as major parts of Randstad, school size has hardly been maintained or has grown to reflect population patterns. This is the result of the competition between private (mostly denominational of various kinds) and state school systems, the minimal requirements to start a new school, and the free school choice parents enjoy.

Secularization increased strongly during the 1960s and 1970s but probably not in the 1980s. One of the main growth areas of secular lifestyles are the suburbanizing parts of the Randstad. There, the stated principles of schools hardly coincide with denominational backgrounds of the population anymore. The strong identity of the schools has very often subsided, despite their official allegiance to one sector of the system or another. Parents of all persuasions send their children to schools of differing original backgrounds. Major parts of the Randstad are among the regions with the least correspondence between shares of denominational preferences in the population and shares in the traditionally accompanying types of schools (Knippenberg & Dekwaasteniet 1987).

A dense pattern of schools and free choice allow for easier black/white segregation at school level in city areas with a significant proportion of recent immigrants. The designation 'black' is in fact erroneous as a large part of the children is of Turkish or Moroccan origin. Most of the neighborhoods with segregated schools are in the Randstad. This has become a much debated problem in educational policy (Van Breenen & Dijkstra 1989, Migrantenstudies 1990, Clark & Dieleman 1990). As we pointed out above, social housing and the distribution system have prevented sharp segregation of immigrant communities in cities. At the same time the school system tends to encourage such division. In addition the rules allow new state-financed schools to be established by immigrant communities themselves, and a small number of these schools have appeared.

Non-compulsory education is in a process of cautious deregulation. Tertiary education is still concentrated in the Randstad. Particularly Amsterdam and Utrecht have a very large student population (proportionately those in the small towns of Delft and Leiden are even larger). These concentrations contribute to the highly visible and dominant youth culture in the inner parts of these cities.

A major part of our second field, that of social welfare services, has recently been decentralized to a very large extent. As we mentioned, the initial experience suggests higher budgets in larger municipalities but no systematic Randstad effect. The same applies to comparable funds to be transferred under the new program of 'social renovation'. In the selection of initial target municipalities, as well as in the negotiations with these local authorities, there is a big-city bias but no specific Randstad effect. It should be added that some of the early examples of such policies originate in big cities. In the case of social renovation the municipality of Rotterdam clearly played an initiating role (Terhorst & Drontmann 1991).

Market elements will be allowed in health care provisions in the near future. As a consequence supply will follow demand more quickly and in a more finely tuned fashion. The culturally diverse population of the Randstad will have more varying needs. Wealthier people may demand more specialist care and immigrant communities at various positions in the social hierarchy may require somewhat different health services. Another case in point where specific population concentrations do produce specific challenges to the health care system is the problem of AIDS. As homosexual males have a much higher risk of infection and Amsterdam has a sizable homosexual community, about 25 percent of all Dutch AIDS cases are found in and around the inner city, mainly among the patients of four general practitioners (Haarlems Dagblad 8 May 1991).

There are already more medical specialists in the Randstad than elsewhere (cf. Chapter 9). And the top-ranking facilities concentrated in the university hospitals are to a large extent found there as well. This pattern will continue and probably even become more pronounced. This is due to a reinforcing set of factors, which will become more vigorous with privatization. Top facilities are located in this area, and population profiles induce extra demand. At the same time the availability fosters demand, as general practitioners refer their patients more frequently to specialists where facilities are available. This has recently been illustrated by the differential frequency of use of temporary rest homes in case of psychic complaints; use is dependent on the availability of the facility. In this case it was clear from circumstantial evidence that the establishment of the facilities was quite independent of demand factors (Knippenberg & Ruisendaal 1990). Even before the health insurance system introduced more market elements, it was found that Randstad companies have more liberal policies. These pertain to special care arrangements that enable patients to stay home and not be institutionalized too early (SCP 1990b). Consequently, these insurers have a more flexible approach to the imminent changes in the health care system.

In the longer term, the Randstad's health care facilities may be confronted with sizable deviations from their population predictions. In other highly developed societies considerable outflows of retired people from the major cities towards more convenient surroundings have occurred. In the US such migration processes have been observed at least since the 1950s. They have resulted in resort towns along the sunny beaches, whose economies thrive on older people (Longino & MacNeal 1991, Wiseman & Roseman 1979). They have tended to relocate to ethnically more or less homogeneous neighborhoods, often planned for the purpose, and have stayed there permanently, although many have kept one foot in their former place of residence. For that reason, Florida has become one of the major concentrations of Jews in the US, as a split-off from Jewish concentrations in and around New York (Sheskin 1991). The quintessential New York City author I.B. Singer died in a Miami hospital in 1991. Comparable though not quite identical experiences have been reported with respect to Paris (Cribier 1990).

For Dutch pensioners the province of Zeeland has recently also become a preferred location for retirement. In fact, a recent paper describes Zeeland as a Dutch Florida (Thissen & Mayling Wong 1990). That is an obvious exaggeration, if only for climatic reasons. It can do no harm to broaden the perspective. Europe is becoming more and more a single economic and political space. More than all other Europeans, Dutch tourists have for decades explored the treasures of foreign places in such numbers that parts of the Spanish coast have large numbers of Dutch commercial services (SCP 1990b). It is conceivable that the trickle of wealthy pensioners along the Mediterranean coast in France and Spain and in Portugal, plus the numerous trips made by old-age pensioners of modest means to Spain in the winter to populate the empty hotel rooms and apartment complexes (Verhey & Van Westerloo 1984) will grow into a wave of Dutch third-age migration to southern coasts. Such migration waves may hit various destinations along the Mediterranean, depending on political stability, tax regulations, price levels, and the like. But first-chance encounters are also important, as the American example has demonstrated (Sheskin 1991, Longino & MacNeal 1991).

Depending on numbers and concentrations, all this may well have substantial consequences for private service patterns, and also for public services in the field of health care and social welfare. Will Dutch insurance companies bargain with foreign medical institutions about provisions for these migrant populations? At what level of concentration would Dutch service institutions be tempted to relocate among retired compatriots? These are questions that can not yet be answered. Their potential importance calls for research efforts in this direction.

10.4   Final comments

The Randstad is, in some respects, different from the rest of the country, but only slightly so. Recent research (Castenmiller & Knol 1989) indicates that people in larger as well as smaller urban places within the Randstad use cultural services, public as well as private ones, in larger numbers and more frequently than people elsewhere (cf. Chapter 9 of this book). This applies to membership of public libraries, visits to the theater, and reading national newspapers. Many of the initial differences between areas are due to differing composition of populations. Education and income (cultural and economic capital in Bourdieu's terms) and also age account for a large part of the variation. Many places in the Randstad also offer more facilities. This again explains part of the variation. But after controlling for all these features, there still remains an extra Randstad effect. The Randstad functions to some extent as a distinctive cultural milieu. This might serve as a more general background factor for the interpretation of differences in the functioning of public services.

Interestingly enough, however, the different orientation towards services is not accompanied by similar opinions on all counts. Opinions with respect to cultural innovations, political activism, and self-identification as modern/traditional differ primarily between larger and smaller, or more and less urban places. Here the Randstad is more often split in its component urban and suburban parts. If any distinction in two milieus can be made, it is an urban versus a surrounding suburban and rural milieu, but parts of each are differently colored by varying religious backgrounds. It should be stressed that the differences in opinions are not large and that the context as operationalized does not seem to be very important (Castenmiller & Knol 1989).

Both cultural participation and some of the opinions mentioned can be described as levels of modernization. There is hardly any question that these levels slope gently downward from the major cities in the Randstad, but they may sometimes first pass the nearby suburban places and in other instances the other nodes in the national urban network. The future is uncertain, but on past evidence it seems that differences in values and orientations are pretty stable, whereas levels of modernized behavior tend to become similar. If stated migration intentions are taken seriously, differences might even level out, more than they already are according to the authors of this study. However, they may have overlooked selectivity as to activities and opinions in the event of migration.

Comparative studies in a number of West European countries indicate similarities in values and orientation (though by no means identical scores) and in their determining factors (SCP 1990b). In that sense European unity has largely been achieved, at least for this part of the continent. The international differences that remain suggest a Dutch position near Denmark and West Germany and somewhat at a distance from more Southern European countries. In contrast, the use and impact of service provision in these countries can hardly be compared so far. One example is education (SCP 1990b). This reflects the large part that national history has played in shaping these systems. However they have been designed or have evolved, they all assist in forming national populations that are by and large modernized in the same fashion, be it at slightly different levels and with minor variations.

The Netherlands appears to be a country where post-materialist values are comparatively widely accepted (SCP 1990b). It is a hypothetical question in what way this relates to the peculiarly Dutch model of public service provision. We can only conjecture whether there is a relation and what the driving factor may be. Whatever differences there may have been in these services so far, they may well diminish a great deal with further European integration. Even for those policy areas that for the time being remain largely outside the scope of the European integration process, the increasingly frequent contacts between policy-makers induce similarities of outlook that leave traces in the policy-making processes of the different countries.

References

Breenen, K. van & H. Dijkstra (1989), De Amsterdamse basisschool, een buurtschool?: een verkennend onderzoek naar de ruimtelijke segregatie van Amsterdamse basisschoolleerlingen langs etnische scheidslijnen. (doctoraalscriptie) Amsterdam:

Faculteit Ruimtelijke Wetenschappen, Instituut voor Sociale Geografie, Universiteit van Amsterdam.

Castenmiller, P. & F. Knol (1989), Convergentie of divergentie. Sociale en culturele ontwikkelingen in stedelijke en landelijke gebieden. Cahier 72. Rijswijk: SCP.

Clark, W.A.V. & F.M. Dieleman (1990), 'Zwarte' en 'witte' scholen in Nederland gezien vanuit de Amerikaanse ervaringen. Geografisch Tijdschrift 24, pp. 139-147.

Cribier, F. (1990), Two generations of retired Parisians and their town. In: L. Deben, W. Heinemeyer & D. van der Vaart (eds), Residential Differentiation, pp. 87-106. Amsterdam: CGO.

Council of Europe (1990), Types of Financial Control by Central or Regional Government over Local Government. Strassbourg: Council of Europe.

Giddens, A. (1987), The Nation-State and Violence. Volume Two of A Contemporary Critique of Historical Materialism. Berkeley: University of California Press.

Gedeputeerde Staten van Zuid-Holland (1988), Planningsronde Algemene Ziekenhuizen. 's Gravenhage.

Haarlems Dagblad, 8-5-1991, 'Aids heeft ons allemaal overvallen'.

Knippenberg, H. & M. Dekwaasteniet (1987), De nieuwe schoolstrijd in geografisch perspectief: de spreiding van openbaar en bijzonder onderwijs 1973-1984. In: H.H. van der Wusten (ed), Postmoderne aardrijkskunde, pp. 150-168. Muiderberg: Coutinho.

Knippenberg, H. & T. Ruisendaal (1990), Het gebruik van herstellingsoorden en de Wet van Jarvis. Tijdschrift voor Sociale Gezondheidszorg. Gezondheid & Samenleving 68, pp. 173-178.

Laslett, P. (1989), A Fresh Map of Life. The Emergence of the Third Age. London: Weidenfeld & Nicolson.

Leering, T. & W. Relou (1990), Verkenning van de veroudering in Nederland. Bevolkingsprognoses ten behoeve van de planning van voorzieningen voor ouderen. Delft: INRO-TNO.

Longino, Ch. & R.B. MacNeal. (1991), The elderly population of South Florida. In: Th. D. Boswell (ed), South Florida: The Winds of Change, pp. 181-194. Miami: Association of American Geographers.

Marshall, T.H. (1973), Class, Citizenship and Social Development. Westport: Greenwood Press.

Migrantenstudies 1990, 2, Special issue on white-black schools.

Sheskin, I.M. (1991), The Jews of South Florida. In: Th. D. Boswell (ed), South Florida: The Winds of Change, pp. 163-180. Miami: Association of American Geographers.

Soja, E.W. (1991), The Stimulus of a Little Confusion. A Contemporary Comparison of Amsterdam and Los Angeles. Amsterdam: CGO.

Terhorst, P. & I. Drontmann (1991), Sociale vernieuwing: een schijnbeweging. Amsterdam: CGO.

Thissen, F. & Mayling Wong (1990), Ageing and residential differentiation in the Netherlands. In: L. Deben, W. Heinemeijer & D. van der Vaart (eds), Residential Differentiation, pp. 164-185. Amsterdam: CGO.

Toonen Th.A.J. (1987), Denken over binnenlands bestuur; theorieën van de gede-centraliseerde eenheidsstaat bestuurskundig beschouwd. 's-Gravenhage: VUGA.

SCP (Sociaal en Cultureel Planbureau) (1984), Trendrapport kwartaire sector 1983-1990. Rijswijk: SCP.

SCP (Sociaal en Cultureel Planbureau) (1989), Doelmatig dienstverlenen. Rijswijk: SCP.

SCP (Sociaal en Cultureel Planbureau) (1990a), School en schaal. Rijswijk: SCP.

SCP (Sociaal en Cultureel Planbureau) (1990b), Sociaal en Cultureel Rapport. Rijswijk: SCP.

SCP (Sociaal en Cultureel Planbureau) (1991a), Rapportage welzijnswerk, deel 2. Rijswijk: SCP.

SCP (Sociaal en Cultureel Planbureau) (1991b), Sociale en culturele verkenningen 1991. Rijswijk: SCP.

UNESCO (1988), Statistical Yearbook 1988. Leuven: UNESCO.

Verhey, E. & G. van Westerloo (1984), De wintertrek. Ouderen op overwintering in Benidorm. In: E. Verhey & G. van Westerloo, Ons soortmensen. Portret van de ruggegraat van Nederland, pp. 128-157. Amsterdam: Raamgracht.

Wiseman, R.F. & C.C. Roseman (1979), A typology of elderly migration based on the decision-making process. Economic Geography 55, pp. 324-337.

WRR (Wetenschappelijke Raad voor het Regeringsbeleid) (1990), Van de stad en de rand. 's-Gravenhage: SDU-Uitgeverij.

Dr. A. Nauta
Scientific Council for Government Policy
P.O. Box 20004
2500 EA The Hague
The Netherlands

Prof.dr. H. van der Wusten
Faculty of Environmental Sciences
University of Amsterdam
Nieuwe Prinsengracht 130
1018 VZ Amsterdam
The Netherlands

11.   THE RESTRUCTURING AND GROWTH OF THE RANDSTAD CITIES: CURRENT POLICY ISSUES

A. Kreukels

11.1   Introduction

This chapter concentrates on central policy themes relating to the development and restructuring of the Randstad. The period ahead and the relevant developments in policy form the basis for this exploratory enquiry. This is all set against an international background.

Many of the characteristic features of policy and the dynamics of development can only be understood against the specific Dutch historical background. This applies particularly to physical planning within the broader framework of Dutch societal and administrative organization. For this reason, the second section provides an overview of this specifically Dutch institutional context.

The third and main section gives an overview and more detailed interpretation of the new ideas, proposals and policies with respect to the Randstad. It focuses on the Fourth National Physical Planning Report (1988/1990) as the central source of the issues and arguments involved.

In a fourth and concluding section these developments are subsequently judged from a wider institutional perspective than that of physical planning. The reason for this is that the developments in the Randstad - also in spatial terms - are largely determined by other lines of policy besides physical planning and also by various developments beyond the direct influence of the policy concerned. It is in this assessment of current developments and policy that international comparisons are made.

11.2   The traditional content and context of the Dutch policy system, with particular regard to urban planning

Taking the long history of the Netherlands as the point of departure, it would appear that this country has had a reputation in the areas of urban development and spatial planning since the early days. The involvement of Dutch military engineers in the construction of urban fortifications and the broader urban planning developments in the Scandinavian countries are a striking example of this.

F. M. Dieleman and S. Musterd (eds.), The Randstad: A Research and Policy Laboratory, 237–262.
© 1992 *Kluwer Academic Publishers. Printed in the Netherlands.*

Figure 11.1   The fortified city of Naarden (Source: KLM Aerocarto N.V.)

With his pioneering work in this field, recorded in 'Van de ordeningh der steden', Simon Stevin was a prominent exponent of this influence in seventeenth century Europe (Konvitz 1978). The Dutch city became celebrated. Its characteristic administrative system, partly related to control of the water situation, was one way in which the country had clearly distinguished itself as early as the seventeenth century (Mumford 1970; De Vries 1978; Schama 1987).

In the nineteenth century this tradition received new impetus. The Netherlands was gradually being forged into a tight national unity, in connection with industrialization and modernization of its infrastructure. Attention for the environment - land use, water management, land reclamation, but also urban planning - received considerable stimulation and gained international recognition (Van der Woud 1987).

   The Netherlands subsequently went on to play a dominant role in the area of town

Figure 11.2   The Rietveld Schröder House in Utrecht, circa 1925; famous example of Dutch architecture of the Stijl Group (Source: Central Museum Utrecht)

and country planning on an international scale during the inter-war period (1918-1940). With respect to architecture, this was via the Amsterdam School; for architecture and town and country planning, the 'Nieuwe Bouwen' group (De Wit 1983; Rebel 1983). Van Eesteren was chairman of the 'Congrès Internationaux d'Architecture Moderne' (CIAM), which introduced the division of functions as a standard element in 'modern' urban planning. During this period Dutch architects and planners were extremely influential on the international circuit, with its new movements and art geared towards a modern society, centered largely in England, France, and Germany. 'De Stijl' group, with Mondriaan, Van Doesberg and Rietveld as its most notable exponents, is a striking example of this broader platform (Friedman 1988).

  Following the Second World War, the Netherlands again adopted a high profile internationally. Investments in national physical planning, the draining of land and its subsequent use, and particularly the development of the Randstad (with its four important urban centers: Amsterdam, Rotterdam, the Hague and Utrecht) now attracted

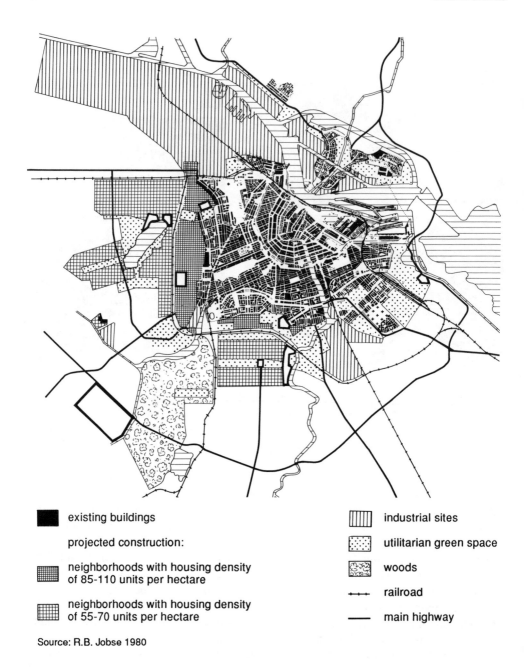

	existing buildings		industrial sites
	projected construction:		utilitarian green space
	neighborhoods with housing density of 85-110 units per hectare		woods
	neighborhoods with housing density of 55-70 units per hectare		railroad
			main highway

Source: R.B. Jobse 1980

Figure 11.3   The Amsterdam Extension Scheme of 1934

Figure 11.4   Polder landscape in the municipality of Hazerswoude in the Green Heart; an example of the Dutch tradition of land reclamation in which farmers and landowners themselves played an important role (Source: KLM Aerocarto N.V.)

most attention and played the leading role in international exchanges (Burke 1966).

In order to characterize the policy associated with this typically Dutch form of urban planning, from the very early period of the Republic of the United Netherlands, the following elements are of significance:

1) The care for the physical environment is remarkable. Remembering the compact setting of the country and the rather unique condition of its soil and water, this has manifested itself throughout the country's history in the Dutch societal and administrative framework, with its wide variety of specialisms within the dimensions of spatial management.

2) This involvement was initially centered on the local, and in certain cases regional, level (for instance on groups of farmers and landowners directly related to each

particular urban or rural area). This form of decentralized self-regulation only gradually spread to the provincial and national level during the nineteenth century. In accordance, the national and provincial authorities took on an increasingly important role.
3) From the end of the Second World War onwards the Netherlands distinguished itself more and more from other West European countries (in particular Great Britain, France, and West Germany) with respect to physical planning, not only in its characteristic tradition, but also in the way planning at the national and provincial level became so pronounced (exceptional when viewed internationally). National efforts aimed at controling the urbanization process in general, and of the Randstad in particular, and regarding such important matters as land use in rural areas and land reclamation, are quite remarkable (and just as exceptional from an international perspective). The impact of national government on physical planning is certainly impressive. The government involvement, particularly following the Second World War, provides a sturdy national framework, radiating its effects to the provincial and regional levels.

This profile of physical planning becomes clear when one looks at the Netherlands in general, or the Randstad in particular.

Societal involvement, professionalization, government interference, and a strong emphasis on the national and provincial policy efforts in the post-war period - all of these factors appear to distinguish the Netherlands from other countries when it comes to physical planning.

However, this initial characterization of spatial policy conceals a more general institutional pattern. This broader setting of societal and administrative arrangements makes it easier to understand the nature of Dutch physical planning. One can speak of a typical Dutch welfare state. In the second half of the nineteenth century - during the genesis of the modern state - there was a need to accommodate the pronounced variety of relatively insular regional and religious cultures in a small country. This required, more than ever before, a common human and physical infrastructure. This accommodation gradually became (not forgetting a climax following the Second World War) closely tied up with the denominations (the so called pacification system) and subsequently the well-organized interest groups, related to specific policy fields. At the core of this representation system of interests in the various policy fields were the strong national-level coalitions between the central units of the interest groups concerned and their counterparts within national government. These coalitions were also connected to the national political parties. This system and representation and its core coalitions can be seen as the basis of the pronounced Dutch national centralized and bureaucratic - administrative framework. This is decisive when it comes to the pronounced national physical planning.

This general societal and administrative framework is what distinguishes the Netherlands from other Western countries, even those in which the welfare state is well developed. The unique character of this Dutch administrative and policy set-up is recorded in international political science literature (Lijphart 1968, 1984).

The heyday of this Dutch welfare state can be traced to the seventies. In this period the motor behind an increasingly strong and centralized government was the ambition to strengthen the coordination and integration of policy from a national perspective. It was physical planning in particular, together with social and economic planning, that played a central role here. The seventies - a period of climax for the welfare state, with a focus on centralized arrangements in the form of national plans and programs - represented a golden age for physical planning. At that time physical planning was the most highly developed planning system and as such formed the natural center for planning and coordination in general.

However, the economic recession, the societal and political reaction to this 'central rule approach' system, and last but not least, the changes in the political parties and their electorate finally had an impact in the Netherlands, albeit more gradually than in many other countries. This resulted, in the seventies, first in an attack on the 'hypertrophy' of national government policy-making and planning, and subsequently in a search for alternative structures in which market and sub-national administrative units became more important.

Since the eighties, this 'Dutch adaptation for the nineties' can be seen as an uninterrupted and ongoing effort to counter the highly bureaucratic and centralistic government interference, without a new equilibrium having been found. The value of the primary involvement of society itself, of market processes, and of the private sector is currently being discovered. The administrative overemphasis on national policy in relation to nationally organized interests is recognized as an obstacle to achieving greater dynamism and flexibility on various fronts and within various circles. This is expressed in pleas for more latitude for sub-national territoral (local and regional) and functional relationships.

Since the eighties, physical planning in the Netherlands, and especially investments and policy efforts regarding the Randstad, must be seen in light of these considerations. This is well illustrated by the policy development in the context of the Fourth National Physical Planning Report policy since 1988. It also highlights how a new equilibrium has in no way emerged and how the presence of the 'establishment' of the sixties and seventies is still strongly felt, even if the extreme forms of this state-dominated system have, in the meantime, been modified.

A detailed sketch of this recent development in policy, in the third section that follows, provides a suitable departure point for a discussion on the necessary modifications to policy and policy systems.

The fourth section returns to a discussion of the necessary policy adaptations based on present and future tasks, in light of developments in and the dynamism of the Randstad of the nineties. It will then become clear that relevant Dutch policy is, in the historical and international perspective, due for a change. This will involve a drastic alteration in the pattern that previously characterized the institutional framework of this country.

**11.3   The Fourth National Physical Planning Report as illustration of the recent
policy program with respect to physical planning in general and the Randstad
in particular**

Post-war national planning was dominated by a policy of dispersal, first of the general
population and then of business and industry. This policy evolved from the fifties
onwards. It gradually acquired the tenor of a sophisticated strategy for controlling the
growth of population and industry in the Randstad and other urbanized areas. The
main impetus behind this policy was the threat of congestion in the highly urbanized
western part of the country. It was complemented by the target of reinforcing regions
in other parts of the country whose growth and development had remained rather
stunted.

One can view this policy program, which really determined the picture prior to the
Fourth Report, as the Dutch version of the British policy of 'urban containment'. To
put it briefly, the same criticism can be made of this Dutch program as Hall et al.
made in their analysis of British urban containment. The pronounced tension between
the ambitions involved in this program on the one hand, and the diversity of forces
in society, the economic market, the real estate market, and those active in various
government sectors on the other, severely limited the success of this policy. This was
also largely related to the fact that the designers and directors of this policy failed
to fully recognize, or even totally overlooked, this tension. Ultimately, the real
determining factors in the new spatial pattern were such trends as the increasing mobility
and the dominant residential needs of those in a position to satisfy their preferences
with respect to housing and business location. As research has revealed, powerful Dutch
policy efforts via national planning policy left something to be desired, as was also
the case in the British planning system. In addition to the influence of social and
economic forces, the fact that the policy had long been thwarted by policy emanating
from other sectors with other objectives, in the field of public housing in particular,
also played an important role here (cf. Hall et al. 1973; Glasbergen & Simonis 1979).

This implies that, from the second half of the sixties onwards, a main current of
suburbanization continued to determine the picture, despite policy efforts to systematically channel this flow. The policy program in general as formulated in the First (1961),
Second (1966) and Third (1974 -1985) National Physical Planning Reports, was not
a success when measured against the stringent and detailed targets of 'urban containment' in these reports. From the seventies onwards, the cornerstone projects of growth
locations within this program; growth nuclei and growth cities (a Dutch version of
'new town' programs) were successful in the sense of accommodating both quickly
and systematically, by way of specific procedural conditions and strong financial support
to cover infrastructure at these locations. However, a more precise assessment must
conclude that there was a negative aspect to this controlled growth policy, as it resulted
in gradual erosion of the four main cities of the Randstad: Amsterdam, Rotterdam,
The Hague, and Utrecht. They became less diversified in terms of composition (these
four main cities had to sacrifice a large proportion of their upper- and middle-class

inhabitants, as well as young families) and their populations fell. This applies especially to the period from the mid-sixties to the mid-eighties.

Looking at the situation retrospectively, one can conclude that the national program of physical planning between the sixties and the eighties - as an example of controlled growth - failed to have a proportional effect, especially when one considers the intensity of national planning. In as far as it was successful in concentrating growth at selected locations within cities and in suburban settings, there was still a lack of awareness of the side effects of this form of controlled growth, especially with respect to the four main cities.

The conclusion on the disproportionality between the national program and its implementation supports the conclusion of the prominent German policy researcher Fritz W. Scharpf. His statement that the surplus value of, in this case, West German national physical planning decreases the more the restrictions of its effects in relation to other policy sectors and market processes are underestimated and granted insufficient latitude, rings true (Scharpf & Schnabel 1978).

In most international odes to Dutch (national) physical planning, and in considerations of the Randstad in particular, this reality behind the ideal picture of Dutch national physical planning is not, however, sufficiently recognized. That applies to general studies (e.g. Dutt & Costa 1985), but also to more specialized work (e.g. Hall 1977). There are exceptions; namely where a keen eye in case studies discovers, recognizes, and subsequently records these contradictions. In this connection reference must be made to the astute analysis of the 'Hoog Catharijne' project in Utrecht made by an American administrative lawyer, and a comparative study of development policy in relation to a university town in the Randstad (Leiden) and a British university town (Oxford) by an international research team (Lefcoe 1978; Thomas et al. 1983).

In the meantime, the main societal trends and housing policy (with a strong emphasis on public housing, particularly in cities) both continued to encourage the process of increasing and selective suburbanization in the Randstad and from the Randstad towards the directly surrounding area. This led to a decrease in the growth of the four major cities from the end of the sixties onwards; a pattern which only showed some sign of change in 1984. Not only the Randstad but the whole country gradually became urbanized. Within this system of urbanization the decisive elements are not only the Randstad with its four big cities (Amsterdam, Rotterdam, The Hague, and Utrecht) but increasingly a number of strong middle- sized towns scattered across the country, such as Eindhoven, Arnhem/Nijmegen, Enschede/ Hengelo, Groningen, Breda, Zwolle, and Amersfoort with their own suburban areas. This controlled diffusion of urbanization on a nation-wide basis is characteristic for the Netherlands at the moment. It is a pattern that has brought the Netherlands (even if somewhat delayed) into line with other comparable Western countries, via the (sub)urbanization of not only people but also of economic and other functions.

Does the Fourth Report represent an answer to these recent developments? To what extent is it indicative for a restructuring of current policy in terms of a new planning

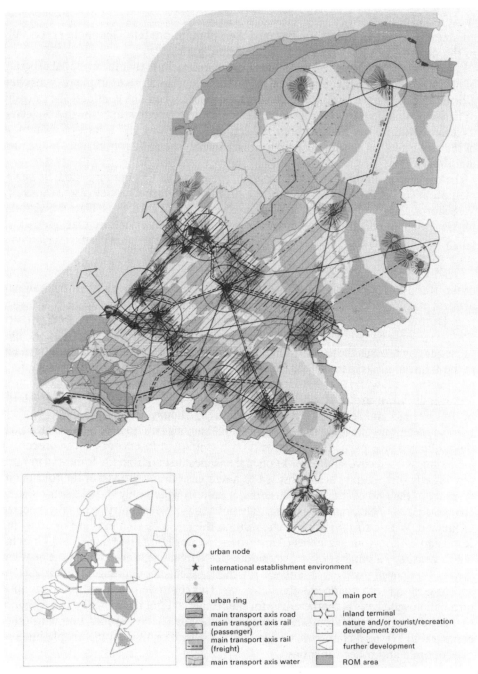

*Figure 11.5   Spatial development perspective; Fourth Report on Physical Planning, Extra
(Source: Ministry of Housing, Physical Planning and Environment 1991)*

and market paradigm? Which about-turn does the Fourth Report - in its initial 1988 version - reveal?

Much of the content of the Fourth Report can be seen as a continuation of what are considered to be the fixed features of national planning policy in the Netherlands from the fifties onwards: the development of a dispersed metropolitan environment with four major cities and associated metropolitan areas instead of a concentration in one capital city; securing and protecting the open middle area of the Randstad, know as the Green Heart.

Another characteristic feature is the coordination of spatial planning and the transport/traffic infrastructure via exchanges during the administrative preparation of both programs. In comparison with the Third Report, more attention is now paid, in the connection with the main transport and traffic infrastructure, to rail links (a system of interrelated national (intercities) and regional rail links, from which the urban areas of the Randstad in particular will benefit). However, one must not overlook the fact that investments in rail infrastructure over the previous 15 to 20 years had been insufficient. It is clearly a question of making up for lost time.

The Fourth Report is also characterized by an alignment of the physical planning program with the ambitions inherent in the building programs, particularly with regard to housing. In this way, the first version of the Fourth Report assumes that the Randstad as a whole needs to expand by some one million dwellings. This number was later reduced. In the latest version of the Fourth Report (December 1991) an estimate is made for each of the four metropolitan regions (Amsterdam, Rotterdam, The Hague, and Utrecht) for the construction of approximately 485,000 dwellings to house some 1-1.5 million people. There is still some difference of opinion regarding the effects on the Randstad's Green Heart. In the Autumn of 1991 the national government took the position that no more than 15,000 dwellings can be built in that area between 1995 and 2005. Then the three Randstad provinces set the maximum at 21,000.

It must be noted here that the decrease in the huge scale of building programs (the emphasis is shifting from new construction to management, maintenance, and reconstruction and from the social rented sector to (in a number of cases subsidized) building and housing by the private sector) means that the relations between public housing policy and planning - how important they might still be - now carry less weight than at the time of the Second or Third Report.

Also, the significance traditionally attached to a differentiated spatial design in the Reports, whereby the metropolitan area with a variety of residential and working environments forms the most important link, can also be traced in the Fourth Report. Here it is dealt with appropriately, on the basis of broad current demographic developments. However, little is specified at the more detailed level: the increase in suitable accommodation for the elderly, for those on a double income, for single persons etc.

In addition to all these examples of continuation, the Fourth Report (1988 - 1992) above all represents a shift to a program emphasizing urban regeneration and revitalization in particular. Although there was evidence of a strong and successful effort to improve housing and stimulate urban rehabilitation in the residential areas of the four big cities from the seventies onwards, with the Netherlands distinguishing itself internationally, little attention was paid to the major cities or metropolitan development beyond this. This not only applies to planning and housing policy. In the period 1965 - 1982/1983 there was limited evidence of administrative involvement regarding metropolitan infrastructure or the restructuring/expansion of the urban economy. This restricted general concern for the specifically urban also appears to characterize other policy sectors. In city councils as well as higher authorities, concern for specifically urban matters was also at a low ebb.

By way of contrast, the Fourth Report focuses on the main urban centers and the metropolitan outline of the Randstad. This means a reinvestment in urban areas and the related main infrastructure after a long period of neglect. As mentioned above, this meant that the four major Randstad cities had experienced decreasing expansion since the second half of the sixties, with suburbanization of the residential and then of the industrial sector determining the picture of spatial growth. The four big cities, the Randstad, and the infrastructure needed to support this metropolitan area, and Dutch urban areas in general, are for the first time given the attention they deserve.

The other side of the coin is the sudden withdrawal of the policy of dispersal, which emphasized the shift of residents and industry to regions beyond the Randstad and the concentration of growth in growth nuclei within existing towns and new growth towns in and around the Randstad. These latter projects, aimed particularly at managing the extreme top of the overspill within the Randstad and from the Randstad to other regions, have been terminated. The various expansion programs at the new urban and suburban 'growth' locations are even being phased out.

This reorientation is linked with, and is almost an extension of, the political and administrative pleas in favor of the compact city. The big cities themselves have been making such pleas since 1978. They had been battling, since the sixties, against a fall in population and consequently an even more serious weakening of their economic foundations. The offensive to combat these trends and the related policy of dispersal was started in Amsterdam. With a change in the City Executive in 1978, a program to strengthen the city with respect to population and facilities was launched. It was believed that this could be achieved by rerouting the overspill to the new growth locations and other suburban areas back to the city. The city could cope with more inhabitants by condensing and by building closer to the city edge. This was the so-called new policy of the 'compact city'.

The Fourth Report can be seen as a broader, national version of this policy program. There are, however, a number of important differences between this new national urbanization program and the original compact city programs devised by the four big cities themselves. There are also a number of additional aspects.

The first striking difference is that in the Fourth Report the economic aspect plays a more determining role than in the compact city program. In the early stages (1978 - 1983) of this latter approach the social aspect certainly tended to dominate. In this emphasis of the economic aspects the Fourth Report differs also from the previous national planning reports, where one sees little evidence of this economic aspect. In such a way, Dutch national policy is following (even if somewhat later) the process of urban revitalization as initiated in other Western countries since 1973 (The United States), France (1979), and Great Britain (1980) (Fosler & Berger 1982; Shalala & Vitullo-Martin 1989; Parkinson, Foley & Judd 1988; OECD 1987).

A second striking difference between the Fourth Report, on the one hand, and the previous National Physical Planning Reports and the original compact-city program drawn up by the city councils of the four big cities, on the other, is the emphasis on the involvement of the market and the plea for government withdrawal. Physical planning should be selective. Some things should be left alone. Certain aspects should be emphasized, also in relation to locations and areas that deserve top priority. Public-private partnerships are embraced as an expression of this shift from a government-dominated to a more combined approach involving state and market parties. The authorities should concentrate on providing impetus to the developments they support. However, action in the direction of this reorientation towards a government that does not organize and determine everything itself but seeks, with others, to realize the desired effect, is still hesitant, despite encouragement from many projects (Kreukels & Spit 1989). The change mentioned here is also expressed in the content and form of the Fourth Report itself. It is a report written in a canvassing style, supplemented by a great number of visual aids. The presentation of the Fourth Report was a professional affair, with press campaigns etc. It soon became a bestseller.

A third point of difference is the attention paid to what is referred to as spatial quality. Although this concept is never clearly defined, it forms the basis in the Fourth Report for the belief that the Randstad and the big cities are in need of extra reinforcement, particularly when it comes to quality, in order to be able to compete with metropolitan areas in other Western countries. As a consequence, the classification of urban areas in the Randstad and of the Randstad in relation to other urban areas and, finally, between the other urbanized areas themselves is being accentuated.

Attention should be paid to the quality of existing and new urban areas, making them attractive for living, working, and leisure. This is the criterion behind the emphasis on high-quality urban design in town and country planning. It also figures importantly in the pilot- and key projects by means of which the Fourth Report considers it stimulates urban revitalization. To name one example, the quality of urban public space, including parks and gardens, receives the necessary attention, after a long period of neglect. Jo Coenen's design for the Sphinx Ceramics site in the city of Maastricht is the most famous example in the urban planning sphere. Another significant difference is that prominent foreign designers and architects are receiving commissions for the first time since the war (Ricardo Bofill, Richard Meier, Robert Krier in The Hague; Alessandro Mendini, Daniel Libeskind in Groningen; Luigi Snozzi, Aldo Rossi in Maastricht). At the same time, Dutch architects, designers, and planners are again beginning to look towards examples from abroad (De Boer et al. 1990). The first really meaningful exchanges with other countries since the Second World War have only taken place from 1986 onwards, and with some reticence. Examples are the symposia: 'Intercities '87: Barcelona, Milan, Rotterdam' in Rotterdam in 1987 and 'City Center, Amsterdam, Brussels, Copenhagen, Milan, Frankfurt a/M, Hamburg, Munich' in Amsterdam in 1990.

This trend also extends into experiments in the landscape sphere: the Randstad parks and gardens program (a draft plan for recreation and landscaping in the Randstad as metropolitan unit) and for the 'Nederland-Waterland' design program, in which, in the same way, recreation on and alongside the water, landscape and utilitarian functions of the 'water' sector are programmed, taking the Randstad as focal point and working outwards (Blue Zone).

However, the Netherlands has not, as yet, managed to equal a number of other Western countries, for example the United States, France, Spain, Italy, and Germany, in the way in which design and qualitative landscaping has flourished, to set the criterion for top locations and exclusive residential and business environments. In this sense no famous Dutch program has emerged to compare with the period between the Wars when people like Van Eesteren, Rietveld, Van Doesburg, Duiker, Oud and so on were active.

With respect to infrastructure in the broadest sense - as a new element in spatial planning - (the fourth difference with regard to the previous National Reports) the program of the Fourth Report comes a lot closer to operationalization than those of previous National Reports. However, comparisons with other metropolitan areas abroad reveal the limitations of this section of the Fourth Report when taken in combination with the latest National Report on Traffic and Transport. The comparisons are most revealing in regard to telematics-logistics; a traffic-transport system, in which the various modes of transport are interrelated; the strategy for mainports (strategic air-and sea ports) and inland terminals (strategic transshipment, rail and road distribution centers).

In operational policy terms the only things that seem to be of any great importance are the two important 'mainports' in the Randstad: Amsterdam Airport (Schiphol), hoping to stand a good chance in the contest to become Western Europe's top intercontinental freight and passenger terminal; and the port of Rotterdam, hoping to continue as the world's number one port and Europe's most important transport center. In the case of these two mainports, the Fourth Report also fails to offer anything really substantial, let alone guarantees, in the form of references to policy priorities regarding conflicting interests (for example with respect to the economy and environment) or via basic financial agreements.

Within the national program for the urbanization of the Randstad (a fifth difference with regard to the previous national reports) the focus is now on Amsterdam (mainport) and Rotterdam (mainport), supplemented by The Hague as the third metropolitan center. Utrecht disappears from the picture as the fourth big city in the Randstad when it comes to national priorities for metropolitan reinforcement. The national government provides the necessary stimulus for urban regeneration, particularly economic, via pilot- and later key projects, for which extra funds are made available. The focus subsequently

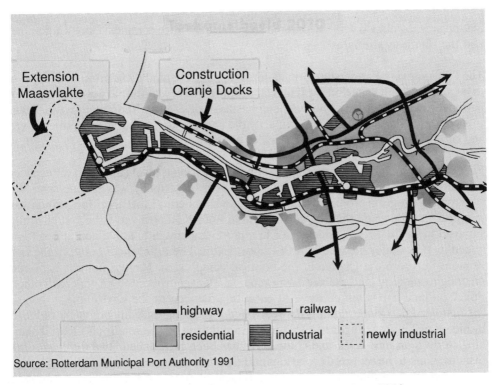

Figure 11.6 Future vision of a mainport; the port of Rotterdam 2010

radiates out from the Randstad to the surrounding areas (the so-called Central Netherlands Urban Ring). Finally, a number of cities, scattered throughout the country, have been granted special status: 'urban nodes'. This number was originally quite small but it ultimately reached eleven. The effect in the relevant political decision-making process can be compared to that in the sixties when, in the United States, cities had to be chosen to participate in the Model Cities program (Warren, Rose & Bergunder 1974).

In the Randstad the following projects in the four big cities are involved. Financing for the three largest cities differs from that for the fourth, Utrecht. It is a question of priorities. The projects are: in Rotterdam the 'Kop van Zuid' project (reinforcing the area on the southern bank that is separated from the rest by the Nieuwe Maas); in Amsterdam the 'IJ-oever' plan, another example of a waterfront plan, whereby the capital city gains access to an extra location for expansion right next to the city center where the opportunities to expand and restructure were considered limited due to the historic character of the ring of canals; in The Hague the plans involving a wide area around Central Station; in Utrecht the City Plan, the restructuring of the Central

Station area, combined with the covered shopping and office complex 'Hoog-Catharijne' and the 'Jaarbeurscomplex'.

The Public-Private Partnership formula forms the ideal behind these projects. It appears to be an important criterion for financial support from the national government. The national government does, however, emphasize its desire to withdraw from the scene. In its opinion, these projects are primarily the concern of the major cities themselves and of the parties involved with the cities at that level.

First of all, this new policy on urbanization at the national level (the main differences compared with previous policies have now been described) was in line with the government program produced by the Christian Democrat/Liberal cabinet, which was in power in 1988 when the first version of the Fourth Report was issued. It basically survived in its final form, which the Christian Democrat/Social Democrat coalition issued in 1990 under the title Fourth Report Extra. The differences between the two versions illustrate the change in the political complexion. More emphasis is placed on bringing physical land use and environmental management into line with each other. Policy on land use is aimed more at curtailing damage to the environment than in the first version. Congestion on the roads and increasing mobility are to be reduced by means of a more stringent policy on traffic and transport in relation to spatial planning. A division into A, B, and C locations has been introduced. The developments in industry are to be centered on various nodal points, the locations being distinguished by their access to public transport (A and B locations) or to main roads (C locations), depending on the transport flows generated by the industry in question.

There is in this period also some movement on another front. This is of great significance to the Randstad and the development opportunities of the four metropolitan areas within it. After holding the discussion on modifications to metropolitan administration on ice for the first half of the eighties, more pressure began to be felt from the major cities. They had been increasingly plagued in the eighties by economic malfunctioning, high unemployment, and the accumulation of social problems, connected with the concentrations of large numbers of people on welfare. The decline in the big cities began in the early seventies and continued into the eighties, reaching an all-time low in 1984. Even after 1984, growth in the major cities remained relatively low in comparison with other parts of the country.

As mentioned earlier, a start was first made in 1978, but more seriously from 1982/1983 onwards, on developing a policy of urban revitalization. This began in Amsterdam and Rotterdam, followed in 1985/1986 by The Hague and Utrecht. It soon became obvious that the policy opportunities, partly dependent on the administrative relations for their success, were inadequate, particularly for the four metropolitan areas in the Randstad and with respect to the Randstad as an entity. The Christian Democrat-Liberal cabinet of that period instigated a commission (the Montijn Commission, named after its chairman, ex-Shell director Ir. J.A.P. Montijn) to look into these problems. The report 'Major cities, Major Opportunities', which this commission issued in the first half of 1989, provided a stimulus to social and economic consciousness regarding the necessity to strengthen policy on the big cities and the related modification of the administrative organization (Kreukels & Wilmer 1990).

While the Fourth Report was being touched up (1988-1990), welcome use was made of this line of administrative reinforcement. The solutions were sought primarily via strengthening the administrative framework of the metropolitan agglomerations (the four big cities and surrounding municipalities). Since 1990 this has been extended to seven regions, in an operation aimed at modifying metropolitan government under the leadership of the Minister of Internal Affairs: 'Upgraded Local/Regional Administration for Urban Agglomerations I' (1990) and 'Upgraded Local/Regional Administration for Urban Agglomerations II' (1991). Outside the Randstad the agglomerations concerned are: Eindhoven, Enschede/Hengelo and Arnhem/Nijmegen. Final decisions will not be taken until 1993.

Despite considerable efforts on the part of the Ministry of Internal Affairs, no final administrative or political agreement between the Christian Democratic and Social Democratic parties constituting the present cabinet has yet been reached, even though the necessity for at least minimal modifications to metropolitan administration is generally recognized.

In order to conclude this overview of recent changes in and content of spatial planning and the related policy and administrative context - with a particular view to the Randstad and the four metropolitan areas it contains - a summary of the most important reactions to this report follows. The reactions come from the political world, professionals, and the general public.

Initial reactions in the press revealed that a number of members of society as well as specialists were troubled by the one-sided emphasis on economic, at the expense of social aspects, although there was general support for the attention paid to economic factors.

The attention paid to the economic aspects of internationalization received support. But statements were subsequently made to the effect that this trend had become little more than a trend. It had not, in any case, been sufficiently actualized for application in, for example, an EC policy context. Research on and keen insight into foreign developments were felt to be lacking.

In a number of other reactions the Fourth Report was felt to have a visionary and somewhat electioneering character, while its investigative foundation was felt to be weak, as was the elaboration in financial terms, particularly when it came to the necessary infrastructure.

It was also felt that the Fourth Report failed to take a sufficiently detailed look at the differentiation at regional level with respect to the divergent areas of the Netherlands. This is even more so if the differentiation, for example between the Randstad, the four metropolitan areas within it, and the remaining urban concentrations, are viewed in relation to the transport and traffic infrastructure. According to comments from interested parties and experts in the field, this infrastructure is not sufficiently well thought out and its relation to spatial planning and the priorities involved, for example the emphasis on the Randstad and the major cities within it, is not made clear enough.

In the same way, reactions from the environmental protection people suggest that the 1988 version of the Fourth Report provides insufficient guarantees for even minimal safeguards regarding essential environmental values.

The greater selectivity in the Fourth Report and its more pronounced priorities provoked reactions from those cities and regions that considered themselves to be under-rated in the Randstad pecking order (the city of Utrecht) or as urban center (Breda and Zwolle). The two latter cities were to be recognized as special status centers, or 'urban nodes' in the revised version of the Fourth Report.

The proposals for rural areas were not considered sufficiently up-to-date by representatives of the agricultural and land-use sectors, especially with regard to the restructuring of agriculture in the context of the European Community. These same people do, however, support the abandonment of the area typology of the Third Report, concerning the zoning of agricultural, landscape and natural environment functions per area unit. This typology appeared not to be operational and caused a lot of tension and friction among the various rural interest groups. In contrast to the precise specification of how the agricultural and natural elements of the landscape were to be divided and interwoven per area unit in the Third Report, the targets for the rural areas in the Fourth Report are more roughly outlined and flexible.

This array of reactions to the Fourth Report in the period 1988 until the autumn of 1991 gives an indication of the ongoing discussion in our country on themes related to urbanization in the broadest sense. When one uses the most advanced developments in metropolitan areas elsewhere as a measuring rod, the following conclusions can be drawn, with the Randstad and its four metropolitan areas, in particular, in mind.

For the future of metropolitan areas, the high level of financial and professional investments related to the quality of the main infrastructure and the main urban projects is decisive. The outline and setting of the majority of such projects as described in the Fourth Report for the Randstad and the four major cities within it generally fail to demonstrate enough of this high quality. There is also insufficient evidence of timely implementation or of guarantees of adequate financial resources.

One of the constants in the Fourth Report, going back to the basic schemes in the previous National Reports, is the continuing division between the policy programs for urban areas and those for rural areas. There might well be a move away from two separate memoranda, one for the urban areas and one for their rural counterparts, but the whole design betrays this division. It is related in the Netherlands, as in a number of other Western countries, to divergent interests and, professional differentiation. This is particularly pronounced in the profile of agriculture and the related infrastructure of knowledge and development emanating from the Agricultural University of Wageningen. It is precisely this division, which features in separate plans for rural and urban areas in a number of countries, that will have a decelerating effect. That effect can emerge in a period in which interrelations between the metropolitan centers, the surrounding municipalities and the string of more distant centers, as well as the rural areas, are becoming more important with respect to the coordination of facilities and infrastructure over an increasingly large area. Urbanization now involves both rural and urban areas, bringing them together. Those countries that do justice to this in their planning policy will be at an advantage in the years ahead.

A similar observation can be made with respect to the pronounced division created in the Fourth Report between the everyday (residential) environment and the main infrastructure. The latter is largely seen as determined by economic functions. This caesura is explicable against the background of differentiation of interests and the related specialisms in the past. Yet it also leads to a division that must be considered dysfunctional, bearing present-day and near-future dynamics in mind. In the qualitative development of metropolitan areas in the period ahead, the combined quality of home and work, recreation, traffic and transport are increasingly responsible for the quality of the metropolitan areas as a whole, be it from the viewpoint of resident, employee, employer, or economic investor.

With the overall quality of an urbanized country in mind, there is a certain conflict between granting the Randstad a high urban profile and taking sufficient account of the Randstad in relation to the rest of the urbanized country. A too distinct division between the Randstad, the central ring of cities, and the rest of the Netherlands, as indicated in the Fourth Report, does not coincide with the complex interrelations involved in urbanization now and especially in the near future. This is particularly relevant in a small country (the Netherlands as one urban field).

One can question the creation of a category of 'urban nodes' throughout the country, given special status and facilities by the Fourth Report. Will this serve, in any functional way, the natural process of differentiation and the dispersal of facilities and accommodation related to this complex and interrelated urban field?

Finally, one must conclude - bearing the examples of urban revitalization abroad in mind - that there is a serious gap, particularly in the Netherlands, between the proposals and intentions, not only economically but also socially, as formulated in the Fourth Report, and the reality of the institutional framework of vested interests in the public and private sector. Even if there is a current movement away from the 'central rule approach' of the seventies, no really new balances between national and local/regional level, between government units and between the public and the private sector have emerged.

The climate and setting are still strongly dominated by (central) government policy, notwithstanding the adherence to the new planning and policy-making paradigm. The main recent projects, in both the local and regional setting, can be considered as showcases for the incongruity between the language of the Fourth Report and the real world.

11.4   A concluding characterization of the policy and context of physical planning for the Randstad, with a view to the period ahead

With respect to policy on the Randstad, with particular emphasis on the spatial planning of this most urbanized area, the most important point of tension can be extracted from the above, especially with a view to the period ahead.

On the one hand, there is evidence of a distinct government system of physical planning, originating in a tradition of social and administrative involvement in spatial planning in a small, densely populated country with an exceptional system of land-and water management. This was expressed in the post-war period in the form of an unusually powerful national regime (internationally speaking), which laid down stringent terms for enterprise, residence, and general existence in the Randstad metropolitan area.

On the other hand, a metropolitan concentration area such as the Randstad is increasingly expected to be dynamic, adaptable, and quick to react with respect to initiatives and activities in the economic-technological and therefore also social-cultural spheres. An important determining factor here is the fact that the metropolitan regions and their related infrastructures become competitors for power on the international scene.

This tension links up to the following point. The pronounced awareness of and care for the physical environment, characteristic of Dutch physical planning, becomes even more functional in the exclusiveness of the Dutch system - not forgetting the specific composition of our country and the advantage which this affords us in relation to other countries - and has to be safeguarded. However, this focus on the physical environment, including the location and space requirements, must now, more than ever before, relate to the continuous adaptation to new challenges in the socio-economic and socio-cultural sphere. This largely involves a return to more open relationships between metropolitan areas across national boundaries, both today and in the near future. In other words: the strength of the Dutch regime (safeguarding and bringing into line divergent interests and functions in a balanced system of physical planning) must not become a weakness. (The danger lies in not reacting satisfactorily to the demand for dynamism, flexibility, and modifications due to a centralized and overorganized government system, particularly with regard to physical planning).

In the Fourth Report reference is made to the desirability of such an about-turn; at least the intention is there. However, as demonstrated in the previous section (11.3), there is still no evidence of real change in ultimate policy and even less in the policy system.

Behind references to the importance of the market, of decentralized involvement of municipalities and provinces, the most recent implementation route formulated in the Fourth Report seems to provide another option. The Ministry of Housing, Physical Planning and the Environment, the Ministry of Transport and Public Works and (to a certain extent) the Ministry of Economic Affairs continue - via the new metropolitan district authorities in the form of New Metropolitan Umbrella Administrations for a selected number of major city areas - attempts to encourage the coordination of various policy sectors at the national level *in a very centralized way*. The metropolitan district land-use policy acts as a pivot here, with the divergent internal claims from the various areas needing to be brought into line with each other. Such a cumbersome and non-specific 'top-down' system is at odds with the demands of segmental administration and direct relations of responsibility within the nation-state. The latter involves those in the front lines of the complex and dynamic policy systems typical of modern western countries.

Dynamism, flexibility, and the capacity to adapt, on the one hand, and stable basic qualities on the other will be the key to optimal development opportunities for an urbanized center such as the Randstad. Such a center in such an affluent country (rich in both human and physical capital, but at the same time failing to fully utilize the potential due to institutional rigidity) seeks to evolve at the same rate as its international counterpart. To attain that goal, a far reaching and consistent division of effort, responsibility, and risks (functional and territorial) is necessary in the metropolitan centers and agglomerations.

The WRR (Netherlands Scientific Council for Government Policy) has followed up on an analysis of the relative strengths and weaknesses of the four metropolitan areas within the Randstad. The Council assesses the Randstad in relation to other countries and analyzes the Dutch institutional system. Their Report to the Government 'Institutions and Cities', elaborates on such a modification of administrative and financial relations (Netherlands Scientific Council for Government Policy 1990). To activate the local authorities in relation to the interests manifest in the urban areas, emphasis is placed on the recovery of financial autonomy and tax revenues by local and regional authorities. This area had suffered a somewhat distorted development (Peterson 1981; Page & Goldsmith 1987; Paddison & Bailey 1988; Clarke 1989; Kreukels & Spit 1989).

In order to motivate the divergent parties involved (territorially and functionally), the national government will have to present a more distinct profile internationally when it comes to strategy (strategic locations, main infrastructure, mainports) and finance. This forms a natural complement to the locally and regionally more differentiated efforts, linked with more autonomy for subareas and subfunctions. That aspect of national government is increasingly determined by the fact that strategic backing is crucial to success and to the existence of extra opportunities when competing internationally as a metropolitan area. More than ever before, this implies a direct and powerful role for the Ministry of Trade and Industry in development policy for the Randstad, the four metropolitan areas within it, and its mainports: Amsterdam Airport and the seaports of Rotterdam. Despite a slight policy shift in the recent Ministry of Trade and Industry Report, 'Regions without Borders' (1990), there is still no evidence in the Netherlands of such powerful action being taken. The ministry in question also lacks such a tradition.

It is apparent from the above that the initial impulse for a Randstad development policy, also in physical planning terms, demands a modification of the general administrative and financial relationships. Changes in planning policy are both pointless and meaningless unless combined with this necessary, more general administrative change, whereby societal impulses, market processes, and governmental intervention are brought together.

The modification of physical planning itself consists of two aspects. The first has already been discussed. Leading on from what has been said above, the character of national physical planning will have to change to allow more latitude for functional subsections and local and regional initiatives and considerations.

This greater elasticity of physical planning also implies a step backwards, for the benefit of other policy sectors. This step backwards is connected, in the first instance, to a greater understanding of the fact that spatial planning is ultimately the result of the combined action of a series of spatially relevant policy fields, each with its own motivations and methods: housing, land reclamation, traffic and transport, regional economic policy and, last but not least, the environment. Within Dutch physical planning, this multi-sectoral heterogeneity is too quickly written off in diminished and therefore less meaningful policy proposals via national and provincial physical planning reports. In everyday practice these diverse sectoral interests tend to return in full vengeance. An explicit return to this multi-sectoral approach in relation to spatial planning, based on divergent interests, is a prime example of one step backwards, and two steps forwards, in planning policy.

A similar, but at the same time more drastic shift in the relative position of planning policy is connected to the relationship of this policy sector with other policy sectors (for instance: health, education, manpower services) in general, but the social and economic sectors in particular. Physical planning in the Netherlands will, with particular reference to the Randstad, have to take Fritz W. Scharpf's conclusion for West Germany seriously. The more national physical planning tries to promote itself at the national level at the expense of other policy sectors and lower government levels, the less actual meaning it will have. That is to say, more reticence is required when seeking coordination than suggested in even the Fourth Report, as well as a greater reliance on the adjustment mechanisms inherent in society itself.

As far as policy on the Randstad is concerned, this means, in more concrete terms, that the economic and social policies for this area deserve to be granted relatively more weight, locally, regionally and also nationally. Subsequently, physical planning has to adapt itself to these policies. Then it is possible for the Randstad to develop strongly, measured against international standards on the quality of an area and judged according to the utilization of available potential. This is all based on the assumption that the quality of an area is directly proportional to how it functions in general.

The second major modification in physical planning implies a keener sense of responsibility and commitment on the part of national government when it comes to the strategic national elements (mainports, main traffic and transport infrastructure) involved in such a complex and dynamic area as the Randstad. It is more important than ever that national physical planning, seconded by national transport planning and together with national policy on trade and industry, guarantees the necessary financial and professional resources for high quality development, taking metropolitan areas abroad as a measuring rod. This new strategic role for national physical planning will imply, in a number of cases, a limitation of the jurisdiction of other authorities and of the private sector. However, this can be defended when linked to clear procedures and parliamentary control. This type of strong, independent procedure of national physical planning for strategic projects can be seen as a good alternative to the existing complex and time-consuming procedures, serving only indicative, noncommittal programs.

At the moment, the Randstad still lacks a policy regime with the characteristics necessary to react quickly and adequately in the competitive market of metropolitan areas at the level which such an affluent and well-equipped country as the Netherlands warrants. Such a regime should also serve to safeguard basic environmental and social values.

The dual modification is: a) a general adjustment of primarily financial, but also partly administrative, relationships that will help to distribute the impulses for activities and responsibilities; b) a planning policy that explicitly takes account of relevant policy sectors and, more generally, takes a step backwards for the benefit of direct social and economic policy, becoming at the same time more powerful with respect to national strategic issues.

In this way, the Randstad's chances of measuring up to other prominent metropolitan regions abroad, not only in the economic-technological sense but also in a social-cultural context, are optimal. As so often in the history of this country the quality of, and opportunities to develop within, the central urban area would again be well served by a really effective planning policy. Then, the Netherlands will again be in a position to consider itself one of the international forerunners.

The above-mentioned modifications to policy and policy systems involve - without suggesting a return to the past - the restoration of a number of features characteristic of the quality and power of the Dutch city of the seventeenth century. The relevance lies in the fact that the city at that time was involved in a system in which the preconditions for management and development were emerging and being implemented within various circles and at various levels of the republic.

References

Burke, G.L. (1966), Greenheart Metropolis. Planning the Western Netherlands. London: MacMillan.

Clarke, S.E. (ed) (1989), Urban Innovation and Autonomy. Political Implications of Policy Change. Newbury Park: Sage Publications.

Boer, M. de, W. Janssen, D. Lambert & B. Colenbrander (eds) (1990), Architectuurbeleid in acht steden: San Francisco, Chicago, New York, Toronto, Barcelona, Parijs, West-Berlijn, Londen. Rotterdam: Nederlands Architectuurinstituut.

Dutt, A.K. & F.J. Costa (eds) (1985), Public Planning in the Netherlands. New York: Oxford University Press.

Fosler, R.S. & R.A. Berger (eds) (1982), Public-Private Partnership in American Cities. Seven Case Studies. Lexington Mass.: Lexington Books.

Friedman, M. (ed) (1988), De Stijl: 1917-1931; Visions of Utopia. Oxford: Phaidon.

Glasbergen, P. & J.B.D. Simonis (1979), Ruimtelijk beleid in de verzorgingsstaat; Onderzoek naar en beschouwing over de (on)mogelijkheid van een nationaal ruimtelijk beleid in Nederland. Amsterdam: Kobra CV.

Hall, P. (1977), The World Cities. Londen: Weidenfeld & Nicholson.

Hall, P. (1973), The Containment of Urban England (two volumes). London: PEP.

Jobse, R.B. (1980), Van kelderwoning tot hoogbouwflat. Honderd jaar bouwen en wonen in Amsterdam. In: Wonen, werken en verkeer in Amsterdam 1880-1980. Bijdragen tot de sociale geografie en planologie 1. Amsterdam: Geografisch en Planologisch Instituut, Vrije Universiteit.

Konvitz, J. W. (1978), Cities and the Sea; Port City Planning in Early Modern Europe. Baltimore: The Johns Hopkins University Press.

Kreukels, A.M.J. & T. Spit (1989), Fiscal retrenchment and the relationship between national government and local administration. In: S.E. Clarke (ed), Urban Innovation and Autonomy; Political Implications of Policy Change, pp. 153-181. Newbury Park: Sage Publications.

Kreukels, A.M.J. & H.J.T. Wilmer (1990), Metropolitan government in the Netherlands. Tijdschrift voor Economische en Sociale Geografie 4, pp. 299-306.

Lefcoe, G. (1978), When governments become land developers. Urban Law and Policy 1, pp. 103-160.

Lijphart, A. (1968), The Politics of Accommodation; Pluralism and Democracy in the Netherlands. Berkeley: University of California Press.

Lijphart, A. (1984), Democracies: Patterns of Majoritarian and Consensus Government in Twenty-One Countries. New Haven: Yale University Press.

Ministerie van Volkshuisvesting en Ruimtelijke Ordening (1966), Tweede Nota over de Ruimtelijke Ordening. 's Gravenhage: SDU-Uitgeverij.

Ministerie van Volkshuisvesting, Ruimtelijke Ordening en Milieubeheer (1974-1985), Derde Nota over de Ruimtelijke Ordening. 's Gravenhage: SDU-Uitgeverij.

Ministerie van Volkshuivesting, Ruimtelijke Ordening en Milieubeheer (1988-1991), Vierde Nota over de Ruimtelijke Ordening. 's Gravenhage: SDU-Uitgeverij.

Ministerie van Volkshuisvesting, Ruimtelijke Ordening en Milieubeheer (1991), Sleutelprojecten Ruimtelijke inrichting; Rol van het Rijk en Tussenstand 1991. 's-Gravenhage: SDU-Uitgeverij.

Ministerie van Binnenlandse Zaken (1989), Grote steden, grote kansen. 's Gravenhage: SDU-Uitgeverij.

Ministerie van Binnenlandse Zaken (1990), Besturen op niveau, deel 1. 's Gravenhage: SDU-Uitgeverij.

Ministerie van Binnenlandse Zaken (1991), Besturen op niveau, deel 2. 's Gravenhage: SDU-Uitgeverij.

Ministerie van Economische Zaken (1990), Regio's zonder grenzen; het regionaal-economisch beleid voor de periode 1991-1994. 's Gravenhage: SDU-Uitgeverij.

Mumford, L. (1970), The Culture of Cities. (first edition 1938). San Diego: Harvest, Harcourt Brace, Jovanovich.

OECD (1987), New Roles for Cities and Towns. Paris: OECD.

Paddison, R & S. Bailey S. (eds) (1988), Local Government Finance; International Perspectives. London: Routledge.

Page, E.C. & M.J. Goldsmith (eds) (1987), Central and Local Government Relations; A Comparative Analysis of West European Unitary Systems. London: Sage Publications.

Parkinson, M., B. Foley & D. Judd (1988), Regenerating the Cities; The UK Crisis and the USA Experience. Manchester: Manchester University Press.

Peterson, P.E. (1981), City Limits. Chicago: The University of Chicago Press.

Rebel, B. (1983), Het nieuwe bouwen; Het functionalisme in Nederland 1918 -1945. Assen: Van Gorcum.

Rotterdam Municipal Port Authority (1991), Draft Plan for the Port 2010; Future Vision of a Mainport. Rotterdam: Port Authority.

Schama, S. (1987), The Embarrassment of Riches; An Interpretation of Dutch Culture in the Golden Age. London: Collins.

Scharpf, F. W. & F. Schnabel (1978), Durchsetzungsprobleme der Raumordnung im öffentlichen Sektor. Informationen zur Raumentwicklung, Heft 1, pp. 29-48.

Shalala, D.E. & J. Vitullo-Martin (1989), Rethinking the urban crisis. Journal of the American Planning Association 55, pp. 3-13.

Thomas, D. et al. (1983), Flexibility and Commitment in Planning; A Comparative Study of Local Planning and Development in the Netherlands and England. 's-Gravenhage: Martinus Nijhoff Publishers.

Vries, J. de (1978), Barges and Capitalism; Passenger Transportation in the Dutch Economy. Wageningen: Landbouwuniversiteit Wageningen.

Warren, R.L., S.M. Rose & A.F. Bergunder (1974), The Structure of Urban Reform; Community Decision Organizations in Sta-bility and Change. Lexington Mass.: Lexington Books.

Wit, W. de (ed) (1983), The Amsterdam School; Dutch Expressionist Architecture 1915 -1930. New York/Cambridge Mass.: Cooper-Hewitt Museum/ The MIT Press.

Woud, A. van der (1987), Het Lege Land; Ruimtelijke orde van Nederland 1798 - 1848. Amsterdam: Meulenhoff Informatief.

WRR (Wetenschappelijke Raad voor het Regeringsbeleid) (1990), Institutions and Cities; The Dutch Experience. Rapporten aan de Regering 37. Herziene uitgave. 's-Gravenhage: SDU-Uitgeverij.

Prof.dr. A. Kreukels
Faculty of Geographical Sciences
University of Utrecht
P.O. Box 80.115
3508 TC Utrecht
The Netherlands

LIST OF CONTRIBUTORS

Prof. dr. F.M. Dieleman
Professor of Urban and Rural Geography and Applied Demography, Faculty of Geographical Sciences, University of Utrecht; Chairman of the Dutch Urban Networks Research Program

Prof. dr. R.E. van Engelsdorp Gastelaars
Professor of Urban Geography, Faculty of Environmental Sciences, University of Amsterdam

Prof. dr. A. Faludi
Professor of Physical Planning, Faculty of Environmental Sciences, University of Amsterdam

Dr. H. Floor
Associate Professor of Research Methodology, Faculty of Geographical Sciences, University of Utrecht

Drs. R.B. Jobse
Senior Lecturer of Urban Geography, Faculty of Geographical Sciences, University of Utrecht

Dr. R.C. Kloosterman
Fellow of the Royal Dutch Academy of Sciences, Regional Economics and Economic Geography, Faculty of Economic Sciences, University of Amsterdam

Prof. dr. A. Kreukels
Professor of Physical Planning, Faculty of Geographical Sciences, University of Utrecht; Member of the Netherlands Scientific Council for Government Policy

Prof. dr. J.G. Lambooy
Professor of Regional Economics and Economic Geography, Faculty of Economic Sciences, University of Amsterdam

Drs. G. Molenaar
Urban and Policy Researcher, City Council of Ede; Former Researcher in Urban Geography, Faculty of Geographical Sciences, University of Utrecht

Dr. S. Musterd
Associate Professor of Human Geography, Faculty of Environmental Sciences, University of Amsterdam; Coordinator of the Dutch Urban Networks Research Program

Dr. A. Nauta
Executive Secretary of the Netherlands Scientific Council for Government Policy

F. M. Dieleman and S. Musterd (eds.), The Randstad: A Research and Policy Laboratory, 263–264.
© 1992 *Kluwer Academic Publishers. Printed in the Netherlands.*

Prof. dr. P. Nijkamp
Professor of Regional, Urban and Environmental Economics and Economic Geography,
Faculty of Economics, Free University of Amsterdam

Prof. dr. ir. H. Priemus
Professor of Housing, Faculty of Architecture, Delft University of Technology; Director
of the Research Institute for Policy Sciences and Technology, Delft; Member of the
Board of the Dutch Urban Networks Research Program

Prof. dr. P. Rietveld
Professor of Traffic and Transport Economy, Faculty of Economics, Free University
of Amsterdam

Prof. dr. M. de Smidt
Professor of Economic Geography and Regional Economic Planning, Faculty of
Geographical Sciences, University of Utrecht

Drs. W. Stam
Staff Member in charge of Policy, Ministry of Transport, Public Works and Water
Management; Former Senior Researcher at the Research Institute for Policy Sciences
and Technology, Delft University of Technology

Prof. dr. H. van der Wusten
Professor of Political Geography, Faculty of Environmental Sciences, University of
Amsterdam; Member of the Board of the Dutch Urban Networks Research Program

The GeoJournal Library

1. B. Currey and G. Hugo (eds.): *Famine as Geographical Phenomenon.* 1984
   ISBN 90-277-1762-1
2. S. H. U. Bowie, F.R.S. and I. Thornton (eds.): *Environmental Geochemistry and Health.* Report of the Royal Society's British National Committee for Problems of the Environment. 1985   ISBN 90-277-1879-2
3. L. A. Kosiński and K. M. Elahi (eds.): *Population Redistribution and Development in South Asia.* 1985   ISBN 90-277-1938-1
4. Y. Gradus (ed.): *Desert Development.* Man and Technology in Sparselands. 1985   ISBN 90-277-2043-6
5. F. J. Calzonetti and B. D. Solomon (eds.): *Geographical Dimensions of Energy.* 1985   ISBN 90-277-2061-4
6. J. Lundqvist, U. Lohm and M. Falkenmark (eds.): *Strategies for River Basin Management.* Environmental Integration of Land and Water in River Basin. 1985   ISBN 90-277-2111-4
7. A. Rogers and F. J. Willekens (eds.): *Migration and Settlement.* A Multiregional Comparative Study. 1986   ISBN 90-277-2119-X
8. R. Laulajainen: *Spatial Strategies in Retailing.* 1987   ISBN 90-277-2595-0
9. T. H. Lee, H. R. Linden, D. A. Dreyfus and T. Vasko (eds.): *The Methane Age.* 1988   ISBN 90-277-2745-7
10. H. J. Walker (ed.): *Artificial Structures and Shorelines.* 1988
    ISBN 90-277-2746-5
11. A. Kellerman: *Time, Space, and Society.* Geographical Societal Perspectives. 1989   ISBN 0-7923-0123-4
12. P. Fabbri (ed.): *Recreational Uses of Coastal Areas.* A Research Project of the Commission on the Coastal Environment, International Geographical Union. 1990   ISBN 0-7923-0279-6
13. L. M. Brush, M. G. Wolman and Huang Bing-Wei (eds.): *Taming the Yellow River: Silt and Floods.* Proceedings of a Bilateral Seminar on Problems in the Lower Reaches of the Yellow River, China. 1989   ISBN 0-7923-0416-0
14. J. Stillwell and H. J. Scholten (eds.): *Contemporary Research in Population Geography.* A Comparison of the United Kingdom and the Netherlands. 1990
    ISBN 0-7923-0431-4
15. M. S. Kenzer (ed.): *Applied Geography.* Issues, Questions, and Concerns. 1989   ISBN 0-7923-0438-1
16. D. Nir: *Region as a Socio-environmental System.* An Introduction to a Systemic Regional Geography. 1990   ISBN 0-7923-0516-7
17. H. J. Scholten and J. C. H. Stillwell (eds.): *Geographical Information Systems for Urban and Regional Planning.* 1990   ISBN 0-7923-0793-3
18. F. M. Brouwer, A. J. Thomas and M. J. Chadwick (eds.): *Land Use Changes in Europe.* Processes of Change, Environmental Transformations and Future Patterns. 1991   ISBN 0-7923-1099-3
19. C. J. Campbell: *The Golden Century of Oil 1950–2050.* The Depletion of a Resource. 1991   ISBN 0-7923-1442-5
20. F. M. Dieleman and S. Musterd (eds.): *The Randstad: A Research and Policy Laboratory.* 1992   ISBN 0-7923-1649-5

KLUWER ACADEMIC PUBLISHERS – DORDRECHT / BOSTON / LONDON